SAS FORGED IN HELL

Damien Lewis

SAS

FORGED IN HELL

FROM DESERT RATS TO DOGS OF WAR: THE MAVERICKS WHO MADE THE SAS

QUERCUS

First published in Great Britain in 2023 by

QUERCUS

Quercus Editions Ltd
Carmelite House
50 Victoria Embankment
London EC4Y 0DZ

An Hachette UK company

A CIP catalogue record for this book is available
from the British Library

HB ISBN 978 1 52941 382 3
TPB ISBN 978 1 52941 383 0
Ebook ISBN 978 1 52941 385 4

10 9 8 7 6 5 4 3 2 1

Typeset by CC Book Production
Printed and bound in Great Britain by Clays Ltd, Elcograf S.p.A.

Papers used by Quercus Editions Ltd are from well-managed forests and other responsible sources.

For Lieutenant Colonel R. B. Mayne DSO,
The Pilgrim

Picture Credits

'Twas there I first beheld, drawn up in file and line,
The brilliant Irish hosts; they came, the bravest of the brave'

THE BLACK HACKLE

Frae a' the crack regiments, came our men,
The flower o' the Highlands and Lowlands and a'
And the lads of the Shamrock, frae peat moor and glen
And Corps troops and cavalry, gallant and braw.
And noo we're awa lads, to meet with the foe
We'll fight on the mountain, the shore or the plain
And though we've no honours at present to show,
They'll ken the Black Hackle when we're home again.

George Duncan MC
(The marching song of No. 11 Scottish Commando)

'It was forged in hell, forged behind the lines'

David Stirling DSO, describing
the founding of the SAS

Contents

ADRIATIC SEA

ROME

ITALY

Anzio

Termoli

Naples

Salerno

Chiatona

Taranto

Pisticci

Scalea

TYRRHENIAN SEA

1 SAS (SRS) and
2 SAS Operations, Italy 1943

Bagnara

Gallico

IONIAN SEA

Mount Etna

SICILY

Catania

Augusta

Syracuse

Capo Murro di Porco

Pantelleria

N

0   100 miles

0   200 km

Author's Note

There are sadly only a handful of survivors from the Second World War operations told in these pages. Throughout the period of researching and writing this book I have been in contact with as many as possible, plus surviving family members of those who have passed away. For those contributions and input, I am hugely grateful. If there are further witnesses to the stories told here who are inclined to come forward, please do get in contact with me, as I will endeavour to include further recollections of the operations portrayed in this book in future editions.

The time spent by Allied servicemen and women as Special Service volunteers was often traumatic and wreathed in layers of secrecy, and many chose to take their stories to their graves. Memories tend to differ and apparently none more so than those concerning operations deep behind enemy lines. The written accounts that do exist tend to differ in their detail and timescale, and locations and chronologies are sometimes contradictory. Nevertheless, I have endeavoured to provide an accurate sense of place, timescale and narrative to the story as depicted in these pages.

Where various accounts of a mission appear to be particularly contradictory, the methodology I have used to reconstruct where, when and how events took place presents the 'most likely' scenario. If two or more testimonies or sources point to a particular time or place or sequence of events, I have opted to use that account as most likely, while also considering the relative verisimilitude of each of those accounts.

The above notwithstanding, any mistakes herein are entirely of my own making, and I would be happy to correct any in future editions. Likewise, while I have attempted to locate the copyright holders of the photos, sketches and other images and the written material used in this book, this has not always been straightforward or easy. Again, I would be happy to correct any mistakes in future editions.

As it was originally conceived of as an airborne unit – using parachutes to drop behind enemy lines – the unit was named the Special *Air* Service (my emphasis). In due course many other forms of insertion to target were adopted – on foot, by vehicle, and by submarine and landing craft. During the period covered in this book the Special Air Service went through various iterations in terms of its official name and identity – including Special Service (SS), Special Raiding Squadron (SRS) etc. This plethora of names can be confusing, and for ease of reference and comprehension I have tended to stick to the words Special Air Service or SAS to describe the unit portrayed. The SAS's training base in spring 1943 was located on the shores of the eastern Mediterranean at a small village variously called Azzib, Az Zib, Az Zeeb, Al-Zaib and Zib. For ease of reference, I have used the first of those spellings in this book.

To preserve the authenticity of quotations and extracts from primary sources such as SAS war diary entries, letters, telegrams etc., I have reproduced spelling and grammatical errors as they appear in the original. Where explanation of specific references in the sources is required, a note is included in square brackets.

Preface

THE WAR CHEST

A decade ago, I was invited to visit the home of Fiona Ferguson and her husband, Norman, in Northern Ireland. Fiona (née Mayne) is one of the nieces of Colonel Blair 'Paddy' Mayne DSO. Upon his early death it fell to Fiona to become the keeper of the flame, safeguarding the Mayne family archive and wartime memorabilia – especially what became known as the 'Paddy Mayne War Diary' and her uncle's war chest. In the loft of the family's Mount Pleasant home, in Newtownards, Fiona and Norman discovered a trove of wartime memorabilia, secreted behind a water tank, as if it had been placed there to be overlooked and forgotten. This included Mayne's uniform, carefully wrapped in brown paper, plus a large wooden chest, with the words 'Lt. Col. R. B. Mayne DSO, Mount Pleasant, Newtownards, C. Down, N. Ireland. 39247. HOLD. C.O. 1st SAS' stamped on the lid.

Visiting Fiona and Norman's home, I was able to study the extraordinary contents of that war chest at first hand. It proved to be brimful of SAS wartime reports, diaries, letters, photographs and film – both developed and undeveloped – plus various eclectic and compelling wartime memorabilia. I was also able to study at first hand the gutted skeleton of the original *Chronik*

1

of Schneeren, a massive leatherbound volume that Mayne and his raiders had purloined from the town of Schneeren, in north-western Germany, and which they had transformed into a diary-cum-scrapbook embodying the SAS's wartime history (what became known as the *SAS War Diary*). There were also heaps of other wartime mementoes – those items that Mayne had brought back to Ireland, after five years of waging war across two continents. Needless to say, all of this constituted a treasure trove of SAS wartime history.

As I sifted through the contents of the war chest, the war diary and all the related materials, I came across a feast of behind-enemy-lines Second World War history. Simply incredible. The first book I wrote based upon that rich store of materials was *SAS Brothers in Arms*, which tells the story of the first eighteen months of the SAS at war. In many ways this book, *SAS Forged in Hell*, follows on from that, picking up where *Brothers in Arms* left off, though it is equally capable of being read as a standalone story.

Fiona and the wider Mayne family offered me access to Colonel Mayne's wartime memorabilia generously and freely, in the spirit that this wartime story might be written.

To tell it has been a privilege and an honour.

Damien Lewis
Dorset, March 2023

Chapter One

THE SACRED SCROLL
October 1945, Britain

The tall, erect figure stood before the ranks of his men, and by his very bearing it was clear that momentous events were afoot. He began speaking, his quiet, somewhat shy-seeming voice appearing sombre and half-choked with emotion. So it was that Lieutenant Colonel Blair 'Paddy' Mayne delivered the news to the men of the SAS that all had been expecting and dreading – that they were being summarily disbanded.

It was October 1945, and many of those who stood before their revered leader had waged war together for five brutal and bloody years. Together, they had braved repeated back-to-back operations behind enemy lines, seeing their closest comrades wounded, captured, maimed and killed, and losing so many dear friends in the process. Towards the war's end they had witnessed unimaginable horrors, being the first troops to enter the Bergen-Belsen concentration camp, at a time when few in Allied forces had the barest clue what a 'concentration camp' might be, let alone of the unspeakable nightmares they harboured.

Despite all of that, as Mayne was now informing his troops, the fellowship was about to be broken, their proud regiment – one that had pioneered special forces soldiering – being consigned to the dustbin of history. In short, those who stood before him, including his closest and dearest friends, faced two stark options: they were either to be sent back to their parent unit, whatever that might be, or to be returned to civvie street. For most of the war, Mayne had been forced to fight a battle on two fronts: one against the Nazi enemy, but another against those who had sought to do away with the maverick, free-spirited Special Air Service and its ranks of warriors. He had triumphed in the former fight, but today he was forced to accept that the latter had been lost.

Typically, Mayne – the most highly decorated British soldier serving in the Army in the Second World War, with four Distinguished Service Orders to his name – rounded off his speech by quoting some lines from 'The Boys of Killyran', an Irish folk song:

> Some they went for glory,
> Some they went for pillage,
> Pillage was the motto,
> Of the boys of Killyran.

He followed that, as if in afterthought, with a few final, self-deprecating words replete with a wry and bittersweet humour, which embodied what would then have seemed to be the epitaph of the SAS: 'We came for the pillage, but maybe we got a wee bit of the glory as well.'

Though beloved of Winston Churchill and a few senior generals, the rank and file of the SAS had never been popular with many on high. Though they had been tolerated during a time of war – desperate times had called for desperate measures – few seemed to want to keep these piratical raiders in the British Army, now that peace had been declared. They had become something of an inconvenience; an embarrassment even. As Sergeant Albert Youngman, one of Mayne's stalwarts, would describe it: 'The war was over . . . we were still alive and had had a good time. And then the next day a parade and you're not wanted any more. You're all split up and back to your unit. Thank you very much, goodbye. And that was so demoralising . . . Unbelievable thing to do and I think Paddy took it to heart.'

As all knew full well, during the war years the SAS had been branded as 'raiders of the thug variety', and few on high seemed to want their types serving anymore. They didn't like the SAS, Youngman explained, 'and they didn't like Paddy, that's for sure, because he had a complete disregard for the chair-borne bastards who never saw a shot fired in anger'. Or, as Alec 'Boy' Borrie, another of Mayne's veteran warriors, would recall, 'They couldn't get shot of us quick enough. We'd never been popular. We did things our own way. Didn't pay much attention to what they told us on high . . . So they did away with us just as soon as they could.'

The long years at war had taken a relentless and heavy toll. Many of those men ranged before Mayne were battling deep-seated trauma and their inner demons. During the closing months of the war, Major Harry Poat – Mayne's second-in-command and his right-hand man on innumerable missions – had written to Mayne, warning how an entire SAS squadron 'must come home at once, they are totally unfit bodily and mentally'. The squadron's commander, Poat had added, was 'completely played out, and quite unsuitable for the job . . .' Or, as long-standing SAS veteran Captain Roy Close would put it, 'There were unpleasant memories to be supressed, [sic] frightening dreams to be exorcised, and

5

the war's legacies were everywhere . . . It was not an easy transition . . . It took time to get used to, to feel part of the civilisation we had fought to protect. Some never did.'

In short, those who had made it through to October 1945 had suffered greatly, while many had made the ultimate sacrifice, yet the SAS was now to be consigned to the scrapheap. Of one thing Mayne and his comrades were certain: they would not allow the proud history of this regiment to die with its dissolution. Indeed, sensing the way the wind was blowing, Mayne and his stalwarts had put in place measures to ensure that the legacy of the SAS would not be buried, no matter what their detractors might decree from on high.

Six months earlier, in early April 1945, Mayne had led a convoy of heavily armed Willys jeeps, as the forces of 1 SAS had made a forty-eight-hour dash from Britain, across Holland and into Germany, snatching a few hours' precious sleep by the roadside. Placed under the operational command of a Canadian armoured division, the SAS was slated to serve at the very tip of the spear, its vehicles – bristling with rapid-firing Vickers-K machineguns, plus here and there the heavier Brownings – punching a way through the enemy frontline. As the German defenders fought ferociously to hold back the forces of the Allies, so the SAS was ordered to 'achieve deeper penetration . . . attack enemy lines of communication and pass back intelligence'.

Crossing the Rhine, the men of 1 and 2 SAS combined forces, forming a potent body of men at arms. But the signs of fierce and fanatical – some might argue suicidal – resistance were everywhere. As the Allied spearhead thrust into the lands of the Reich, so Nazi Germany's diehards – teenage soldiers of the

Hitler Youth, elite SS units and paratroopers, with here and there the elderly men of the *Volkssturm* 'home guard' – fought tooth and nail for every inch of ground. 'The journey . . . was bloody awful,' recalled Lieutenant Charlie Hackney, a man who'd served with the SAS from the earliest days. 'We kept encountering these pockets of SS soldiers concealed by the roadside who were quite happy to fight and die . . . We never took prisoners on those occasions.'

It proved hard to distinguish friend from foe. Some of the enemy were 'wearing British and French uniform', while others were disguised as civilians. To make matters worse, the terrain was atrocious, at least for a unit intent on classic 'jeeping' operations. 'The area was crossed and recrossed by dykes and canals, making it extremely difficult for jeeps to operate with any degree of freedom', read an SAS operational report, 'and there were very few places in which vehicles could reverse and turn around . . . there were innumerable culverts and bridges which were prepared for demolition by the enemy. The majority of the fields were of a "boggy" nature, even in dry weather, but . . . with fairly heavy rainfall, it made conditions very much worse.' As a result, the SAS columns were increasingly channelled onto the few roads.

Before leaving Britain, these elite warriors had been ordered to 'sanitise' themselves, discarding their SAS berets for less distinctive headgear, and blanking out all references to their unit from their pay books and other papers. Over the radio they were to refer to themselves only in code, to try to further obfuscate their true identity. As all had learned, Hitler had issued his notorious 'Commando Order', which condemned all captured Allied parachutists and special forces troops to certain death. 'The presence of SAS troops in any area must be immediately reported . . .', the Fuhrer had declared; 'they must be ruthlessly exterminated.'

Typically, one of the first patrols into action in Germany was commanded by Major Bill Fraser, a veteran raider who had served on the very first SAS operations, along with Mayne and David Stirling, the SAS's founder. Wounded several times during the war – twice in Italy, one time being blown up by an artillery shell – Fraser had earned a towering reputation for being at the forefront of battle whenever he wasn't being patched up in hospital. Moving through a battalion of battle-worn Canadian paratroopers, Fraser was warned that an enemy position lay up ahead. With the German forces holed up in thick woodland, the Canadians had been driven back by 'heavy Spandau [the belt-fed MG34 machinegun], bazooka and infantry fire, losing eight men'.

Fraser figured his patrol could possibly break through, by sneaking up on the enemy using the cover of some dead ground. Riding in their jeeps, they got to within a few dozen yards of the German positions, when a 'well camouflaged machine-gun opened up at Major Fraser's jeep, which ran into a ditch'. With Fraser hit and wounded, the patrol split into three spearheads, their vehicle-mounted weapons blasting enemy machinegun pits, bazooka nests, plus a group of fighters that were holed up in some houses, silencing them 'one by one'. Even as the battle raged, one jeep managed to drag Fraser's vehicle out of its ditch, after which the SAS advanced into the woods on foot, clearing it of any further resistance. Ten of the enemy had been killed, and thirty-two prisoners taken.

Typically, Bill Fraser – shot in the hand – 'didn't seem relieved to get such a wound', one of his men remarked. 'I think he wanted to see it through.' Even at this late stage of the war – the

8

dying days of six years of a worldwide struggle – Fraser hungered to soldier on to the bitter end. But he was to be denied such a wish, being evacuated to a casualty clearing station. In his stead, Captain Ian Wellsted, Fraser's deputy, stepped forward to take over command. As they pushed east towards the heavily wooded, hillocky terrain of the Grinderwald – the Grinder forest – again and again they were forced to run the gauntlet. 'At times it was like hitting a brick wall you could never penetrate, and of course it was ideal country for ambushes.'

Heavy weaponry was also in play in this fast-moving and confused battle. At one stage a three-jeep patrol approached a phalanx of tanks, presuming them to be some of the Canadian armour. It was only when they had drawn dangerously close that they realised their mistake, as the tanks opened fire. Caught in the onslaught – they carried no weaponry able to take on such targets – one jeep was 'completely crushed under a tank', even as the others were abandoned. The men of that patrol were listed as missing in action, but amazingly all would make it back to friendly lines. In another daring mission, an SAS unit captured a train 'loaded with V2s', the V2 being Hitler's much-vaunted *Vergeltungswaffe 2* – Retaliation Weapon 2 – the world's first long-range guided ballistic missile.

Pushing further into the Grinderwald, Wellsted's eleven-jeep convoy found itself surrounded by the impenetrable oak forests and wetlands that fringe the Steinhuder Meer, the largest lake in north-west Germany. Dense, dark vegetation crowded in from all sides, making it impossible to deviate from the road. The route stretched ahead, cutting a narrow swathe south-west, linking the town of Nienburg to that of Neustadt am Rübenberge. The patrol of jeeps came across a Daimler armoured car. It was flying British colours, and it turned out to be one of a reconnaissance unit of the British Inns of Court regiment, a light armoured unit which also used Daimler Dingo scout cars.

The column of jeeps pulled to a halt, to confer. From the Daimler's commander, Wellsted learned that the woodland up ahead was thick with the enemy. Undaunted, he issued his battle orders, leading the jeeps into combat. Thundering ahead, some two dozen Vickers sparked into 'full-throated life', the onslaught tearing into the suspected enemy position, making the woodland literally 'dance' with fire. Though it seemed as if nothing could survive such a ferocious barrage, stabs of flame among the dark trees revealed where 'Spandau' gunners were holding firm, and then there came the fierce flashes of *Panzerfäuste* – a single-use anti-tank grenade – being unleashed.

Wellsted led his men in a wild charge on foot, as battle at close quarters was joined. But it proved 'absolutely impossible to see the enemy, as the woods were too thick'. By the time Wellsted ordered his patrol to withdraw, they'd grabbed two German captives, but in the process one of their jeeps had taken a direct hit from a *Panzerfaust*. The blast rocked it back on its springs, triggering a blinding flash and a plume of smoke. More *Panzerfaust* operators broke cover, hefting their stubby broomhandle-like launchers, a burst of flame and a shroud of smoke engulfing the operators as they let fly. Several were cut down, even as they tried to blast the SAS jeeps all to hell.

With fierce fire from the enemy's machineguns kicking up dust on the road and ripping into the vehicles, Wellsted led his column in a helter-skelter retreat, their every weapon belting out covering fire. Roaring out of the 'valley of death', as Wellsted would name it, the one wrecked jeep had to be left behind. The burning vehicle lay where it had been hit, the bloody figure of its gunner face down on the tarmac. That man was John 'Taffy' Glyde, a former factory worker from Pontypridd, who was married with one son. All had grown used to Glyde's catchphrase, uttered in his thick Welsh accent, whenever an enemy soldier was killed: 'Another one bites the dust.' But it was Taffy himself who had done so now. As the SAS report would note: 'German Bazooka [*Panzerfaust*] landed about 2 yards from his jeep. His head nearly blown off.'

Forcing the two 'very arrogant' German prisoners to sit on the bonnet of the lead jeep, 'so the Germans wouldn't fire', the patrol managed to get away. Pulling back to a crossroads, Wellsted and his men paused to take stock. Glyde was dead, two others were injured, and they'd lost one jeep. But it could have been far worse. Then Wellsted realised that he was himself hurt. There was blood dripping from his hand. With Bill Fraser out of action, he knew that he had to remain in command, and especially as they were far from out of the worst of the trouble yet. Someone yelled out a warning. There were enemy troops advancing from the opposite direction. In short, they were in danger of becoming surrounded; of getting boxed in.

Two more jeeps roared into view, the lead vehicle carrying Harry Poat, Mayne's deputy. Joining forces with Wellsted, Poat could see how the SAS patrol was at a 'terrible disadvantage, standing up high on the road', while 'the enemy were lying low in the undergrowth'. Yet with their line of retreat cut off, they had no option but to stand and fight. Opening fire with all the vehicle-mounted weaponry, plus their Bren light machineguns and the small, 2-inch mortars the jeeps also carried, for fifteen minutes the battle raged. Even as they began taking casualties, a message was received that a column of armoured cars was inbound to relieve them. Sure enough, from the direction of a gravel track that branched off south – signposted to the town of Schneeren – they heard the grunt of powerful engines, and three armoured vehicles hove into view.

Presuming them to be friendly, it wasn't until the approaching vehicles were some thirty yards away that all learned otherwise. The nearest armoured car opened fire, its 20mm cannon ripping into the closest jeep, which took several direct hits and burst into flames. From the burning ruins of that vehicle, which had been 'shot out from under' its occupants, three figures stumbled clear – Lieutenant Denis Wainman, and Troopers Jim Blakeney and Alec Hay. As SAS and German gunners traded savage fire at close range, a round from an armoured car struck Blakeney, cutting him down. To their rear, the jeep commanded by Sergeant Jeff DuVivier was 'hammering away at this armoured car', but moments later DuVivier felt a stabbing pain in his leg as he too was hit.

The SAS kept pouring in the fire, but the Vickers rounds ricocheted off the armoured cars' flanks, doing little appreciable harm. As the enemy drew closer, those riding in their armoured vehicles started to unleash grenades. A third jeep was hit, a desperate figure crawling beneath it in an attempt to take cover and avoid the murderous onslaught. It was Trooper Roy Davies, and he was badly injured. Both Davies and Blakeney had been captured on the SAS's first ever mission, the ill-fated Operation Squatter, in North Africa in the autumn of 1941. Subsequently they had managed to escape from an Italian POW camp, making it back to Allied lines. Rejoining their unit, they were viewed as iconic figures in the SAS.

Spotting their plight, Wellsted dashed forward, trying to 'advance through a hail of bullets', as Poat would report it. He reached the third jeep in line – smouldering and peppered with cannon fire – to find Davies lying beneath it, covered in blood and in terrible pain. He had been hit in the back and, Wellsted feared, was mortally wounded. He managed to inject the injured man with a shot of morphine. But even as he was busy doing so, the third enemy vehicle rumbled closer, and from its open rear began to disgorge hordes of enemy fighters. It was a half-track armoured personnel carrier, and those riding in it proceeded to dash into the woods before opening fire.

Yelling to Davies that he would be back, Wellsted made a break for his jeep, but he made only a few yards when the first bullet found its mark. Shot in the left leg, he staggered onwards for a good twenty yards, before another round struck, hitting his other leg and knocking him to the ground. Badly injured, Wellsted was dragged back towards the road junction by others in his troop. But when those same men returned to try to retrieve Davies from under his vehicle, Trooper Dougie Ferguson, one of Poat's key deputies, was gunned down, and left lying on the track, wounded.

Back at the crossroads, Poat – typically 'very quiet and very calm' when in the heat of battle – signalled the Inns of Court Daimler armoured car forward. When it was within sight of the nearest enemy vehicle, Poat directed the gunner to 'bolt it with its two-pounder, which [he] did with great success'. The British 2-pounder was a 40mm anti-tank gun, and the Daimler's main armament. Once the lead enemy armoured car had been blasted with one of those shells, the second was also hit, and it was forced to pull back into the cover of the woodland. But the trees were now alive with enemy troops, and Poat and his men were forced to 'fight like devils, firing everything they had'.

Still the enemy kept coming.

Unbeknown to Poat, Wellsted or the others, here at the Schneeren crossroads they had stumbled into the rump of the 12th SS Panzer Division Hitlerjugend (Hitler Youth). Realising they were 'outnumbered . . . and with casualties mounting rapidly', Poat gave the only order he could. They were to grab whatever jeeps remained driveable and pull out, taking any wounded with them. Poat sent a first contingent off with the injured, as the remainder held the enemy at bay. Then, with the German troops just yards away, Poat and the remnants of the patrol turned tail to run. 'I never thought the old jeeps were so slow,' he would note; '30 miles an hour seemed a snail's pace.'

Accelerating back along the highway, the first of their own vehicles they ran into was a field ambulance. It was a stroke of good fortune. Into that they loaded Wellsted – 'wounded in both legs below the knee, but very cheerful' – Trooper Owen – 'shot through both arms' – Sergeant DuVivier – 'wounded in leg . . . drove jeep back' – and Trooper Blackhouse, also 'wounded'. With the injured offloaded, Poat turned right around again, and together with the unit's padre, he returned to the scene of the battle, to ascertain if any more of his men might be rescued. There, they discovered some '80–100 SS' gathered at the Schneeren crossroads, together with five armoured fighting vehicles, so there was nothing more they could do.

They had left behind four comrades: Glyde, killed in the initial ambush; Davies, lying injured beneath the jeep: he would die of his wounds; Ferguson, injured, who had been captured: he was almost certainly executed by the enemy under Hitler's

Commando Order; Blakeney, hit in the initial onslaught by the enemy armoured cars, was also missing, believed killed. As the SAS's report on Blakeney's death would subsequently conclude, he had been shot through the stomach and the head. In a day or two the padre of 1 SAS, J. Fraser McLuskey, would manage to retrieve the bodies of the fallen. They were buried locally after a short and sombre service.

As Wellsted – then recovering in a field hospital – was fully aware, the battle for the Schneeren crossroads had constituted his single greatest setback during the war. Four of his patrol had been killed, several more were wounded, plus four jeeps had been lost, one of which, nicknamed 'Homer', had been captured by the enemy. A reckoning was called for. This was true in more ways than even Wellsted appreciated, for in recent weeks Schneeren had become the temporary base for a section of the 12th SS Panzer Division, teenage boys as young as twelve being press-ganged into their ranks.

Headquartered at the nearby town of Neinburg, in light of the Allied advance the 12th had sent its forces into the towns and villages thereabouts, with orders to give no quarter. One unit had ended up in Schneeren, based at what was a First World War-era barracks. Outside of the barracks, together with its imposing war memorial, there was parked the hulking great form of an E-V/4 *Panzerkraftwagen* Ehrhardt, a seven-tonne armoured car of First World War vintage. It symbolised the long martial tradition of the Schneeren townland, which, with its quaint half-timbered houses and ancient churches, was also known as the 'place under a thousand oaks'.

On 12 April 1945 the SAS returned to the area and took Schneeren, en route blowing up a former SS headquarters and an ammunition dump. By then, most of the 12th SS Panzer Division had been defeated, or had melted away. But still, dozens of prisoners of war were seized, including 'marines attached to the SS' who were winkled out of the woods at gunpoint. Some attempted to sneak away in civilian clothing. One, a teenage boy, tried to attack the British troops. He was quickly taken captive. When he burst into tears as his captors loaded him aboard one of their jeeps, the SAS relented and decided to let the young boy go. But there was to be no such reprieve for something else that the town harboured.

Secreted in Schneeren the SAS discovered a huge, heavy, leatherbound tome. Embossed in thick gothic lettering on the cover were the words *CHRONIK der Gemeinde Schneeren, Kreis Neustadt a.Rhge* – 'Chronicle of the Municipality of Schneeren, District of Neustadt am Rübenberge'. On its spine were engraved four portentous symbols, which had come to epitomise so much during the long years at war: the first, the distinctive icon of Nazi Germany, an eagle with outstretched wings grasping a swastika; the second, a dagger superimposed over an oak branch; the third, a Thor's hammer coupled with an oak leaf; and lastly an Odal Rune, an ancient Anglo-Saxon symbol co-opted by the Nazis, set atop a plough tilling the dark German soil.

In 1936, the Interior Ministry of the Third Reich had issued an order that all *Gemeinden* – councils – were to maintain such a chronicle, 'in the spirt of our Führer and Chancellor'. One such tome was to be given to each district, in which to record the history of the area 'from its beginnings up to the World War'. On its massive pages were to be kept a record of the glories of the Third Reich, 'in accordance with the wishes of our Führer and Reich Chancellor, Adolf Hitler'. Each *Chronik* was to document local life, from cultural traditions and farming to large political rallies – the kind of things that welded the people together under the credo of Nazism. In time, the finest *Chroniken* from across the nation were to be amalgamated into *The Book of the Germans*, but before that gripping tome could be produced the tide of the war had turned.

Those war-bitten SAS veterans who had conquered Schneeren – this place that had cost them so dear in blood and death – decided that they would seize the town's *Chronik*. Even as the invasion of Nazi Germany was in its final, desperate stages, so much human life had been needlessly wasted. By way of payback, they would steal Schneeren's very identity, its Nazi-era heart and soul. With that in mind, the weighty leather tome – the *Chronik* of Schneeren town – was loaded aboard one of the jeeps and spirited away.

That same day, 12 April 1945, Major Poat penned a letter to Colonel Mayne, outlining their recent battles (Mayne was even then deployed on another eleventh-hour thrust into Nazi Germany). In his letter, Poat spoke of how 'the chaps have fought magnificently, and killed many S.S. and captured a large number'. A little over three weeks later VE Day was declared. The war in Europe was over. A column of battle-torn jeeps made their way towards a port in Belgium, to catch a ship bound for Britain. The spirit of victory was in the air, and the procession was striking, with 'each jeep, battle-scarred and dirty . . . flaunting its peculiar individuality'. Some were flying giant swastikas – the ultimate symbol of Nazi's Germany's demise. All were loaded with war booty, one piled so high it looked like 'an enormous mobile cat's cradle'.

In recent weeks, Mayne had commandeered a fine-looking

maroon Mercedes Benz saloon car. He'd asked his long-standing stalwart, Sergeant Bill Deakins, a Royal Engineer by trade, if he might work his magic, stencilling an SAS badge onto each wing. 'I was no sign writer, but who was I to argue,' Deakins would remark. Shortly, Mayne was also to be presented with what was to become the ultimate symbol of their march into Germany, and the resulting cost in human lives – the *Chronik* of Schneeren town. During Operation Archway, the codename for the push into Germany, all four of 1 SAS's fatalities had been suffered during the battle for Schneeren, and there were many more wounded.

One of the injured men was Alec Borrie. Even then he was recovering in hospital, his jeep having been blown up by a mine. As Borrie would relate, 'Mayne seized that book [the *Chronik*], a massive leather-bound thing. He wanted it to hold and to bind up all of the SAS's war records. It was to be the unit's diary of the years at war.' In due course the *Chronik* was eviscerated. The heavy brass studs that held it together were removed, the Nazi-era pages carefully taken out, and in their place was assembled the detailed, blow-by-blow account of the SAS at war, from inception to disbandment. Part official history, part scrapbook, it included mission reports, orders, strategy documents, maps, photos and profiles of the key figures involved, plus choice newspaper cuttings from the war years.

After the SAS's disbandment in October 1945, Lieutenant Colonel Blair Mayne would return to the family home, Mount Pleasant, a fine Georgian country house situated in the rolling, forested country outside Newtownards, in Northern Ireland. There, the former *Chronik* of Schneeren, now packed full of the most detailed and compelling records of the SAS's wartime history, would be quietly secreted away under his personal care. This clandestine record – the SAS's diary of its time at war – would have to be kept well hidden, for this was a unit that had been disowned and disavowed by many on high.

Decades later, long after the tragic early death of Mayne, in 1955, in a car accident, what had become known as the 'Paddy Mayne Diary' emerged from the shadows. The SAS had long been re-formed and brought back into the light, for the realities of modern-day warfare called for a unit such as this, and by then its future survival was beyond all doubt. The Paddy Mayne Diary was offered to the SAS Regimental Association by Mayne's younger brother, Douglas. In that way, and renamed the 'SAS War Diary', the precious founding history of this legendary unit was preserved for posterity.

And so, fittingly, the legacy had been saved and the story could be told.

Chapter Two

THE WINGED-DAGGER WARSHIP

July 1943, the Mediterranean

The chiselled prow of the tall-masted vessel cut through the seas, the waters all around her as calm and as sunlit as all had wished for. With her twin funnels emitting faint whisps of smoke, and her diesel boilers throbbing away gently below decks, the scene had all the hallmarks of a classic summer's day steaming the balmy waters of the Mediterranean. Indeed, there was almost the feeling of a cruise liner about the vessel, but certain distinctive features would give the lie to any such peaceable impressions.

First and foremost was the grey-and-white zigzag camouflage pattern painted on the ship's hull, with a view to breaking up her profile and better conceal her from any marauding U-boats or warplanes. Secondly, the pair of cannons mounted on raised pivots on the ship's prow signified a distinctly warlike intent. So too did the angular forms of the landing craft – each like a giant shoe box – lashed to the ship's sides, and cradled in davits, a crane-like device used for lowering heavy objects to the sea. But mostly what drew the eye was the utterly distinctive badge that had been affixed to the ship's bows, indicating how this former passenger ferry had been transformed into a vessel armed to the teeth and primed to wage war.

It was Sergeant William 'Bill' Deakins, the foremost explosives expert then on board, who had been ordered to fashion the first of several such striking emblems. Being a Royal Engineer by trade, it was said of Deakins that he could craft pretty much anything by hand. The task he'd been given typified that attitude. With little more than a battered New Zealand butter box as his raw materials, plus a multi-purpose knife, some colouring kit and a broken mirror with its sharp, scraping edges, Deakins had set to work, carving with infinite care a 'winged dagger, with the motto "Who Dares Wins"'. Received with great enthusiasm by the ship's captain – 'a bearded skipper who had a reputation for skill and daring' – it was a highly unusual crest to grace the prow of any Royal Navy warship, let alone those three iconic words.

Yet, of course, in July 1943 that emblem – *that motto* – was entirely fitting, for those riding in that vessel had entirely piratical, do-or-die intentions in mind. Right at this moment the stakes could not have been higher, for they were embarked upon an undertaking which, if successful, might prove to be the turning point in the entire war. Not only that, but this small force of 287 raiders were to form the very tip of the spear – being first into action, among what was then the largest amphibious invasion fleet ever assembled, one that would rival even the 'D-Day' landings in Normandy.

Conversely, if they failed in their mission, a force of some 3,200 warships carrying just shy of half-a-million men at arms might be blown out of the water, and the entire daring enterprise face calamity and ruin. In short, failure was not an option, as each and every man aboard knew, and as had been drilled into them relentlessly by their tireless and unforgiving master and commander, during the long weeks of training.

Deakin's orders to craft the ship's iconic badge had come from that self-same commander, a man who was as revered and loved and cherished by those he led, as he was at times feared. Just twenty-eight years of age, Major Robert Blair 'Paddy' Mayne had already earned a Distinguished Service Order (DSO) – awarded for outstanding service during combat – on operations in the North African desert. Striking-looking at well over six feet tall, powerfully built and seemingly fearless - a born warrior who led from the front – there were two sides to Mayne. There was the quietly spoken, almost shy-seeming Irishman, who eschewed cussing and foul language, and was rarely to be found without a book of poetry at his side. And then there was the hidden, dark side, when drink seemed to seize him and possess his very soul, and unleash the demons that lay within.

That part of Mayne was rarely seen, and never when he was on duty. The business of war-fighting and all that went with it – honing his unit to be the fittest, most intensively trained and closest-knit band of brothers of any in the Second World War – was never to be interrupted by the demon drink and the chaotic wildness and excess it could bring. For sure, Mayne had his reasons to hit the bottle: to wish to drown the memories; to bury the images of the injured, the lost and those who had fallen by the wayside – not only the bloodied forms of the dead and dying, but also those who had simply seen their nerve crack, 'crapping out' as the men called it, never to return to the field of battle. Like many, he sought to banish the images of dear friends gone for ever – those who had fallen victim to the savage vicissitudes of operating deep behind enemy lines.

But where they were heading now, steaming towards the steel shores of Nazi-held 'fortress Europe', the casualties, and the troubling memories that they triggered – the ghosts that drew ever closer – were sure to pile up.

In truth, the distinctive badge that graced the ship's prow wasn't actually a 'winged dagger', as Deakins would describe it. It was either the flaming sword of Damocles, or King Arthur's Excalibur, but even by then, the summer of 1943, its origins seemed to have attracted a growing weight of legend. For months now the exploits of this small unit – for most of its short but exalted history it had been no more than a few hundred strong – had been whispered across the trenches. Wild stories had been swopped in the bars and clubs where Allied troops tended to gather, often exaggerated in their telling, and especially as good news had been so hard to come by early in the war.

These few hundred raiders were rumoured to have destroyed more enemy warplanes on the ground at their desert airbases than the entire might of the RAF in the air over North Africa. One man – a figure of towering repute – was reported to have accounted for more than a hundred aircraft by his own hand. If true, it made him a greater 'ace' than any RAF fighter pilot in the war (it seems uncertain who holds that title, but no single RAF pilot is believed to have achieved more than sixty such kills). Both rumours were true, of course. The Special Air Service had notched up 367 confirmed 'kills' of enemy aircraft, and very likely as many as 400, Mayne himself having bagged his hundredth warplane by as early as June 1942. But that was a year ago . . . and how things had changed in the interim.

In the summer of 1942, the men of the SAS had ranged across the wide-open, dust-dry expanse of the North African desert, operating largely at will and striking targets mostly as they saw fit. Emerging from the supposedly unnavigable wastes of the Sahara, they had taken their adversaries by utter surprise, striking fear and desperation into their hearts, before melting away again just as quickly. In addition to the material losses suffered by the enemy, the impact on their morale had been incalculable. Even German general Erwin Rommel – Hitler's favourite commander for much of the war – had seen fit to acknowledge the achievements of the SAS, hailing 'the desert group which had caused us more damage than any other British unit of equal strength'.

Offering somewhat more fulsome praise, Brigadier Sir Robert 'Bob' Laycock, a driving force behind the formation of the Commandos, and in turn the SAS, would write of the unit: 'For initiative and resource, for endurance, for faultless training and fearless action which culminated so often in grievous loss to the Germans of valuable men and material, I would put them second to none. Their casualties were small because they were well-disciplined, well-trained and well-led . . . When they walked out they looked like soldiers and they were proud of it. But one never heard them brag.' Laycock's words captured the very spirit and essence of the unit – peerless elite soldiering, coupled with a discipline and humility that were the hallmarks of the force and those who commanded it. In time, the high-born and famously well-connected Laycock – himself a future honorary commander of the SAS – would write to Mayne, expressing his 'sincerest admiration and deep sense of honour' for having served alongside the man who would lead the SAS for most of the war.

Yet in February 1943 – eighteen months after the SAS's formation – it had all come crashing down. The first nail in the coffin was when the unit's founder, David Stirling, had been captured.

The second, perversely, was the defeat of the German and Italian enemy in North Africa. They were perennially unpopular with many in high command – disparaged as being 'raiders of the thug variety' by those on high – and the victory for which the SAS had so long fought was seemingly to sound their death knell. Born of the desert, these self-possessed, free-thinking warriors were to be brought to heal once the desert war was done. There was to be no place for their kind – their brand of soldiering – when marching on Nazi-occupied Europe, where combat would return to a more accepted, traditional, gentlemanly form of fighting. Such was the argument presented to Mayne and a handful of surviving fellow officers. Mayne had been forced to fight tooth and nail to win the unit even a temporary reprieve. He'd secured it via the present, July 1943 mission, arguing that his battle-hardened force was the perfect instrument by which Allied forces could bludgeon their way through Europe's defences to gain a vital foothold.

A few days earlier this massive Allied invasion fleet had set sail under the codename Operation Husky. Though few if any of the raiders knew it yet, their destination was to be Sicily, the intensively fortified island lying off the toe of the southern Italian mainland. Almost the same size as Belgium in area and with 5 million inhabitants, in recent months the island population had been swollen by some 400,000 troops. These consisted of mixed Italian infantry, plus two crack German outfits – the Panzer-Division Hermann Göring, a powerful armoured force, and the 15th Panzergrenadier Division. While the former had seen fierce action on the Eastern Front, battling Soviet forces, the latter consisted of troops withdrawn from North Africa. They had been dispatched to Sicily, to face the Allied fleet that the Axis feared was coming, with orders to hurl the invaders back into the sea.

With typical cock-pheasant bluster, Italian leader Benito Mussolini – whom Churchill had branded the 'Fascist hyena' – had vowed to make Sicily another Stalingrad, a reference to the six-month grinding siege of that Russian city. If the Allies dared set foot on Italian soil, the invaders would be resisted with a fanatical fury, Mussolini trumpeted, his troops driving them from the Italian fatherland. Though not blind to the dangers, Churchill, together with US president Franklin D. Roosevelt, had decided that the 'soft underbelly' of Europe simply had to be opened up, and that seizing Sicily was the key. Equally, the two foremost Allied leaders were painfully aware of the need to relieve the pressure on the Soviet Red Army by starting a second front in Europe.

In attempting to do so – in launching the entire Operation Husky venture – a degree of risk was inevitable. Writing in December 1942 of the 'actual spear-head of assault', Churchill pointed out that awaiting the perfect conditions to strike would 'render operations of this character utterly impossible'. Lord Louis Mountbatten, the Chief of Combined Operations – under which the SAS now sat – feared that grave dangers would bedevil any such amphibious assault force, facing 'conditions other than practically flat calm'. Landing at night in rough or storm-swept conditions would mean that vessels and men 'would simply pile up on shore, or collide, or lose their way . . .' Churchill had countered with a pithy riposte: 'The maxim "Nothing avails but perfection" may be spelt shorter "Paralysis."'

There was an added impetus to Churchill's driving sense of urgency. The 'U.S. Chiefs of Staff . . . consider that "HUSKY" should have absolute priority,' he was informed, 'and say they have "stripped themselves to the bone to provide the extra craft . . ."' Husky was such a gargantuan undertaking, it would monopolise British and American amphibious resources, rendering any 'cross-Channel operations' – Operation Overlord, the Normandy landings – impossible, at least for months to come. Even so, the American view was absolutely 'to put "HUSKY" first'. Churchill was of the same mind. In June 1943, shortly before the invasion fleet set sail for Sicily, he'd written again to Mountbatten, acknowledging that 'all your tackle has been taken away for HUSKY', but that was just the way the cards had fallen. Everything the Allies had was to be thrown against Italy's defences, and the landings simply had to prevail.

With the stakes being so inconceivably high, so much rested upon the shoulders of a few hundred brave souls – those serving at the tip of the spear. Not that any of them were quite aware of it yet. As HMS *Ulster Monarch*, the ship that carried Mayne and his men, had set sail, few knew where they were headed, or where they might make landfall. Operational security had been vice-tight, only those with an absolute need-to-know being apprised of their objectives. As Deakins, the creator of the *Ulster Monarch*'s decidedly dashing badge, noted in his diary, 'We knew we were part of an invasion force. But where?' Where would they land? Lieutenant Peter Davis, a relatively fresh recruit to Mayne's raiders, would echo such sentiments, writing in his diary of how none of them had the 'slightest idea where we were bound'. Indeed, the first few days aboard ship were spent 'guessing wildly about our immediate future'.

There had been clues, of course, and most often as a result of their exhaustive training. From their Azzib base, perched on the shores of the eastern Mediterranean, they'd engaged in repeated dry-runs, landing from assault craft and scaling the heights, to attack clifftop positions, and with various friendly forces serving as stand-in 'enemy'. Honing their seaborne assault skills had proved a particular challenge. Just about every man of Mayne's force was parachute-trained and fit for airborne operations, as well as being a dab hand at vehicle-borne missions. Landing by sea from a Royal Navy ship was an entirely different kind of war-craft. But with all that training now behind them, they were left to speculate as to just where the 'coast or island might be' – their elusive target – even as the *Ulster Monarch* steamed onwards, some 3,000 kilometres of Mediterranean lying between their port of departure and point of intended landfall.

Fortunately, with such a lengthy voyage before them, there was a great deal to like about the *Ulster Monarch*. Chiefly, the daily tot – 'we were now on a naval ship and were served the rum ration,' declared Deakins, gleefully. But equally, the com-paratively luxurious accommodation made a very welcome break from their tented camp at Azzib, their home of recent months. There was nothing about the *Monarch* that suggested 'a dirty little crossing steamer', Davis noted, and in proper Navy fashion she was 'clean and orderly, giving out an air of quiet efficiency'. The men of 'Paddy' Mayne's SAS and the crew of Lieutenant Commander Nigel Adrian Kingscote's vessel were set to spend many weeks together as shipmates. They were well-matched. As the vessel's winged dagger crest intimated, soldiers and sailors alike were keen to dare all in battle, and in the most audacious – some might argue suicidal – of ways.

Mayne had a very special bond with their adopted floating home. Laid down by Harland & Wolff, the Belfast shipbuilders, in 1929, the *Ulster Monarch* hailed from the same part of Ireland as did Mayne, who was as fiercely proud of his Ulster heritage as he was of being from the Emerald Isle. Before the war, Mayne was already a sportsman of international renown, having been capped numerous times for Ireland at rugby. In 1938, he'd been selected for the British Lions. During their tour of South Africa his standout performances had prompted even that nation's sports commentators to hail him as 'one of the greatest forwards of the world'. As if that were not enough, he'd also earned the crown of being the Irish Universities heavyweight boxing champion.

All who served with Mayne knew of his pre-war sporting prowess, and that he was a spirited Irishman to the core. For Deakins, a salt-of-the-earth Devonshire lad who'd been serving an apprenticeship with his father's building firm, their union with the *Ulster Monarch* 'could not have been a better assignation or omen'. In one sense he was right – much good fortune and glory lay at the end of the *Ulster Monarch*'s journey. But so too did untold calamity, heartache and bitter bloodshed.

In the SAS War Diary – the unit's own record of its history throughout the Second World War, delineating the 'cold, blunt facts . . . of British soldiers who preferred to fight in a technique of their own' – there is what amounts to an official photograph of Mayne. It shows him staring somewhat combatively into the camera, his lips pursed and tense - a coiled spring primed for action. Below runs the caption 'Lt. Col. R. B. Mayne DSO', while above lies the title 'DESERT RAT', a nickname harking back to his North African days. Beside it lies a photo of David Stirling – the SAS's great strategist – eyes downcast, pipe jammed pensively in his jaws. It is entitled '"Phantom" Major', the nickname the Allied and Axis press had coined for Stirling before he was captured. But by now, of course, Stirling was gone – a veritable 'phantom' – the enemy spiriting the SAS founder into a series of ever more heavily guarded prison camps, in an effort to foil his escape attempts.

Where Mayne and his men were heading would require true desert-rat-like cunning, if they were to stand a chance of winning through. Italy – Europe – offered no wide open spaces from which to strike, and into which to melt away again just as swiftly. Generally, guerrilla-style operations required two key aspects to make them feasible. The first – vast expanses of terrain devoid of humans. The second – where lands were inhabited, to be populated by those who were friendly. In Italy, neither factor applied. In Sicily, with its rural, agrarian economy, every inch of available land was cultivated, and Mayne's raiders would be operating among the population of those who were the enemy. Worryingly, they would be going in en masse, to a rigorous and exacting timescale, giving just a few hours to seize their targets.

Originally formed of small units of between four and twelve men, and designed to strike at a time and place of their own choosing, the SAS had been conceived of to maximise flexibility, opportunity and surprise. In many ways, the coming mission sinned against every founding precept of the unit. Mayne knew this. He was acutely aware that to secure their survival, he had been forced to commit to a form of warfare for which they were entirely unsuited. It was a heavy sacrifice, but an inescapable one.

As it was, the Special Air Service was much reduced. Faced with disbandment – the men slated to return to their parent units, or to be subsumed into the Commandos – Mayne and his fellows had fought desperately to salvage what they could. First, a few hundred men had been syphoned off into a separate, water-borne raiding unit, the Special Boat Squadron (SBS), under Earl George Jellicoe's command. Then, a few hundred more were spirited away to a camp in Algeria, to train under Bill Stirling, David Stirling's elder brother. As for Mayne, he had managed to retain a rump of the desert-hardened originals, in a unit officially rebranded the 'Special Raiding Squadron', though most would pay bare lip-service to that name.

As the *Ulster Monarch*'s bow-badges epitomised, Mayne's raiders cherished their founding identity, and their emblems, more now than ever. The daily record of the unit during the summer of '43 reflects this: 'WAR DIARY of Special Raiding Sqn., 1 S.A.S. Regiment.' The SAS was still very much in play. Mayne, certainly, intended for it to rise from the ashes, proving in Italy, as they had been forced to do before, that they could punch well above their weight. Those summer '43 War Diaries are stamped with the red insignia of the 'tactical investgation directorate, war office', a unit that studied individual battles with a view to future operations. If successful, the Husky landings should constitute a blueprint for how Operation Overlord would be spearheaded. In many ways this was a dry-run. If Mayne's raiders could get ashore and achieve their objectives, a similar force could win the Normandy beaches. No pressure, then.

Aware of the stakes – and that the *Ulster Monarch* was something of a pressure cooker – Captain Kingscote employed various foils, designed to lighten the spirit and the mood. In time this would earn him the nickname 'Captain Cheery', before the cold steel of his spirit would come barrelling to the fore, at which point he would be dubbed 'Captain Crash'. His vessel had a long history of war operations. Having been requisitioned in 1939 as a troopship, she had steamed for France as part of the British forces sent to stand against the Nazi onslaught. Further duties as far distant as Iceland and West Africa had followed, at one stage the ship suffering engine failure in ferocious seas. She'd weathered that storm and gone on to serve on Operation Torch, in November 1942, landing American Rangers – a unit modelled upon the British Commandos – in Algeria, so enabling the British and American-led forces to trap Rommel's Afrika Korps in a pincer movement, securing victory in North Africa.

To underline the impression that the *Ulster Monarch*'s voyage was something of a pleasure cruise – for now, at least – the ship's captain ensured that music was piped continuously through the Tannoy system. If a certain individual was wanted on the bridge, rather than his name being called, a song was broadcast which typified his character, with distinctly teasing undertones. A man who had failed to complete his parachute course prior to departure was heralded with the song 'If Only I Had Wings', the 1940s hit that had become the RAF's de facto anthem. There were plans to broadcast the 1941 jazz tune 'Someone's Rocking My Dreamboat' on behalf of the captain, if and when the *Ulster Monarch* came under attack from enemy aircraft.

Even the dress and dash of Mayne's raiders had a distinctly jaunty, Mediterranean air about it. His men 'looked dammed smart', Mayne would write home to his elder sister, Barbara, with whom he'd keep up a regular correspondence for much of the war. Sporting 'blue shirts with our parachute wings on the left breast', their navy flannel tops had a distinct touch of Italian style, as future events were to prove. With rubber-soled commando boots, white socks, khaki drill trousers and their signature sandy-coloured 'winged dagger' berets, they stood out from the mass of the British Army. Card games flourished aboard Captain Kingscote's ship – gin rummy being the favourite – with the stakes being a penny a point. By the time they were a week at sea, Mayne's raiders had added another catchphrase to their more famous motto, this one being 'Train hard, rest easy'.

Even the expected scare of passing the German-held island of Crete failed to come to much. It was bristling with enemy garrisons, and dotted here and there with Luftwaffe airbases, so anxious eyes scanned the skies above Crete for that 'first German reconnaissance plane', related Lieutenant Derrick Harrison, another of Mayne's newer recruits. But not a single aircraft hove into view, the lead vessels of that massive armada steaming ever onwards. In truth, across the length and breadth of Crete, Earl Jellicoe's SBS had been at work, blowing apart enemy airbases and keeping the Luftwaffe firmly on the ground. The success of those daring operations could be gauged by the fact that the entire Husky armada would slip past under the 'very noses of the Germans'.

But shortly, the 'dark cloud of impending action' seemed to lurch suddenly closer. A booklet was circulated bearing the catchy title *The Soldier's Guide to Sicily*. A quick browse revealed all. 'We are about to engage in the second phase of the operations which began with the invasion of North Africa,' announced General Dwight D. Eisenhower, the Supreme Allied Commander for Europe and the Mediterranean. 'We have defeated the enemy's forces [in North Africa] . . . However this is NOT enough . . . and as this book falls into your hands we are about to pursue the invasion and occupation of enemy territory . . . as such we must expect extremely difficult fighting.'

Page two got down to brass tacks. Their target – Sicily - was revealed, with its 'dozen-odd aerodromes', and hosting 'Air Marshal Kesselring's HQ . . . who invented the word "Coventrize" after his too successful raid on that place . . .' It was a timely and deliberate reminder. On 14 November 1940 the Luftwaffe had launched the first mass fire-bombing of the war over Coventry, destroying 4,300 homes and killing and wounding 1,800 of its citizens. Hailing their so-called success, Nazi Germany coined the term '*Koventrieren*' – to totally annihilate a city. Seizing Sicily would put Allied bombers within '2 hours range of Rome', the booklet continued, 'the nearest we have ever been'. Vengeance would be within the Allies' reach. On the far side of Sicily only 'two miles of water' separated it from 'Italy itself', which would then lie well within the Allies' grasp.

By 8 July briefings were in full swing, as maps, aerial reconnaissance photos, orders and passwords were produced. A call went out over the ship's speakers – no teasing jazz tune this time – 'All officers report to the briefing room.' There, Mayne oversaw an intensive and detailed series of planning sessions, as he sought to hone every last detail. A large-scale model of the target, rendered in minute detail, was studied. Meticulous, exacting and precise, Mayne went over the minutiae of the where, when, how, what and why of the coming assault repeatedly, until no man, no matter his rank, had the slightest doubt as to his individual role. The plan was so well briefed, it could be executed without any need for orders on the ground, so maximising silence, stealth and surprise.

A complex, multifaceted character, Mayne was possessed of the seemingly contradictory qualities of being able to operate completely on the fly, striking by opportunity and instinct alone, as they had in North Africa, or the exact opposite, as of now, striving to plan, rehearse and gameplay every minute detail. For the SAS, never had the stakes been higher. Success or failure at an Axis airfield deep in the Sahara desert had helped determine the course of the conflict in North Africa. Here it might determine the fortunes of the war, deciding the fate of millions of Allied and Axis souls.

With his mission orders in hand, Mayne revealed to his officers – newbies Davis and Harrison among them, but including long-standing stalwarts Major Bill 'Skin' Fraser, Captain Robert 'Bob' Melot, Lieutenant John 'Johnny' Wiseman, and more – exactly what lay before them. 'The task of your Squadron is to destroy the Coast Defence Battery at 183239,' read the orders, giving the map coordinates of the target. The raiders were to put ashore under cover of darkness 'on the southern coast of Capo Murro di Porco', a tongue of land lying on the south-eastern tip of Sicily. A bare, rocky bastion, with towering cliffs plunging into the sea, the name translates fittingly as the 'Cape of the Pig's Snout', for in profile that was exactly what the promontory looked like, and as the air recce photos clearly showed.

Winning the confidence of higher command, Mayne had secured huge leeway for the coming mission. 'The method to be adopted is left to your discretion,' the orders continued; it was up to him and his men as to how exactly the objective should be seized and destroyed. The key priority was to get his men back 'on board the *Ulster Monarch* as soon as possible . . . for further seaborne operations'. While busy on Capo Murro di Porco, Mayne and his raiders also needed to remain utterly vigilant, for any surviving gun positions could still blast the Allied invasion fleet out of the water. If he or his men made 'contact with other hostile Batteries or defended localities you will, if the task in your judgement is within the power of your Sqdn, destroy them'.

Until 'H Hour', the moment to launch the assault, strict radio silence was to be maintained, in an effort to hide their presence from the enemy. Once the mission was under way, a set of code-words were to be used to alert headquarters to their fortunes. 'Deduction one' would signal 'Task complete'. The coastal battery had been destroyed. 'Loudwater' would signify that Mayne and his men were heading back to the *Ulster Monarch*, while 'Judas' would indicate they were advancing on foot, to link up with the main body of Allied troops that would even then be surging ashore.

With a large map pinned to the briefing room wall, they studied the enemy positions, comparing them to the air-recce photos. These were incredibly detailed, and even individual bushes and trees were visible. But the single most striking feature was how bare the terrain looked; that, and the fact that the headland was criss-crossed with a latticework of drystone walls. The entire expanse was a chequerboard of walled-in fields, only the sea cliffs being free from any such obstructions. One crucial factor was deduced from the careful study of those photos. Apart from the 'barbed-wire entanglements' that lay in their way, the path to the guns looked to be free of minefields. A horse could be seen grazing in and around the very terrain that Mayne and his men would have to cross. If there were mines, the horse would have been blown to pieces; ergo, it had to be free of those deadly encumbrances.

Another detail was far less easy to fathom, causing real trouble and debate. They'd been briefed that Sicily was the most heavily fortified island in the entire Mediterranean, and this feature was interpreted as some form of military structure. But of what kind no one could be certain. Someone noticed the figure of a man beside it. With an Allied reconnaissance aircraft buzzing over-head, it stood to reason that he would be taking cover from what he feared was a hostile warplane. If he was running towards the unknown feature, it had to be a bunker or air-raid shelter. If he was running away from it, it must be a bomb or fuel dump. The trouble was, no one could decide in which direction the figure was headed. The debate remained unresolved, and in due course the mystery feature would prove to be nothing more than 'an innocent haystack!'

To his immense relief, Bill Deakins – Royal Engineer by trade, and Mayne's explosives expert – was passed an actual photo of the guns themselves. Perched atop the bare cliffs, the batteries menaced the sea to all sides, while remaining ensconced within a steel and concrete sarcophagus, rendering them immune to attack from the air. The RAF had tried to bomb them, with little effect. The cape was a 'veritable fortress', equipped with machinegun nests, searchlights, range-finders to vector the big guns onto targets, and with the defenders outnumbering the raiders 'by 50 to one'. Apprised of their objective – *apprised of the odds* – there was little doubt that the *Ulster Monarch*'s pleasure cruise was over.

Deakins studied the photo he'd been given: it showed three massive guns, the barrels of each of which were as wide as a man's torso, and many times a standing man's height in length. At least now he 'had a guide to an approach on setting charges'. Deakins led two other Royal Engineers – Roy Chappel and Jock Bowman – making up a team of sappers, or combat engineers. Each would carry three explosive charges, so a total of nine in all. That way, if only one of them made it to the guns, that man should still be able to blow them sky high. For that was the mission objective, of course. It wasn't enough simply to capture the guns. A fierce counter-attack was expected, and if the enemy retook those batteries they could turn them on the invasion fleet, blasting apart ships crammed with soldiers before they had a chance of getting ashore.

The target was doubly important, for the guns covered neighbouring Syracuse and its all-important harbour. A crucible-like feature, the narrow entranceway was guarded by the Pig's Snout headland on the one side, and an equally dramatic promontory on the other, on the tip of which perched the Castello Maniace, a massive-walled Byzantine fortress dating back to the thirteenth century. Only four ports on Sicily could accommodate an invasion fleet of the size and potency of Husky: Messina, Catania, Palermo and Syracuse. It was the last that the Allies had decided to wrestle from enemy hands. For Husky to succeed, Syracuse needed to fall to the invaders within the first twenty-four hours. That harbour was to be the artery via which the supplies required by an invading army were to flow, but only if the spearhead were got safely to shore.

Aware now of their mission and the awe-inspiring stakes involved, so much fell into place. First and foremost the long months of training just passed, which were of an intensity that few had ever thought possible. Secondly, the brutal attrition rates: so many had been RTU'd – returned to their parent unit – for being found wanting. As several brief entries, scribbled in pencil in the SAS War Diary, recorded: 'Nothing to note. 2 ORs [other ranks] returned to unit for disciplinary reasons.' *Nothing to note.* Over the spring and early summer of 1943, being RTU'd – the single greatest threat to any man who sought to join this exalted force – had become a routine occurrence. In this Mayne showed little mercy. Even as late as 2 July 1943, with his men aboard the *Ulster Monarch* and poised to depart, another entry had been made: '1 Sgt sent ashore under escort to be placed in close arrest and subsequent RTU, for disciplinary reasons.'

By now, the attitude and demeanour of their commanding

officer was starting to make sense. During the long months of training, Mayne had seemed possessed by a maniacal and unforgiving zeal. It was all because *he had known*. He had known exactly what was coming; what he'd volunteered his unit for; what was at stake. He'd been gripped by a determination to ensure that his few hundred raiders had every possible chance of success, of winning through. And for that they would need to be the toughest, hardest, most skilled and fittest soldiers ever to head to war. Even so, nagging doubts remained. Had they really done enough? Had the drills and the instruction and the dress rehearsals and the laser focus on fitness, fitness, fitness been sufficient for what was coming?

Only time would tell.

Chapter Three

THE RED QUEEN

At their remote hilltop training camp of Azzib – perched on what was then the Palestine side of the Syrian border (today's Israel) – the day had begun with a highly unusual form of reveille. The unmistakable tones of 'Bugle Call Rag' (a 1920s jazz tune popularised by the likes of Duke Ellington, Glenn Miller and the Chocolate Dandies) rang out across the tented camp. Fast, energising, jarring, it was perfect for a New Orleans dance club, but not exactly typical for a British military camp. Yet in its leftfield, maverick, irreverent sort of way this was vintage Mayne.

As Sergeant Bob Bennett, one of Mayne's stalwarts, would remark of the SAS commander, he 'had this twist about him'. He had a reverse-logic way of seeing the world, being able to think the unthinkable. Why not greet the dawn with 'Bugle Call Rag'? Why not let that set the tone for the coming day? To some this made Mayne unpredictable; to others it was unsettling; but to those with an open mind it was inspirational. And to those who truly understood – *who got it* – this was the founding essence of the SAS. The *raison d'être* of the unit was not only to think unconventionally, but to put that into practice; to hit the enemy in a way and at a time and a place that was utterly unexpected, so maximising the crucial elements of shock and surprise.

Though few of Mayne's men could understand it at the time, at Azzib he'd insisted they go back to the very basics – simple weapon drills, marksmanship skills and focusing on the raw building blocks of physical fitness and stamina. Once they'd mastered those essential foundations, they'd gone on to practise with all arms used by the enemy. Where they were heading, there would be no jeeps or trucks to help carry heavy loads, so they would have to fight and survive solely with what they could manage on their person. They would need to be ready to grab whatever weapons and ammo might come to hand – most likely that of the enemy.

Embracing that mentality, Bob Bennett would be sporting a German '9mm Schmeisser' – more accurately the MP 40 sub-machine gun. It was one that he'd made sure to salvage from a derelict armoured car back in the desert. As an old hand like Bennett well appreciated, 'Tommy guns were no use on this kind of show, because the ammo was so heavy – you couldn't carry enough.' Lieutenant Harrison concurred. 'There were few German or Italian weapons we had not learned to fire. In any prolonged action behind enemy lines, when ammunition might run low, we could always rely on captured enemy weapons to help us carry on the fight.' Mayne even had them train in handling mules and horses, in the hope that they could co-opt some of the pack animals of the enemy.

From that they'd graduated onto punishing cliff-climbs, time and again being forced to scale the dry, rough, friable rock that rose above the nearby shoreline. They did so in the furnace heat of the day, and during the dead pitch of the formless night. They did so laden with weaponry, grenades and crushing loads of kit. They did so with ropes and then free-climbing, which meant they had no safety gear at all. At every juncture Mayne was at their backs, driving them onwards, urging them to ever greater efforts. Cajoling and berating them at every turn, he proved tireless, remorseless and unforgiving, as he challenged them to equal his own indefatigable form.

In keeping with David Stirling's founding ethos, officers and men were subjected to exactly the same rigours and strictures. There was good reason for this. If only one individual made it through to the target, that man had to feel confident enough to go ahead and complete the mission, regardless of his rank. It also fostered the egalitarian spirit such a unit thrived on, one based upon 'mutual respect and real friendship'. This was the essential alchemy of the SAS, welding together the seeming opposites of individualism and teamwork into an unbreakable whole.

Indeed, that concept of 'friendship' – fraternity – underpinned everything. In this unit there would be no blind discipline or following of orders. There were no sheep here. Instead, men were compelled to act due to the deep bonds of brotherhood they had forged, no matter the danger or the odds. No officer got an easy ride. There was no hiding behind rank. To lead in such a way, an officer had to know his men intimately. He had to spend time studying and fathoming each individual character, for status alone would not cut it. But if that special kind of bond could be forged, anything was possible.

Those first few weeks of merciless training were building up to Mayne's ultimate test – a challenge to his men to prove they were the best of the best; the forty-five-mile forced march under a blistering sun. The route would take them from the shores of

Lake Tiberias – the biblical Sea of Galilee; the lowest expanse of freshwater on earth – west towards the coast, crossing a range of jagged, towering peaks. It was to culminate in an attack on an ancient mud-walled fortress occupied by an 'enemy' garrison who were forewarned and forearmed, not to mention well-fed and rested.

Mayne had split his force into three troops, plus an HQ squadron, and the march was to be completed with competition to the fore. Although they would have staggered departures, Nos 1, 2 and 3 Troops would be competing against each other to finish in the shortest time possible. No. 3 Troop went first. They attempted a non-stop dash in the heat of the day; barely a handful made it, for they were 'passing out like flies' under the burning heat of that summer sun. No. 1 Troop, commanded by Bill Fraser, did far better, most making it to the camp still on their feet, but they'd taken a wrong turn and were seriously overdue. No. 2 Troop set out last, hoping to have learned from the others' mistakes.

A convoy of trucks dropped them at the lakeside. At 600 feet below sea level, not a breath of wind stirred. From that furnace-like crucible the snake of heavily laden men began to climb. They were instantly soaked in sweat, which ran into their eyes, half-blinding them. Each ridge proved a false dawn, as yet another hidden crest rose above it, forming a series of seemingly endless steps. Finally, they topped the high point under a scorching midday sun. A valley dropped away below them, with a stream snaking through its depths. Parched with thirst, they longed to drink, but orders had been given that no one was allowed to do so without the troop commander's consent.

That man, Captain Harry Wall Poat, was the comparative

old man of the unit, being all of twenty-nine years of age. A former tomato farmer from Guernsey, Poat's entry in the SAS War Diary trumpeted of his studies before the war – 'Failed, Reading University!' With his cut-glass accent and neatly clipped moustache, Poat was somewhat eccentric, but brave as a lion. In North Africa, he had been forced to grow an 'attractive Santa Claus beard', but mostly he prided himself on maintaining an immaculate appearance, even after weeks on operations. Poat was a veteran of Mayne's A Squadron and their months spent raiding Rommel's supply lines. Superficially, Mayne and Poat seemed to have little in common. Yet in truth, they were so very much alike. They shared an uncanny ability to remain preternaturally calm and laser-focused, even as combat raged all around them. Already inseparable, they would go on to forge one of the longest-lived and most enduring elite forces partnerships of the war.

Poat allowed his men to dip their hats and neckerchiefs into the river, to help cool scorching heads. Even so, as they descended into the knife-cut valley below, men began to drop. Nine went down, then three at once, before Poat finally called a halt. Scrambling for the nearest scrap of shade 'like animals', figures wormed their way into patches of bush or crawled beneath rocky overhangs. Lieutenant Peter Davis was on Poat's march. A student of modern languages at Peterhouse College, Cambridge, prior to the war, Davis chronicled this long march in fine detail in his diary. He wrote of dozing fitfully, 'until the shadows lengthened and the noises of the day grew quiet'. As the evening cool drew in, they took to their feet again and recommenced the march.

Though an eighteen-month veteran of soldiering in the Middle East, Davis had yet to see any action. Frustrated, chafing at the bit, he assumed he'd just been unlucky. Indeed, his entire military career had seemed dogged by misfortune. Born in Calcutta, India, in 1921, he'd signed up in June 1940, a baby-faced recruit with high hopes of 'daring and glory'. But as an officer trainee he'd found himself mired within the 'snobbery and ignorance' that seemed to pervade the officer's mess, and which 'sapped the spirits of the men'. Deeply disillusioned, he'd been spurred to volunteer for the SAS. There, he'd found his true home – 'a small body of men under young and intelligent officers who abhorred routine and spit and polish', and who coexisted in 'harmony and mutual respect'. The youngest officer then serving with the SAS, Davis had yet to fire a shot in anger. He thirsted to do so; to be tested to the full.

Poat's troop marched long into the evening, winding their way down from the heights into the coastal lowlands. There Poat called a halt for the evening meal. Bob Melot, the unit's intelligence officer, had been developing the kind of rations a force such as this, moving on foot, might require. Consisting of oatmeal, bacon, lentils, plus tea, sugar and dried milk, it was highly nutritious while weighing next to nothing. Most of it could be eaten raw. A Belgian First World War veteran and a highly decorated fighter pilot, Melot was at the opposite end of the scale from Davis, being the oldest officer by far in the unit. All of forty-eight years of age, he had been turned down by various nations' militaries for being 'too old', before being scooped up by the Inter-Services Liaison Bureau (ISLD), the cover name for the Secret Intelligence Service in North Africa.

A fluent Arabic speaker, Melot had embarked upon a series of daredevil missions with the ISLD. Those had earned him a Military Cross for 'sorties behind enemy lines', showing 'complete disregard for his own personal safety'. In time, he'd jumped ship, swopping his Arab Bedouin robes – his usual guise when executing espionage missions – for the beige beret and insignia of the SAS. Well-read, fearless and generous-spirited, Melot had struck up the closest of friendships with Mayne. At one stage, during the SAS's ill-fated September 1942 raid on Benghazi, Melot was very nearly given up for dead, so serious were his injuries. He had refused to be left behind. Evacuated to a Cairo hospital, he had discharged himself into his wife's care, and was shortly back on active duty. Unbreakable, indefatigable, he was one of those seemingly legendary figures that Davis could hardly believe truly existed. Yet now, here he was, training alongside them for a mission that might change the course of the war.

Poat's men gathered in twos and threes around the cooking fires to brew up their oat porridge. 'As the darkness deepened, nothing could be seen but these orange glows, with eerie shadows bending over them,' noted Davis. All too soon, they were off again, the narrow valley emptying onto a metalled road. Following Poat's lead, they formed up three abreast, footfalls ringing out as they marched. Spirits soared as they allowed themselves to believe that it was all downhill from here. Eventually, they rounded a bend, only to spy an apparently impossible climb stretching far ahead. The road snaked ever upwards, a twisted hairpin of silver in the 'moon-softened darkness'. Spirits plummeted. The pace slowed. The chat and banter fell away to nothing.

It was then that Corporal William 'Bill' McNinch, one of Davis's men, began to strike up the soft, lyrical tones of a song. McNinch – known as 'Mac' or 'Willie' to all – was worshipped by the younger, more junior ranks. A thirty-one-year-old Glaswegian who'd worked for a wine and spirits merchants before the war,

McNinch shared a common pedigree with the SAS old hands. As with Mayne, Bill Fraser, and any number of other originals, McNinch had volunteered for No. 11 (Scottish) Commando, back in the summer of 1940. He was a veteran of Operation Exporter, the June 1941 Litani River landings, during which Mayne and Fraser had had their bloody baptism of fire. Towards the end of that immensely costly operation, McNinch had been captured by the enemy, as he and a handful of men had tried to make it back to friendly lines.

Overnight, as their Vichy French adversaries stared defeat in the face, McNinch and his fellows had been released. Among them was Lieutenant Eoin McGonigal, a southern Irish Catholic and Mayne's closest friend from well before the outbreak of the war. Having volunteered for 11 Commando together, the two Irishmen had gone on to do the same with the SAS. Sadly, McGonigal – an officer of daring and huge promise – had gone missing on Operation Squatter, the SAS's very first, and calamitous, mission. Ever since then Mayne had been trying to deal with that loss, while searching for the truth about what had happened to his friend. Intensely loyal, he'd travelled alone into the desert in search of clues to McGonigal's fate. If nothing else he'd sought closure, plus a chance to let his friend's mother know exactly what had happened to her son.

Though they had suffered heavy casualties during the Litani River landings, and subsequently on Operation Squatter, McNinch seemed able to rise above such dark misfortunes. A real joker, he was 'always the man in an emergency', as he was set to prove during that long climb, as Poat's troop scaled the last of those brutal, tortuous hills. With McNinch taking up a popular marching song, one by one the others joined in, until the entire troop was giving voice 'from then until dawn. It was a remarkable performance,' observed Davis, as the singing buoyed their spirits and enabled them to eat up the miles.

Come first light, they mustered to assault the 'enemy' position – an old ruined fortress. As matters transpired, they would face little resistance. The 'enemy guard force' had never dreamed that Poat's troop could reach the place so quickly, and had yet to put in an appearance. It was seized without so much as a shot being fired. Ten miles remained to cover. Much of the route followed a narrow, swift-flowing stream, which over the eons had carved out a deep gorge. The easiest path was to follow the river bed itself. It proved a 'blessed relief', as men cooled 'burning feet in the ice-cold water'. But that soon turned to agony, for walking in the water had softened their feet, which broke out into a rash of blisters.

Emerging from that gorge, three miles of an open plain separated the marchers from their camp. But this was 'infinitely the worst'. Every step on blistered feet was agony, as the sun beat down from a sky that hurt the eyes. They 'plodded on in a sullen, tortured silence', barely able to keep the 'tears of exhaustion' from their eyes. Strung out, limping badly, plagued by fatigue, all felt as if they were done for. It was then that Poat seized the moment, passing word back down the line, demanding a 'final, supreme effort'. Now was the time to show the rest what Mayne's warriors were made of. They reached the road leading into camp, formed up three abreast and strode ahead. In 'remarkable fashion everyone's limp had disappeared and the troop must have been an impressive sight,' noted Davis.

They had every reason to celebrate: they had competed the forty-five miles under such punishing conditions in just over twenty-six hours. But for Mayne, this was only the beginning – 'a foretaste of the seriousness of our training and the strenuous days that were to follow'. Further marches ensued, and as Poat's troop had set the benchmark, so all were to be completed within a twenty-four-hour time limit. Increasingly, they were to be executed at night, so as to give them a confidence of movement during the hours of darkness that had been 'bred out of us by civilisation'. In this way Mayne taught his men to feel at home in night, as the coming mission would of course demand.

Some felt that Mayne was overtraining his men; that the regime he had imposed was too severe. John 'Jack' Sillito was himself no stranger to such extreme trials of endurance. In October 1942, while serving in Mayne's A Squadron, he had managed the seemingly impossible feat of completing a 180-mile solo escape across the Sahara, on foot. During one of Mayne's Azzib training marches, Sillito, now a sergeant, was ordered to pull his men to a halt. Sillito understood that Mayne sought to build the toughest unit in the entire British military, in the spirit of the Spartans. But when one individual in Sillito's patrol made the mistake of moving, Mayne was onto that man 'like a ton of bricks'. That struck Sillito as being 'a bit unfair', but this was the level of discipline Mayne demanded, come what may.

Lieutenant Derrick Harrison complained that Mayne was working them 'into the ground'. Harrison, a recent officer recruit, had formed the advance party sent out to establish the Azzib camp, little realising what trials and tribulations it would play host to. Harrison, who'd studied journalism at a London university prior to the war, had enlisted in October 1939, joining the Cheshire regiment, but he'd found himself stuck for months in a training depot in Egypt. Hungering for more, he'd volunteered for the SAS. Not long after doing so, he was warned by Mayne that the SAS was being disbanded. A rump – the SRS – was being kept on. Being a newbie, Harrison felt he stood little chance of being retained. He was 'shocked' when Mayne revealed that he intended to keep him. In time the faith Mayne put in Harrison – 'Very quiet, and soft-spoken, but hard as nails and a leader by nature' – would be repaid many times over.

Harrison had always felt himself to be different, and he had good reason. Abandoned in early life by his opera-singer mother, and with a largely absent father, Harrison had been brought up by his 'Auntie Kathleen' as best she could. That lack of parental love had forged a fiercely independent outlook and mindset. Harrison was noted for his open views, his sympathy for the underdog, and his leftfield kind of approach. Such traits would have been at odds with much of the military, but not in the SAS under Mayne. Within their ranks and fighting the good fight, Harrison would spend his happiest years under Mayne's command.

During another training session, Mayne became incensed about the foul language being used. He called a halt, before unleashing his own extremely colourful string of expletives. 'You see, I know just as many as you do,' he warned his men, 'and even some you may possibly never have heard of.' He understood that men did swear when under extreme pressure, or if pushed to the limits, but if it reached the stage where it threatened the unit's morale and their *esprit de corps*, he would stamp it out mercilessly.

Unsurprisingly, downtime was rare at Azzib, and truly to be cherished. Whenever it was offered, the men had to seize the moment. Mayne's squadron had been allocated a padre to administer to the spiritual needs of the flock. Captain Robert Lunt was comparatively new to the SAS, but to him Sunday mornings meant one thing – church service. The men were formed up in ranks, as the squadron sergeant major called out the first orders of the day: 'One step forward march all Jews and Muslims.' There was nothing prejudicial about such an order. The SAS was a broad church – always had been – and non-Christians were being given the chance to skip Sunday service. To a man all took that one step forward. To their minds, there were far better things to do than spend Sunday in church, especially after the kind of punishment they'd been taking.

The nearest watering holes were a lengthy drive away, their favourite being a cabaret bar known as 'Queen's'. The chief attraction was the beer – which the men quaffed with abandon – and the 'girl crooner' on stage, who happened to be a Belgian. Their shared nationality being an instant bond, she and Bob Melot became inseparable. One day, one of the troopers – SAS-speak for privates – Ken Sturmey, imbibed too much for his own good. Becoming aggressive and belligerent, he turned his ire upon a stuffy-looking cavalry major. Sporting a string of medal ribbons, including that of the Military Cross, the major also had an odd-looking set of parachute wings affixed to one arm. To Sturmey, it didn't add up, and he figured the major was an impostor.

Marching over to his table, Sturmey told him as much, at which stage 'the fat was in the fire with a vengeance'. The Military Police were called, and Sturmey was carted off to the cells. That left Davis, Melot and a third officer, Lieutenant Alexander 'Sandy' Wilson, to try to calm decidedly stormy waters. Wilson, an extremely tall, shy-seeming and apparently ham-fisted fellow, had the largest pair of feet that just about anyone had ever seen. He was forever walking into the officer's mess and knocking over someone's drink, if not an entire table. His clumsiness earned him the catchphrase 'Oh, Sandy!', uttered whenever he stepped into a room. Quiet, apologetic and polite to a fault, Wilson did his best to mollify the irate cavalry officer. Even as he went about doing so, few could imagine the heart of a lion that lurked within.

The following morning, no one could quite believe that Ken Sturmey was present and correct at camp reveille. All had presumed he was locked away facing a court-martial. It turned out that Sturmey had refused to go quietly, demanding the MPs investigate his allegations. They did a quick check on the 'major's' credentials, discovering that the man had indeed inflated his rank. Worse still, he had no right to wear either the MC ribbon or the parachute wings, for he had been awarded no such honours. Such cases of 'stolen valour' rankled with the old hands, for they had earned their wings and their decorations the hard way, at the rough and bloody end of war. It was doubly galling, for they knew that soon they would be heading into the cauldron of combat once more.

The proximity of action was underlined most powerfully when the top brass paid a visit. It was mid-May 1943 when General Miles Dempsey, CB, DSO, MC, turned up at Azzib. Hurriedly, the men were herded to the camp cinema to hear his address. Few had the slightest clue who he was or why he was there, until the general began to speak. They were being placed under his personal command, Dempsey explained, for an undisclosed operation at an undisclosed location. What he was able to tell them was this: they were to land in the first wave of a seaborne assault, and storm and capture a very strongly held clifftop position. Dempsey made it absolutely clear that they would be spearheading the 'invasion of Europe' and if they failed in their mission, the entire Allied fleet 'would be subjected to intense shell fire'.

Oddly, Dempsey seemed to be addressing the men as if they were untested in battle, not the combat-hardened veterans that so many were. Realising this, Mayne stepped in. Taking Dempsey momentarily to one side, the tall Irishman had a quiet word. Dempsey returned to the podium and made his fulsome apologies. He had been led to believe they were raw recruits. Now he understood fully that many were SAS veterans who had been fighting hard for years. From there, the men headed out to show Dempsey exactly what they were capable of. After beach and cliff-climb demos, there followed a live-fire exercise, as figures wormed on their stomachs across the sand and shinned up ropes, 'machinegun bullets zipping a few inches above them'. They were most impressed when they realised that Dempsey had insisted on crawling and weaving his way through the fire right alongside them.

The general appeared struck by one individual in particular, a decidedly diminutive figure. He asked if he might have a private word. Trooper Sydney Davison was called over. Due to his pint-size stature and apparent youth, he'd earned the obvious nickname – 'Titch'. Hailing from Bradford, in Yorkshire, Davison had already lost his two older brothers to the war, both having been killed in action. Consequently, he had every reason to hunger to fight. Upon volunteering for the SAS, he'd been interviewed by Sergeant Albert Reginald 'Reg' Seekings, one of the unit's originals and a self-confessed 'rough, tough so-and-so', who'd been a champion Army boxer at the start of the war.

Seekings reckoned Davison was no more than fourteen or fifteen, which was a tad young even for an outfit that boasted a number of teenage recruits. He'd told Davison as much. They were all about killing in this outfit, Seekings had explained, and he doubted that Davison was a good fit. By way of answer, Davison had pulled a crumpled note from his pocket. It was a recent letter, informing him that his second brother, Herbert, had just been killed, his other brother having died just a few months earlier. Seekings wasn't about to argue with that. In recent days, Titch Davison had been made one of the Bren gunners in Seeking's platoon – the Bren light machinegun being the single most potent piece of firepower that a foot-borne force such as this could muster. Despite the weapon's size and weight, Titch had risen royally to the challenge.

Davison stood before the tall figure of General Dempsey and came to attention. 'How old are you?' Dempsey inquired.

'Twenty-one, sir,' Davison replied, smartly.

'No, no, no,' Dempsey countered. 'Your real age.'

'Twenty-one, sir,' Davison repeated, a little more sharply.

'No, no, no, I'm not going to do anything to you,' Dempsey persisted. 'Just out of curiosity I want to know your real age.'

'Twenty-one, sir,' Davison retorted, 'and if you don't fucking like it you can fucking stuff it.'

There was a moment's awkward silence, before Dempsey started laughing. To all within earshot he remarked: 'This is a bad thing to say, but I wish we had two to three divisions like him.'

Though none had imagined it possible, after Dempsey's visit the pace of training was redoubled. Finally, there was a last wild party, predicated on the adage 'let us eat, drink and be merry, for tomorrow we may die', as Davis noted. Every drop of alcohol in the immediate vicinity was drained dry, and any number of borrowed jeeps ended up in ditches. From there, and with massive hangovers, the men decamped, moving south to Suez, where they boarded the *Ulster Monarch*. To many, the long months of unrelenting training hadn't made much sense at the time. It would only begin to do so once the *Ulster Monarch* set sail for the shores of Sicily, and the nature of Operation Husky, and their role within it, was revealed.

Prior to that there were two further pointers. They executed a series of full-scale mock rehearsals from the *Ulster Monarch*, using the ship's landing craft to assault a clifftop stronghold. Treated exactly as if it were the real thing, each exercise was executed in the dead of night in a tense and febrile silence. During one such dry-run Mayne had seemed unusually on edge, driving them harder than ever. Leaping ashore from the landing craft, Davis noticed a group of shadowy figures 'watching us intently'. Though he didn't know it at the time, this included Field Marshal Henry 'Jumbo' Wilson, the General Officer Commanding (GOC) Middle East. Wilson, a veteran of the First World War – the Somme and Passchendaele – was a highly respected commander, a favourite of Churchill's, and he was there to ascertain if the spearhead of Husky really was up to the task. Mayne was there to ensure that there could be no possible argument made otherwise.

Without a word being spoken, the raiders scaled the dark rocks before them and crept towards their objective. There a contingent of Allied troops – the 'enemy garrison' – were ready and waiting. But with his men moving too slowly for his liking, and with Jumbo Wilson watching, Mayne let it be known that he was 'on the warpath . . . Lashed by his fury,' the raiders stormed in to attack. Fearing more 'the "enemy" behind us than in front,' as

Davis recalled, the target was seized amid a deafening cacophony of blanks firing, Very lights – flare rounds – exploding, and general yells and confusion. They were on top of the defenders almost before they knew what had hit them, after which both Mayne and Jumbo Wilson declared themselves suitably impressed.

Back aboard the *Ulster Monarch*, General Bernard Montgomery, commander of the British Eighth Army, paid a visit. Having witnessed the lightning exploits of the SAS in North Africa – in latter months they had been under his command – 'Monty' was soon in full flood, giving an address to the men from one of the ship's gantries. Promising that they would soon get the chance of 'chasing the Hun still further', he confessed that without the SAS at work deep behind the lines, victory in North Africa may have hung in the balance. A lot of those listening figured that was bullshit. It was just one more example of the kind of hyperbole that Monty liked to deliver to whatever unit he was visiting.

Such an impression was underlined by the passwords that Monty announced, which were to be used for the coming Husky assault. The challenge to be yelled out was: 'Desert Rats?' The answer: 'Kill the Italians!' It was just the kind of theatricality of which Monty was so fond. Initially, relations between the SAS and the British general had been spiky, at best. Monty had declared of David Stirling, 'The boy Stirling is mad. Quite, quite mad,' although he had conceded that 'in war there is often a place for mad people!'

In keeping with their fractious relations, a decision had been taken to hold back the customary applause that Monty was used to receiving. Accordingly, when he finished his rousing speech, he was greeted by ranks of silent, stony faces. He appeared distinctly nonplussed. Not knowing quite what to do, he left the ship for his motor launch, backing down the companionway while muttering: 'Wonderful discipline. Wonderful discipline. Very smart! I like their hats.' But once he was aboard his launch and it began to motor away, a rousing chorus of cheers rang out across the water, the general realising that his visit had been appreciated, after all.

At one stage during the height of their training at Azzib, Mayne had been challenged to explain just why he was pushing his men so hard, not to mention his relentless policy of RTUing those who stepped out of line. He'd done so by referring to his own experience of top-flight sports. When playing as a rugby union international, Mayne explained, he'd reckoned that he and his teammates were at the peak of sporting prowess. But then his eyes had been opened. He'd gone to watch a rugby league match, the rival game to union, which has thirteen, as opposed to fifteen, players, far fewer stoppages, and in which keeping up the relentless intensity of play and sheer physical fitness are key to winning.

Mayne described how he had believed he and his teammates were 'supermen', before watching that Wigan versus Warrington match. In the surprise of his life he realised how either team could have run rings around the Irish team, and 'even the Lions themselves'. It was the sheer 'strength, speed, stamina, cunning and controlled ferocity' that astonished and confounded him. How had they managed this, he'd wondered? What was their secret? He'd asked the Warrington coach those very questions. It was all in the training, the coach had explained, which focused on raw stamina and fitness, combined with targeted strength training. It was then that Mayne had realised there was always a higher level to aspire to.

Those who failed to rise to that challenge had to be rejected, Mayne explained, to give those who remained a better chance of making it through the war alive. There was also a deeper, hidden reason behind Mayne's rigid RTU policy. Beneath his fearsome exterior there lurked a huge heart. Mayne cared about his men deeply, feeling a driving need to bring them home. Those who'd soldiered with him for long enough understood this about him. It was one of the key reasons they would follow him into the very jaws of hell. But equally, if Mayne failed to RTU a man who didn't make the grade, that might well get that man killed, and Mayne would have that on his conscience for the rest of his days.

As a last trial Mayne decided upon a 'sickener' – a final, horrendous route march, designed to test the men's prowess as never before. Ferried to shore in the gathering darkness, they were to march all night long, with only a ten-minute halt allowed every half hour. This close to setting sail, it struck all as being utterly pointless, not to mention 'boring and monotonous' in the extreme. As fatigue set in, 'the fact we disliked what we were doing so much made it decidedly more difficult to carry on,' noted Davis. 'This was undoubtedly Paddy's intention. He wanted to test not only our physical, but also our mental endurance.' Mayne proved indomitable, setting a ferocious pace, then working his way up and down the line, cajoling all. By watching closely all of his patrols, and how they handled 'this most unattractive . . . apparently unnecessary' ordeal, he could work out if any weak links remained.

Mayne had a secret cure in mind for any who flagged. As No. 3 Troop 'were the first to show signs of tiring . . . beginning to shamble along with dragging steps and heads held low,' he passed around a sachet of pills. It was Benzedrine – a euphoric stimulant or amphetamine, better known as 'speed'. One tablet per man, he ordered, to see if that would stiffen their spirits and sinews. In the summer of 1940, a packet of Pervitin had been discovered on a downed Luftwaffe pilot. Pervitin, a drug invented in Germany, was the trade name for methamphetamine, or 'crystal meth' as it's known today. The effects of the drug were studied by Churchill's personal physician, Sir Charles Wilson, who recommended that the British adopt something similar. Benzedrine was the outcome, these so-called 'pep pills' being hailed by the British military as being 'a powerful weapon against the enemy'.

With Churchill's blessing, Benzedrine – 'bennies' – had been given the green light. Mayne for one wasn't surprised as to why. With No. 3 Troop, the 'transformation was remarkable'. Under the influence of the bennies, they began 'swinging along together in grand style, singing and cracking jokes'. On the return leg of this hell-march, all kept up a murderous pace, though Davis was unsure if this was chiefly due to the beginnings of 'Benzedrine addicts in the regiment, or because of Paddy's slave-driving tactics . . . Paddy seemed to be everywhere, and like the Red Queen in *Alice in Wonderland*, kept on shouting "Faster! Faster!" when we were already putting up as fast a pace as we possibly could.' Mayne was unrelenting, driving all to a whirlwind of endeavour, and in the process proving the 'superiority of mind over matter' once and for all.

Despite the haranguing and the bennies, Davis concluded of that final forced march, 'Paddy was terrific that night.' On 5 July the *Ulster Monarch* set sail, the entry in the SAS War Diary reading simply: 'Convoy leaves Port Said for open sea.' Whatever they might face when they hit the shores of the enemy, those riding aboard the *Monarch* knew it couldn't be a great deal worse than Paddy's sickener.

All things for a reason. Who dares wins.

Chapter Four

THE TEMPEST

As the *Ulster Monarch* steamed ever closer to Italian shores, that vital essence of any elite unit – spirit, morale, *esprit de corps* – was at its zenith. As Davis noted in his diary, Mayne's warriors were 'as physically fit as any human beings could possibly be . . . As a fighting body they were perfect.' Being honed to perfection made them all the keener for action. They longed to prove that 'all the trouble they had been taking during this gruelling training had been worthwhile'. The loyalty forged was second to none, but it was a loyalty to each other, 'tempered by a freedom from care, a camaraderie and an unpredictable roguery'. They knew they shared something quite unique. It was what Davis could only describe as 'the gangster mentality', or an 'irrepressible and irresponsible *joie de vivre*'. At one moment appearing as 'nothing more than a band of cutthroats', they shared a 'strange morality, a code of honour', that bound them as one.

These men could be either 'the salt of the earth' or 'the unscrupulous enemies of society', depending on who was in charge. In Mayne – 'one of the outstanding characters of the war' – they had the perfect master and commander, a man who led by example. 'Officers and men alike worshipped him, respected him, cursed him and loved him, and all feared him,' noted Davis. With great care, Mayne had shaped the unit in his own image. He was 'deadly as an enemy, sincere and loyal as a friend, unpredictable and infuriating as a companion', and he 'devoted his whole attention to the unit, imparting to it something of his own amazing character'. At Azzib, he'd forged a 'light-hearted and unorthodox, but nevertheless strangely disciplined and highly efficient fighting unit', which in turn would gain a fearsome reputation with friend and foe alike.

It was time to let battle commence. Weapons were primed, both their own and those scavenged off the enemy. Their explosive charges were made up and good to blow. Their ropes, scaling ladders, radios, rations, charts and passwords were at the ready. All options and possibilities for the coming assault had been rehearsed, brainstormed and prepared for. What else could they have done to ready themselves for whatever lay ahead? In short, what now could possibly stop them?

But even as the *Ulster Monarch* steamed into view of Italian shores – the snow-capped peak of Mount Etna rising ethereal and unreal before them – fate had other ideas in mind. 'Within sight of Sicily', an entry into the War Diary noted simply, for the afternoon of 9 July 1943. But that very day – almost that very hour – the weather turned.

Sunrise that morning had revealed what looked set to be another day in paradise, the happy sun glinting off the mirror-like surface of the Mediterranean. As Mount Etna had come into view – its peak seeming to float upon a cushion of clouds – a frisson of excitement had pulsed around the ship. With enemy territory so close at hand, it was all suddenly so real. Worse than actual combat was the waiting, as the tension grew and the fear of the unknown took hold. Many of the raiders – especially the combat virgins, like Davis – were gripped by it. Furtive glances had been thrown towards 'faces we had come to know so well', as all prepared to head into battle, charged to 'breech this steel wall at one of its strongest points'. As they took one last glance at personal belongings – letters from home, photographs of loved ones, notes scribbled in a diary – everything was stuffed into kitbags, just in case their owner did not make it back again.

At first the glistening peak of Etna, Sicily's tallest, was etched in clear, sunlit skies. Yet almost as if triggered by the sighting of that mountain, the first blasts of the coming storm swept in. The wind began to stiffen, as a bank of clouds blew in across the horizon, angry and dark and tempestuous, and blanking all from view. At the ship's stern, the White Ensign began to flap and snap, caught by the stiffening breeze. Then the calm stillness of the water was pierced by the wind's initial onslaught. As the storm reached the invasion fleet, the waters began to rupture, roar and spit, waves rising up against the *Ulster Monarch*'s steel sides, sea spray hurling skywards and cascading down across the ship's decks.

This was the one thing that all had dreaded, but with the land of the enemy within sight there was no turning back now. For those aboard ship the motion of the *Ulster Monarch* became sickening, and especially for individuals who'd never earned their sea legs. Before long, 'towering waves, white-crested with spume, gave way to . . . troughs into which the ship lurched and twisted dizzily', as the storm 'lashed the seas'. Having never experienced anything other than calm conditions during their time aboard the *Monarch*, no one had been able to practise how to board the landing craft in such perilous conditions.

For Mayne, and many of the old hands, the storm provoked the very worst of memories. Just over two years earlier, in the early summer of 1941, Mayne, Bill Fraser, Bill McNinch and others had sailed into battle aboard HMS *Glenroy* – a cargo vessel converted into a landing ship – when just such a storm had hit. Back then they had learned their lessons the hard way. Going into action at the other – far eastern – end of the Mediterranean, the landings had been aborted, even as they had sailed within sight of enemy shores. But just as quickly that cancellation had been countermanded and the *Glenroy* turned around again, the men of No. 11 (Scottish) Commando – their then unit – being sent in regardless, despite their adversaries being forewarned and forearmed. What had resulted from that dither and delay was little short of a bloodbath, the curse bequeathed by bad weather taking a terrible toll.

Six months later that curse had returned with a vengeance. It was November 1941, and Operation Squatter, the SAS's first ever mission, was under way. It involved a parachute drop deep into the North African desert, to hit a string of enemy airfields. In the hours before mounting up the aircraft, the inconceivable had happened: a ferocious storm, complete with lightning and torrential rains, had torn across the otherwise parched desert. The men of the fledgling SAS had made their parachute jumps anyway, despite the hellish conditions. Of some sixty-odd who had deployed, fewer than two dozen made it back again alive. The disaster of Squatter – none of the targets had been hit, it seemed – almost killed off the SAS before it had even got started.

Now, as Mayne leaned on the *Ulster Monarch*'s rail, he was beset by worries that a similar fate awaited them here, just off Italian shores. They had lost so many fine souls on Operation

Squatter – his best friend Eoin McGonigal included – because no one had had the foresight to call off the mission. Likewise, was his first ever operation in command to be scuppered by the vagaries of the weather? But equally, with the stakes being so high, could he even countenance standing his raiders down? With so much riding on their mission, was the decision even his to make? As the sun slipped below the storm-tossed horizon, Mayne was plagued by such worries.

If David Stirling had still been with them, at least he would have had a touchstone; a sounding board for his doubts. Lieutenant David Lloyd Owen, one of their brother warriors during the desert wars, had observed of Stirling and Mayne that they constituted a perfect partnership – 'the most powerful combination of courage, endurance, bare-faced impertinence, initiative and leadership . . . their combined personalities were almost terrifying in their effect'. In time Mayne would write to Bill Stirling, David's brother, confessing: 'I only wish that D.S. [David Stirling] was around now.' In many ways, with David Stirling's capture had fallen to Mayne the unwanted burden of command.

He turned to face a group of his stalwarts – his experienced fellow warriors. Those who were, like Mayne, former Commandos – Bill Fraser, fellow Irishman Sergeant Chris 'Christie' O'Dowd, Sergeant John 'Johnny' Cooper, nicknamed 'The Kid' due to his striking youth – were seasoned seaborne raiders. They could take pretty much whatever the oceans threw at them. But many were not. Many aboard that storm-tossed vessel were turning green with queasiness, including several of Mayne's officers. Davis was gripped by the all-consuming nausea and listlessness that sea-sickness brings. So too was Harrison, whose stomach was in revolt. The ship's cooks served up a last supper of bacon and eggs and coffee, but the galley remained eerily quiet. Most found their stomachs churning at the very thought of food.

'If this weather keeps up, I'm afraid the little boats won't be able to live in the water,' Mayne confessed, giving voice to his disquiet.

The moon dipped below the horizon. The thin dark pencil line of the Sicilian coast was visible now. At just past midnight on 10 July, a voice rang out over the Tannoy, the ship's captain struggling to be heard above the storm. 'Darken Ship. Rig of the day.' The *Ulster Monarch* was changing onto invasion lighting and invasion mode. The vessel slowed noticeably, as the bright lights were doused, and a series of dull red lanterns began to cast a pale and ghostly glow. Not only would this help hide the ship from any watchers, it would also allow the natural night vision of the raiders to kick in.

As eyes adjusted to the dark, so the enemy shoreline was pulled into better focus. Here and there fires were burning fiercely, and every now and again there were the fierce flashes of exploding bombs. High above the air reverberated to the roar of aero engines, and stabs of red tracer licked through the skies. The RAF was in action, giving the defenders one final pasting, before the raiders went ashore. To one side a searchlight flared into life, probing the heavens for targets. It swept to and fro, and then, for one terrible moment, the blinding beam darted downwards until it was lancing out directly across the waves. It began what appeared to be a methodical search, sweeping back and forth across the angry sea, although the weather was such that it seemed impossible that anyone remotely sane could be out in such conditions.

The beam of light crept closer and closer. The ship's gunners hunched ever more tensely over their weapons, as they took aim and prepared to open fire. It seemed impossible that the *Ulster Monarch* wouldn't be caught, 'limned in the dazzling glare of its arcs'. Then, just as suddenly as it had descended, the beam of light flicked skywards, to meet another wave of bombers.

'Prepare to embark!' came a yell over the Tannoy.

Somewhere, a decision had been taken. They were going in regardless.

On all sides scores of men thundered towards their embarkation points, pausing only to grab their bulging kit and weaponry, and to struggle into backpacks and 'Mae West' life jackets. It was an uncomfortable feeling, pulling on those life vests in the midst of a howling storm, for most were carrying eighty pounds of weight on their backs, not to mention their personal weaponry. If anyone fell in the drink, there was a dead weight to drag them into the depths. The most sensitive kit had been sewn into bags of oiled silk, to safeguard it from a dousing in seawater. For similar reasons, gun muzzles were covered by a 'a certain rubber article designed for a very different purpose'.

Dashing further below decks, the men reached the hatches that had been flung wide along the ship's sides. The oblong apertures opened just above the wildly surging swell, allowing the raiders to leap aboard the Landing Craft Assault (LCAs) as soon as they were lowered. As they waited in the storm-battered darkness, buffeted by the howling gusts, a distinctive figure appeared, crying out a few final words of encouragement. Mayne was doing the rounds. Outwardly, he appeared utterly unperturbed, offering advice and wishing all good luck. But equally, this was his chance to bid farewell – *au revoir* – to so many who were not only his warriors, but his dear friends.

As Bill Deakins, weighed down by his explosive charges, gazed into the seas that raced past, hellish in the 'dim red glow', it struck him that any sane trawlerman would spend such a day as this drinking 'in the Fisherman's Rest', back in his hometown of Torbay. It seemed the height of insanity trying to board the landing craft, to brave such waters. Lieutenant Harrison concurred. There was a distinctly 'satanic' set to the scene, for 'by the light of the red invasion lamps everything seemed to glow with fire', each wave appearing to rise higher than the last, crashing through the open trap and inundating all who stood there.

'Stand by to embark!' The order came blaring over the Tannoy.

On the deck above, the ship's crew began struggling to free the LCAs, but one was stuck fast in its davits. Perched at each of the open hatches below was a long-experienced sailor, his eyes glued to the rise and fall of the ocean, and then the movements of the LCAs, as they came tumbling out of the blackness above, to be halted at just above sea level. As each of the landing craft came to rest, it began to swing like a pendulum, threatening to smash against the flanks of the ship, as she plunged into each giant swell and fought to free herself again.

'SRS, embark!'

The cry was given, and one of the very first to vault across the dark, wave-lashed void was Mayne. Steered by their sailor-guides, more and more shadowy figures made the suicidal-seeming leap, Lieutenant Davis and Harrison among them. 'Staggering under the weight . . . and still feeling weak from seasickness, I fell into the bottom of the landing craft,' Davis confessed. Above him, further figures jumped, one, Sydney 'Syd' Payne, a lance bombardier, ending up teetering on the side of the LCA, before eager hands got a firm grip on his kit and dragged him inside.

Payne had actually been serving with the SBS – the waterborne raiding force commanded by Jellicoe – when he'd decided that the SAS was really more his thing. He'd packed his kitbag, headed for where he knew Mayne was based, and asked, somewhat cheekily, if he might jump ship. Mayne was renowned for making instant, instinctive, on-the-spot decisions about people. Once an impression was formed it was rarely changed ... and rarely wrong. He promised to get it all squared away. Payne was told to climb into a nearby truck and that was it – he was off to join Mayne's raiders. Sure enough, in the course of the coming battles Syd Payne would prove to be a sterling asset.

Right now, he heard a strangled yell from behind, even as he tried to find a place aboard the LCA. The next in line to jump had been Private Ernie Smith, and he'd timed it badly. Payne turned to spy a pair of hands clinging to the edge of the boat, as Smith's body and legs dangled towards the hungry sea. With the weight of his kit, it was all that Smith could do to hang on; there was no way he could drag himself aboard. Reaching out, Payne got a grip, and with the help of some of the others they dragged the hapless Smith aboard.

Davis had just managed to crawl across to one of the LCAs' bench-seats, when a yell went up that managed to pierce even the crashing of the waves and the fearsome thump of their landing craft, as it slammed against the towering mass of the mothership.

'Man overboard! Man overboard!'

Almost simultaneously, a cry went out over the ship's Tannoy: 'Never mind about him! Get cracking and get those boats away!'

A frisson of anger swept around Davis's boat, as those aboard realised they were being ordered to leave a missing man behind, but as further waves forced them into the steel flank of the *Ulster Monarch*, it became obvious that risking a whole boatload for one man was senseless. The longer they remained lashed to the mothership, the greater the danger that all would drown. One LCA had already been holed, due to the repeated impacts, and another had been put out of action completely, its armoured ramp jammed shut.

The man in the sea was Frank Josling, a former Commando. He'd lost his footing as a heavy swell had seized the ship. With no time to save himself, he'd plunged into the churning sea. Weighed down by his kit, he was sucked under and began to 'sink like a stone'. Fighting back the urge to panic, it was now that Josling's training kicked in. As he held his breath – not to mention his nerve – he struggled out of his rucksack and webbing, before kicking out for the surface. Even as he broke through, gasping for breath, he was in danger of being crushed between the landing craft and the ship's side.

The LCAs were certainly no cockleshells – no thin-skinned collapsible canoes. They were three tonnes in weight, being driven by powerful twin engines, and were encased in armour plate that would shield those aboard from small-arms fire. But the mothership weighed in at some 3,000 tonnes, making the contest utterly unequal. Just before Davis's boat cast off, the bedraggled figure of Josling was hauled aboard, those yanking him in timing it perfectly so that he rode high on an incoming swell. Soaked to the skin and shivering uncontrollably, he'd lost his weapon and all of his kit, but he was not about to be abandoned. A quick whip-round, and Josling, the man who'd nearly drowned or been crushed to death, was re-equipped and declared good to fight.

'Come on, Frank, you'll not get out of this one so easily,' one of his fellow raiders needled him.

With the cables cast loose, the LCA's engines roared into life, powering her away from the ship. The men were ranged in three ranks facing forward, those in the middle poised to be the first off, once the armoured ramp slammed down. Open to the elements, the craft were likewise open to enemy fire. With a crew of three and a capacity to carry thirty-six troops, the LCA was designed to leave little wake – no tell-tale whitewash – and with a draft of two feet she could bump right up to the shallows. But with their flat bottoms and shallow drafts, these barge-like craft were ill-suited to such towering seas.

Not all the LCAs would get away scot-free. Bill Deakins's boat failed to unhook itself properly from the ship. With the aft cable refusing to detach, the next swell upended the craft, throwing all aboard into the bows. Wielding an axe, the nearest sailor took emergency action, and manage to smash them free. Normally, at times like this there was always some wit ready with a humorous remark. Not now, not aboard this ship. 'No calls of "Any more for the skylark", this night,' Deakins would note in his diary, ruefully.

In Lieutenant Harrison's vessel matters were, if anything, worse, though none of them quite realised it yet. Leaving the lea of the ship, they motored into the storm, but if Harrison had hoped for an easier ride once they were free from the *Ulster Monarch*, not a bit of it. 'Up and down and around we went. Giddily the stars whirled by us as we were tossed to and fro . . .' The LCA's commander, 'unmoved by the tempest', stood in the bows, eyes to the fore. Without so much as taking a momentary break from his vigil, he cried out an order: 'Rotary pump please.'

Unbeknown to the troops, the LCA had been holed in the bows as she'd slammed against the *Ulster Monarch*, and she was taking in water. They were going to have to pump and bail to keep her afloat. All fears of drowning were driven from Harrison's mind as he groped about in the guts of the vessel for one of the cardboard bowls placed there as DIY sick-bags. Finding them to be soaked in seawater and useless, he turned and jammed his head between the twin Vickers machineguns that the raiders had seen fit to mount on the LCAs' bows. His stomach knotted in agony, his face inches from the waves, which threatened to tear him from his 'precarious perch', all thoughts of the coming operation were driven from his mind.

It was a testament to the skill of the LCA fleet commander, Lieutenant E. Pratt, that all nine of his little ships got away from the *Ulster Monarch* without being sunk or swamped, and that all managed to line up in formation and set a course for shore. In Mayne's report on the mission, he would hail Pratt's achievements in getting his flotilla away 'perfectly . . . with no confusion, no hurry, no noise . . . His boats were kept cleaner and more workmanlike than any other flotilla I have worked with or seen. There was never a case of mechanical breakdown.'

After what seemed like an age, but could have been no more than thirty minutes, the line of boats drew into more sheltered waters, where they were shielded from the worst of the wind by a nearby headland. Soaked to the skin and freezing cold, Davis found himself hoping beyond hope that no matter what might await them on the clifftops, 'we would soon be allowed to escape from this hell'. Pulling into calmer seas, all grew 'strangely quiet' as an eerie red glow spread across the water, reflecting the fires that were raging ashore. A light skein of smoke drifted over the surface, and a smell caught the nostrils almost like 'firework nights'.

Staggering to his feet, Davis went to join Harry Poat, who

was standing in the stern of their craft, his eyes glued to enemy shores. The thunder of aircraft cut the night, as the roar of heavy bombs rebounded off the clifftops. Searchlights swept the heavens, bursts of anti-aircraft fire groping for targets. A stick of bombs seemed to bracket the very position where Poat and Davis figured their target had to be – those massive shore guns. Then there was a violent burst of flame in the sky, and moments later a stricken bomber 'dived to extinction in the sea'. Where it crashed, ahead of the flotilla, the spilled fuel caught alight, transforming the water's surface into a sheet of flame. As landfall drew closer, Davis found he wasn't alone in having a quiet word with his God: 'Even the most bloodthirsty found themselves muttering their prayers . . .'

Up ahead, in one of the lead LCAs, Harrison noticed an un-identified aircraft releasing a shower of flares, and within seconds the entire scene before him became 'as bright as day'. This was the very worst. The formation of little ships was bound to get spotted, which risked them falling victim to the very guns they were here to destroy. But as they cowered beneath the craft's thin sides, hoping and praying not to be seen, something struck Harrison most powerfully. Not only was their boat still afloat, despite the hole smashed in her bows, but the trajectory of the flares might even play to their advantage. As they drifted down-wards beneath their mini-parachutes, they were falling between the clifftop gun emplacements and the flotilla, so blinding each from the other, forming 'a curtain between us and our enemies'.

One by one the flares were extinguished, leaving the night 'blacker than before'. A shape, low and hump-backed, darker than the night even, loomed before them. If they hadn't been warned to expect it, these men might have felt a frisson of real fear, mistaking it for a U-boat. A British submarine was riding half-submerged, a dull blue light from her conning tower pointing the way towards shore. Two days prior to the raiders sailing in here, another clandestine force had been at work. Dropped by submarine, a handful of brave men of the Combined Operations Pilotage Parties (COPP), a tiny special operations unit, had paddled ashore.

Keeping hidden from the enemy, lest the entire secret of Operation Husky get blown, they had proceeded to prove the landing beaches. Led by Lieutenant Commander Nigel Willmott, among his four-man crew was one of Mayne's SAS, Private Jack Nixon. Together, they had surveyed the beaches, checking for minefields and obstructions, and for submerged reefs or sandbars lying offshore. It would have been a disaster if the LCAs had run the gauntlet of the seas, only to run aground on hidden obstacles, and to be stuck fast at the mercy of the guns above. Hence the submarine's presence, to act as their guide. Hence Jack Nixon's presence ashore, his torch flashing a rhythmic beat, to steer them in.

With the landing beach no more than a few hundred yards distant, the engines were cut to a dead slow. The flotilla drifted forward silently, blunt prows nosing through the ghostly light. This close to making landfall, it felt almost inconceivable that they hadn't yet been detected by the enemy. Up ahead in the lead craft, Mayne spied something, lying low and dark, silhouetted in the light of the distant flames. There were no more British submarines in these waters, so by rights it could only be the enemy. An E-boat maybe? One of the German Navy's sleek, fast attack craft, similar to the Royal Navy's motor torpedo boats and equally heavily armed?

As all tensed for action, a voice drifted across to the lead LCA.

The words, yelled across the dark sea, were the last thing that anyone wanted to hear right now, as the cliffs loomed above them.

'Have a heart, lads! Have a heart!'

Torches began to flash from the direction of the mystery vessel, and as the LCA drifted closer it became clear what it was. Before them lay an RAF glider, which must have crash-landed in the sea. Already it had sunk up to its wings, and on the upper surface a group of those who had been riding in it were hanging on for dear life. Worse still, as the raiders surveyed the nightmare scene, corpses could be seen floating on the surrounding swell, face down in the sea. Further across the water another such unearthly apparition was visible, as it became increasingly clear that any number of aircraft must have ploughed into the waters hereabouts.

In a flash those aboard the LCA realised what must have happened. Calamity had befallen Operation Husky, and before they'd even put a foot ashore. In the first major airborne operation mounted by the Allies, scores of such aircraft – a mixed force of Airspeed Horsa and Waco Hadrian assault gliders, carrying between a dozen to two dozen men per aircraft – were to be dropped over Sicily, even as Mayne's raiders went ashore. Their objectives were twofold: first, to seize a vital bridge lying inland, along which Allied forces would need to advance; then, to take Syracuse itself, with its all-important port. But if the seaborne invasion fleet had been rocked by the storms, that was as nothing compared to what had beset the airborne forces. In truth, some sixty-nine gliders would plummet to their ruin, crash-landing in the stormy seas. Of those aircraft that did make it ashore, most had been scattered to the four winds.

Mayne slowed his vessel, so as to drag the nearest bedraggled and desperate figure aboard, even while making the terrible decision that they could afford to do no more. The disaster that seemed to have befallen the airborne forces – some 2,500 British paratroopers were supposed to have been dropped over Sicily – meant one thing above all else: the SAS's mission to take out the shore guns had just attained an even greater significance, if ever that were possible. With the sea littered with gliders, together with their hapless passengers and crew, Mayne's raiders might be the only ones among the spearhead to make it ashore, or at least in any sensible numbers.

From all around came further cries for help, as dozens of figures begged to be saved. Though assailed by those desperate voices, Mayne kept his eyes on the light blinking on the shore-line. Much as it might torture him, he knew in his heart he had to press on. Later, he'd write of this moment in a letter home that: 'It was a terrible thing to have to do.' But it had already turned 0300 hours and they were way behind schedule. He couldn't risk 'a further delay of even a few minutes'. First light was barely two hours away, at which point the enemy gunners would spy the mass of Allied ships sitting offshore. 'The main invasion fleet . . . would have been at the mercy of those coastal guns and the casualties would have been enormous.'

As that lead LCA slipped past, Reg Seekings cried out a few words of encouragement, urging the stricken paratroopers to 'hang–on'. Both the Hadrian and Horsa gliders were mostly made of wood, with a stretched fabric skin, so hopefully they should remain afloat for a good while yet. Once the main body of the invasion force came in, these men should get rescued. Already, Seekings could see the squat outlines of the gun emplacements, silhouetted atop the cliffs above. Knowing that those shore batteries had yet to be destroyed, he was equally single-minded: they couldn't afford to delay.

To their rear, Derrick Harrison's craft crept in among the tangle of stricken gliders. Torches flashed, and pleas for help drifted across the sea. It seemed impossible that the enemy might fail to hear the loud yells or spot the flashes of light. Five figures clung onto the nearest plane. One was lying in the sea, just his fingers 'twined in the torn fabric' of the Horsa. The swell threatened to drag him away. He looked to have been 'battered almost insensible by the waves', and as the LCA drifted closer Harrison could see the 'dull despair in his eyes'. Those perched atop the plane could do little for their comrade, other than plead for the men riding in the LCA to come to their aid.

Someone yelled across from the boat: 'Put that bloody light out!'

Another voice cried out: 'Shut up, you bloody fools!'

Then the coxswain killed the LCA's engine, and they nudged in among the wreckage, reaching out and pulling the five desperate figures aboard. Those rescued men lay in the stern of the landing craft, 'shivering with exposure and shock'. The engines sparked into life again, as the boat's prow swung around and turned for the shoreline.

They had no room to take any more and could brook no further delay.

Chapter Five

BATTLE OF THE PIG'S SNOUT

The first salvo in the battle for the Capo Murro di Porco gun batteries was fired by Mayne's raiders, just as they had intended. Five minutes after landing, they had managed to slip into range of the enemy, and to strike by utter surprise. And what a shot it would prove to be – truly one in a million. As the mortar platoon had lobbed up the first round, the muzzle flash ripping apart the dark, storm-lashed night, no one could have imagined its perfect trajectory. Apart from the odd fires still burning in the distance, the headland was cloaked in darkness, and it was testament to Mayne's insistence that they own the night hours, and embrace the dark, that such a feat of arms was even possible.

To either side of the mortar team, there was the silvery glint of starlight on steel. Mayne had decreed that his men go in with fixed bayonets, hoping that they would strike raw, unbridled fear into the Italian defenders. Once the mortar team had done their work, his men were to charge the gun pits and their various defences, cold steel to the fore. As early as the First World War the bayonet charge was viewed as being a 'surprise attack', because in the age of the bullet, the machinegun and artillery no enemy expected to face bayonets. It was Reg Seekings – the

78

champion Army boxer – and Mayne who had cooked up this twist to the basic plan of attack, for desperate times called for desperate measures. The predicament the raiders found themselves in was desperate indeed, for time was against them.

That first mortar round was unleashed at 0330 hours. It was still streaking through the dark skies as a second was readied. Back at Azzib, Mayne had realised a force moving on foot such as theirs lacked punch and firepower. He'd tasked one man, Lieutenant Alex Muirhead, to select and train a mortar platoon. Muirhead – a medical student before the war, who'd been a talented artist, exhibiting at the Royal Drawing Society – had never once fired a mortar. Regardless, he'd set to it with a vengeance, schooling his section 'entirely along his own lines and in complete defiance of the training manual'. After a few near-death experiences, he'd honed his unit so that they could set up the mortar and get the first rounds airborne in eighteen seconds flat.

The SAS War Diary for the early hours of 10 July noted simply: '3" Mortars engaged C.D Bty. [coastal defence battery] with success, lighting fires.' The reality on the ground was somewhat more dramatic. Just the very presence of such a weapon right here was remarkable. The Ordnance ML 3-inch mortar weighed in at 115.5 pounds (52.4kg). Though called the '3-inch' by the British military, its true calibre was 3.209 inches (81.5mm) and each shell was 10 pounds (4.5kg) in weight. The mortar and its ammo had been manhandled by Muirhead and his small team across the beach and up the precipitous cliffs, to where they were now. So crushing were their loads, each man had appeared like a giant tortoise, burdened under a massive shell. Challenging enough to carry over flat terrain during daylight; nigh-on impossible when scaling cliffs in the thick darkness.

But here they were, just minutes after landing, lobbing in the first bombs.

Private George Bass – hands cold and wet, tense with anxiety – had dropped that first round down the mortar tube. They'd selected a phosphorus bomb, for it would explode in a thick plume of smoke and was a perfect 'sighting round'. From where the smoke erupted they could tell how close the shot was to the target and adjust their fire accordingly, just as Muirhead intended. But as luck – or skill and training – would have it, no such adjustment would be necessary. That round landed smack bang in the midst of the big gun's munitions store, the red-hot phosphorus igniting the first of the ammunition.

The resulting blast was stupendous, as fire and rock and debris erupted high above the headland. The burning tongues of phosphorus seared their way into every corner of the bomb dump, cooking off a series of powerful secondary explosions. A thick pall of smoke billowed skywards, which at its base was lit a scorching red, as a series of fierce fires were sparked in and around the battery. Mortar round one – that shot of a lifetime - was followed by several more, as Muirhead's battery began to 'fire for effect', lobbing in further bombs to add to all the devastation, chaos and confusion.

Barely five minutes earlier, Mayne had been the first to leap ashore, landing from his LCA among a stretch of sand strewn with large boulders and rocks. Oddly, there had been no German or Italian troops to greet them, guns blazing. Instead, the few scattered figures that Mayne had discovered hiding among the rocks were the last thing he was expecting – they were fellow Allied troops. They'd mistaken Mayne's LCA for an enemy gunboat, which was why they were lying low. As that landing craft pulled away from the shore, carrying with it the lone airborne trooper they had plucked from the sea, two of the mystery figures explained hurriedly who they were.

One was Lieutenant Colonel Chatterton, the glider force commander, the other Brigadier Pip Hicks, chief of the airborne troops. Having been released over the sea, their aircraft - Glider No. 2 of 147 – had flown into a blinding dust cloud whipped up by the storm raging far below. It had blanked all from view, Capo Murro di Porco disappearing behind a deathly black shroud. Turning into the towering wall of darkness, Chatterton had steered a course for where he hoped land would be, only for their glider to get hit by a barrage of tracer fire. With the fabric of its wing torn to pieces, they had lost height rapidly, coming out of the belly of the dust storm to be met by the onrushing sea. They'd ditched in a blinding explosion of white, as water cascaded over the cockpit, before the glider finally came to rest on the angry swell.

Clambering onto the wings, they'd found themselves pinned in the glare of a searchlight, and moments later a machinegun had opened up, pouring fire into their stricken aircraft. Sensing they were doomed if they stayed put, the survivors jettisoned their packs and weapons and struck out for shore. Barely had they made it, when a flight of RAF bombers had roared in, carpeting the clifftops with violent explosions. One aircraft had been shot down, crashing into the very stretch of water through which Chatterton et al. had just been swimming, transforming it into a sea of burning. He had stared at the fierce conflagration, 'paralysed with fear and shock, watching the flames lapping the shore'. Oddly, it had reminded him of brandy being lit on a Christmas pudding.

Mayne and his men could only begin to imagine what calamity had befallen the rest of the glider-borne force, for all must have faced similarly perilous conditions. For any airborne troops falling into enemy hands, their fortunes would seem grim indeed. Eight months earlier, two British gliders had been released over Norway, the force they were carrying charged to sabotage a vital component of Nazi Germany's nuclear programme, as Hitler strove to build the world's first atomic weapon. Those airborne troops had never reached their target – the Vermork 'heavy water' plant, situated in a remote snowbound wilderness. Sadly, the gliders had crash-landed amid terrible storms, the survivors being taken captive and executed by their captors.

News of their dark fate made it back to London, and in May 1943 a formal complaint had been raised with Berlin. While Britain and Germany might well be at war, murdering bona fide soldiers on a bona fide military operation was against all the rules of combat. Unbeknown to the Allies, Hitler had ordered a decree be drawn up, ruling that all British 'commandos' were to be executed out of hand. For some reason the Führer had developed an 'exacerbated sensibility' to behind-the-lines operations, believing they were 'a personal attack unworthily directed against himself'. From October 1942, all such raiders were to be condemned as 'terrorist and sabotage troops' and sentenced to die.

London's complaint had triggered an 'unseemly scramble' at the highest levels of the Nazi regime, as they sought to alight upon a cover story. But their efforts to 'legally justify' killing legitimate combatants would never stand up. Instead, Berlin had issued a blanket denial, claiming the German government would never dream of executing troops in uniform embarked upon military operations. Though this was a barefaced lie, it was swallowed hook, line and sinker by London. As Major Eric 'Bill' Barkworth, one of the SAS's intelligence officers, would conclude, 'the sand lay thick in Whitehall's eyes.' Worse still, due to Berlin's dissembling, any reports of such a 'Commando Order', or of the murdering of elite forces troops, would be given short shrift.

Even so, the rumours had done the rounds – that only the worst awaited those taken captive behind enemy lines; that such 'prisoners of war should receive no quarter', and that on capture they would be 'sentenced to death'. Such fears had made Hicks and Chatterton doubly glad to see Mayne's force steam into view. Incredibly, all nine LCAs made the beach undetected by the enemy. It was some achievement. Brigadier Hicks, who out-ranked Mayne by several degrees, asked if he might be able to help lead the coming assault. The offer was refused. Mayne, of course, knew exactly what he was about here, and he didn't need any meddling from the top brass, and especially when their own mission had ended so disastrously.

If there was one thing that Mayne's exhaustive training and planning was intended to avoid, it was that kind of a debacle, not to mention the terrible waste of human life. Still, he made it clear to Hicks that he and his men were welcome to tag along. As matters transpired, they would find a very particular use for Hicks and his airborne warriors once battle was joined. But right now, Mayne's focus was on his own bespoke outfit and their mission. It had just assumed an even greater significance, if, as seemed likely, so few of the glider-borne troops had survived. As far as Mayne could tell, his was the only spearhead force poised to go into action against the enemy.

So be it. All the more reason to strike fast and strike hard.

Just as soon as they'd hit the beaches, his men had begun

to scramble up the cliff face. The scale models that they had studied aboard the *Ulster Monarch* paid huge dividends now, for it all seemed so familiar; almost as if they had been here before. They'd clambered up the sheer rocks, 'nervous, trigger-happy, gasping for breath', remarked Bob Bennett, and fearful of what might await at the clifftop. 'Had Paddy bitten off too much this time? Perhaps we were all too edgy . . .' They discovered a single Italian soldier standing guard at the clifftop. As Bennett and others had thundered out of the darkness, like beasts from the depths, that lone sentry had seemed struck dumb. They'd left him where he stood, frozen like a statue, while they hammered onwards towards their target.

Even as Muirhead's mortar platoon opened up with its bullseye of a salvo, so there was a long burst of gunfire to their rear. It had the distinctive bark of a Bren, so it had to mean that another of the sections had joined battle with the enemy. In truth, it was Johnny Wiseman's patrol, and they seemed to have stumbled into a pocket of exceptional resistance. Lieutenant Wiseman – like so many, a veteran of fighting the Vichy French in Syria – had volunteered for the SAS in September 1942. Another of Mayne's Great Sand Sea raiders – those who had harried Rommel's supply lines while based within that vast expanse of desolate, towering sand dunes – he'd grown close to their Irish commander, learning to respect and fear him in equal measure. 'I admired him enormously,' Wiseman would remark. 'I was very proud to be taken on by him.' But Mayne could also be 'frightening. Not a man to get on the wrong side of.'

The twenty-seven-year-old Wiseman – a Cambridge graduate and an arts student; small in stature, voluble and punchy – had realised quickly that Mayne was a warrior-leader without compare, one who didn't tend to suffer fools. He'd found him 'exceptional . . . particularly in action; the calmest quietest man you ever saw, no matter how many shots were going around'. But he knew that Mayne could prove edgy and unpredictable, especially if drink were involved. At one stage in the desert war, Wiseman and some others had been hitting the rum and lime, Mayne among them. They'd been drinking for a good few hours, when someone had annoyed Mayne.

'What shall we do with this chap?' he'd growled, to no one in particular.

Typically, Wiseman had piped up: 'Why not shave off half his beard?'

With no water in the desert to wash or shave, they were all decidedly piratical-looking. Mayne declared Wiseman's a grand proposal, but that he whose idea it was should go first. He'd proceeded to pin Wiseman down, demanding that someone fetch him his cutthroat razor, after which he'd shaved half his face, no water, no soap, no messing. Wiseman had never been so terrified in his life. 'After that nothing in the war ever frightened me! That cured me.'

As Wiseman's patrol had slipped over the clifftop at Capo Murro di Porco and crept into the darkness, he'd felt a very long way from his hometown of Kingston-upon-Thames. More to the point, it would seem they had company. As the first of the mortar rounds had hammered into their target, they'd set the dry grass surrounding the gun emplacement ablaze, silhouetting the entire area in every detail. As Wiseman's patrol began to advance, drawn by the light of the flames, a figure reared before them, etched in the harsh glare - seemingly an enemy sentry poised to fire.

The lead man of Wiseman's patrol stopped dead, all behind him doing likewise. Had they been spotted? No way of knowing. Breathless, they kept stock still, as they waited for the 'silent and motionless figure' to make a move. But the enemy soldier appeared to be utterly fearless and implacable, and to be going nowhere. On Wiseman's word their Bren opened up, raking the figure with rounds. Still he wouldn't go down. Dashing forward, there was utter consternation when they realised what it was in truth – a grand statue lay in their path, commemorating some '"Itie" big-wig'.

That burst of Bren fire was followed by a long moment's silence, interrupted by the rhythmic 'swish and crump' of Muirhead's mortar unit pumping in the rounds. But then a new and entirely unexpected sound cut the night, as if of a 'child crying for its mother'. The blood-curdling wail seemed to come from directly above the heads of Lieutenant Davis's patrol, as they clambered up the cliff face. Coming to shore a good half a mile out of position, they'd scaled the rocks only to discover a tall steel pylon lay in their path, one that they knew from the recce photos marked a corner of the shore gun's defences. In short, they'd been dropped directly beneath the gun barrels, at the single greatest possible point of danger.

As the unearthly sound was coming from somewhere within the gun battery, Davis reasoned, it could only be from one of the garrison. One of the defenders must have realised that the fire and bombardment wasn't another air attack, or even an abortive glider landing. Instead, Allied troops were on the ground and closing in, flitting through the night. It 'cheered us up immensely', Davis would note, for they felt certain they had 'achieved complete surprise', and were hitting an enemy that was 'utterly unprepared'. Between Davis's patrol and the big guns lay a patch of open ground, leading up to the first of a series of entanglements of barbed wire. As he led the dash forward, Davis spied figures up ahead. Outlined against the flames, he could tell right away they were friendly.

Even as they made that run for the guns, Davis's patrol suffered their first casualty, one of his men taking a fragment of shrapnel to the hand. And as Muirhead's mortar bombs fell thick and fast, another force of raiders risked stumbling into their fire. Desperate to get his demolitions experts to the target, Harrison had dashed forward leading his patrol. Feeling 'as naked as a floodlit monument', they'd thundered across the open, fire-scorched terrain. Then, not thirty yards to their front a mortar had ploughed into the dirt, with a 'blinding flash and a deafening roar'. Harrison had flung himself down, as a building to their front erupted in flames. In the harsh light, he'd spied the tangled wire before him, and beyond that the massive gaping gun barrels.

Despite the temptation to surge ahead and seize them – they were so close – Harrison knew they'd be running into their own mortar fire. His key role in the assault was to get Deakins and his sappers to the big guns, not to get them killed. Pulling back from the danger zone, and skirting west around the battery, they would advance from the side set furthest from the sea – which was the agreed plan of attack. As Muirhead's mortar team hammered in the fire, so Harrison and his men scurried ahead, dropping to the ground every now and again to avoid being seen in the 'flash of bursting mortar bombs'.

But it was then that a vicious stab of flame lanced out from the direction of the gun battery. Harrison heard the 'sharp rattle of machinegun fire' as 'streams of green tracer cut through our ranks'. He dived for cover, even as his two Bren gunners swung their weapons around and opened up from the hip, meeting the enemy attack head on with savage bursts of their own. Having trained relentlessly in accurate and instantaneous marksmanship, it was all now coming good, as that first enemy gunner fell silent. Miraculously, not a man of Harrison's patrol had been hit. Moments later they vaulted over a low stone wall and found some basic cover, lying prone among a thick bed of nettles.

But no sooner had they got behind that wall than a second burst of fire had them pinned in its grip, and this time it was sustained and murderously accurate. 'We lay there hugging the earth as bullets chipped the top of the wall,' remarked Harrison. It was no more than a couple of feet high, offering precious little cover or even the chance to move. Noticing that they were pinned under a 'stream of red tracer', Harrison realised what that had to signify. The colour was the key. The enemy fired green or yellow. Red signified that this was so-called 'friendly fire', though it didn't feel much like it right then.

'*Desert Rats!*' Harrison yelled.

'Kill the Italians!' echoed back the answer.

'We breathed again,' remarked Harrison, for it had to mean they'd been recognised. Harrison clambered to his feet, only for another stab of red tracer to lance out towards him, causing him to dive into the nettles once more. This time, it was even more accurate, especially since he'd revealed his exact position. 'Desert Rats! *Desert Rats!*' Harrison yelled, over and over, each time hearing the correct response – 'Kill the Italians!' Yet still the bursts of red fire kept slamming into the far side of the wall.

Harrison's men lost patience now, Bill Deakins and his fellow engineers, laden with their explosives, included. As a boy back home in Devon, Deakins had been subjected to 'friendly fire' once before. He'd been using his ferrets to flush out rabbits on a piece of farmland. A pair of local priests were after a bit of shooting, and willing to pay him five shillings to help. The over-excited clergymen had shot through a hedge, not realising that the teenage Deakins was on the far side. He was peppered with 'scattered shot, earth and wood splinters'. Back then, there were no hard feelings, but this was an entirely different proposition right now.

An explosion of increasingly irate profanities rang out.

'Desert Rats!'

'Kill the Italians!'

'You dirty bastards!'

'Fuck the Italians!'

Still the red tracer kept coming. Belly-crawling along the wall, Harrison reached the far end and their last man in line. He was peering into the darkness, in the direction the 'friendly' fire was coming from. 'They're our chaps,' he hissed at Harrison. 'They keep shouting the challenge and I've answered right each time, but I don't think they can hear me.'

Suddenly, the penny dropped. Harrison locked eyes with the man. 'That was me challenging. We've been shouting to each other. Come on, let's all shout together.'

Yelling at the tops of their voices – 'DESERT RATS!' – they eventually heard a faint answer drift through the darkness. They'd been recognised. The fire ceased. A figure stepped forward from the distant position, and it was instantly clear that he was one of their own.

Waking up to the fact that this was no air attack – they were facing a ground assault – the battery's defenders began to meet fire with fire. As Mayne's raiders prepared for the final assault, 'streams of red tracer glided slowly and surely into the heart of the target area, in ever increasing volume and intensity,' noted Davis, but there was 'answering green tracer which we knew would belong to the enemy.' Vaulting over one line of perimeter wire, Davis, in his desperation to get past it as quickly as possible, had ripped the backside out of his trousers, detecting a 'draughty section around my nether regions'. That was the least of his worries: the 'vicious *psshht* passing over our heads' betrayed the fact that 'a veritable hail of bullets' had them pinned down.

Typically, it was Bill Fraser's troop that seized the initiative, in the face of the enemy's fire. Superficially, Fraser – tall, gangly, boyish-looking, with a frame largely of skin and bones, hence his nickname 'Skin' Fraser – was an unlikely-seeming raider, but he'd more than proven himself on past operations. A veteran of the doomed 1940 defence of France, and of 11 Commando's Litani River battle, during the SAS's very first successful operations he'd managed to blow up thirty-seven enemy warplanes. Since then he had shown himself to be ferocious in battle, famously prone to injury, a born raider and a true survivor, having brought one desert patrol 'back from the dead', spending weeks crossing the sunblasted Sahara on foot and evading the enemy. In short, Fraser was second only to Mayne in terms of martial prowess and spirit.

As Fraser and his men prepared to rush the guns, bayonets fixed, they came under concentrated attack. A machinegun bunker was the source of the threat. The enemy gunner threw out burning tongues of tracer, trying to scythe down Fraser and his patrol. Reacting instantaneously, one of Fraser's Bren gunners, Private J. 'Nobby' Noble, swung his weapon around, pinning the enemy gun emplacement in his metal sights. Hammering out long bursts of highly accurate fire, Noble silenced the enemy gun-post, not only tearing apart the machinegun itself, but killing a dozen of those positioned there. Another of Fraser's men lobbed in a grenade to add to the carnage, but it struck the bunker's concrete wall, bounced back and exploded in their faces. Incredibly, no one was badly hurt.

With the machinegun post out of action, Fraser led the charge, with Johnny Wiseman right on his shoulder. Vaulting their way through the final tangles of barbed wire, they were the first into the inner sanctum of the battery position. Forced to pause momentarily for a break in the mortar barrage – Muirhead's troop were still hammering in the bombs – Fraser and Wiseman were joined by Mayne himself for the final dash. Moments later they were on their feet pounding forwards, bayonets to the fore. Faced with the speed and ferocity of their attack, the first of the enemy garrison began to break and run, those not managing to flee paying for it with their lives.

Harrison's section broke cover from behind their low wall, and together they charged into the battery from the rear side. Even as they cut a path through the wire, Harrison caught a slight movement out of the corner of his eye. Just three or four yards away in a hidden bunker, 'the light gleamed on the barrel of a machinegun pointed straight at us'. Realising no one else had spied the danger, Harrison felt his heart freeze. He tensed for a devastating burst of fire. In the signature way that intense combat appeared to slow down time, Harrison found himself wondering whether he could hurl a grenade, but at this range he and his men would be caught in the blast. He had his revolver gripped in his hand – it would be good for picking off 'one man at a time', but could he get them all? Such thoughts flashed through his mind, before three 'very frightened' Italian troops crawled out of the bunker, with their hands raised. Perhaps they had read the look in his eyes.

Taking them prisoner – they'd clearly decided discretion was the better part of valour – Harrison led his men towards the guns. Heading into the fire-scorched chaos, the acrid stench of burning and smoke hanging thick in the air, it proved a nightmare trying to identify friend from foe. From every side cries rang out: 'Desert rats!' 'Kill the Italians!' Bursts of Tommy gun fire rent the night, as did the crump of grenades, which were being lobbed below ground to clear the bunkers.

At one point, Lance Corporal John 'Ginger' Hodgkinson was creeping around one of the gun positions, when he spied a shadowy force advancing towards him. Wielding his Bren from the hip, he opened fire. Maybe it was because his hands were wet and cold and his grip less than perfect, but the burst of rounds went over the heads of his targets. Yells of alarm revealed the lead man to be none other than Syd Payne – the SBS warrior who'd cheekily asked Mayne if he could jump ship to join the SAS. Payne had been leading a patrol to clear the gun from the opposite side, hence the near-disaster.

Davis – still minus the backside of his trousers – led his section to clear one of the main bunkers. The first blush of dawn was painting the eastern horizon, even as grenades and bursts of Tommy gun fire echoed around the narrow concrete entranceway. Finally, the survivors were forced to give themselves up. They emerged from the bunker, 'a sorry sight', with many looking shocked and bloodied, but clearly glad to still be alive. The biggest shocker were the last figures to appear, for they were what Davis had least expected to find here – a group of women and children. It was truly sobering, and it most likely explained the eerie child-like wailing he had heard as he'd scaled the cliffs.

It turned out that as the mortar barrage had begun, some of the local villagers had fled to the 'safety' of the bunkers, fearing it to be yet another Allied air raid. They appeared 'numb with fear'. After a few questions it transpired that Mussolini's propaganda had been relentless, as he'd warned his people to expect nothing but rape, pillage and murder if Allied troops set foot on Italian soil. The captured troops were gathered against the wooden wall of a hut, one of the few that was still intact. There were scores of them, all Italian; it seemed almost as many prisoners as there were captors. They 'had the unkempt look about them of men who have fought long and hard in impossible conditions', remarked Harrison of the POWs.

Reg Seekings was busy clearing another bunker. This one was big, and it was chiefly an ammunition store. From below ground he and his men could hear the murmur of voices. They were about to go in – 'the blood was running high and we were in real killing mode' – when up the steps stumbled a little girl. Seekings was utterly flummoxed. 'She looked just like my younger sister that I'd left in hospital.' Telling his troops to hold their fire, he got everyone out of the bunker, for if they'd lobbed in a grenade all those sheltering there would have been caught in the blast. Underscoring Seekings's fears, some of the last to emerge from the bunkers at Capo Murro di Porco were British soldiers. They were four of the glider-borne forces who'd been scattered by the storm, crash-landing and being taken prisoner by the enemy.

An Italian officer was discovered, lying wounded in one of

the machinegun pits, his legs lacerated with mortar shrapnel. As they carried him across to join the rest of the captives, he began gesticulating wildly, crying out 'Dottore! Dottore! Dottore!' He claimed to be the garrison medic, and a quick search revealed papers that seemed to back up what he was saying. Once they'd got his legs bandaged he started to calm down a little. He went on to explain that he was the only officer present. He'd sent word to the Germans, positioned on the high ground a little further inland, that the British had landed. None of the German officers had believed him. No one would be able to land on a storm-lashed night such as this, they'd argued. They had refused to come, insisting that no Allied troops could possibly be there. On one level, the storm had been a blessing.

In the midst of the smoke-enshrouded, battle-torn scene there stood Mayne, looking 'amazingly calm and very pleased with himself', noted Davis. He had every right to be. So far, it was mission accomplished and at the loss of not a single man. They had suffered a few wounded, but nothing remotely life-threatening. By anyone's reckoning, it was a remarkable achievement. With the sky rapidly lightening, the urgency was to blow apart the guns, and to let the invasion fleet know that they had done so. Otherwise, the fleet commanders would assume that the SAS had failed in their mission, and the Royal Navy would attack, their salvoes intending to take out the shore guns before they could open fire on the massed ranks of warships below.

Bill Deakins and his sappers were ordered to get to the guns and get to work. As they hurried in to set their charges, there was movement in one of the bunkers behind them – a group of enemy soldiers had evaded capture. A quick lob of a grenade, and 'there was no more sound from that direction'. Shrugging off their packs, they went about laying their charges as quickly as they could, but to their utter consternation they were joined by a couple of Italian soldiers, who appeared eager to help. 'In no way did they hinder us or try to stop us destroying their guns,' Deakins noted. Unsure if this was some kind of a 'ploy or a trick', he had to 'literally kick these Italians out of the emplacements'. Of British manufacture, the guns had required 'continual polishing and maintenance', and as Deakins had imagined, it would take a significant explosive force to destroy them.

Having set the three lots of charges linked to the one fuse, Deakins gave a warning cry. 'Stand clear!'

The prisoners were herded to safety, behind a nearby ridge, the wounded being carried there, as all prepared to take cover. One group of figures were still fussing around the guns. It was Wiseman and his platoon.

Mayne went to warn them. 'Get your men off the site,' he told Wiseman. 'The RE are ready to blow the guns.'

'Sorry, sir,' Wiseman mumbled. 'I've lost my false teeth.' It was true. Somewhere amid the churning melee of battle, Wiseman's teeth had popped out. He and his men were busy searching the ground for them.

'Don't be so bloody silly!' Mayne scolded. A pair of false teeth wasn't worth getting them all blown to hell for.

Mayne was right of course, but just as Wiseman went to leave he spotted something glowing white in the half-light. Snatching up his teeth, he scarpered, along with the rest of his patrol.

As soon as they were out of the danger area, Deakins triggered the fuse. There were 'simultaneous crashes and sheets of horizontal flame', as the gun emplacements were engulfed in a cloud of billowing smoke. Back where the rest of the force had taken cover, 'flying pieces of metal whined eerily above our heads', before the echoes of the blasts died away. Returning to inspect his handiwork, Deakins was able to let Mayne know the good news: 'Guns destroyed.'

It was now breaking dawn. It was one thing having blown the guns and removed the chief danger; it was quite another letting the invasion fleet know. Radios having proved so temperamental during previous missions, the plan was to send up signal rockets. Hurriedly, they broke out the kit to do so. Only then did they realise that during the fraught rush and chaos of the storm, they'd forgotten to bring the sticks to mount the rockets on. They tried propping the first one on a rock. It toppled over and fizzed on the ground, scattering green sparks to all sides. A second did no better. A third and fourth were hurled into the air, where they 'cavorted about like drunken aerial torpedoes', getting no more than twenty feet off the ground.

Fortunately, keen eyes aboard the command ships had spotted their antics, and the Royal Naval gunners were ordered to stand down. Just minutes after the raiders' ham-fisted display of pyro-technics, the fleet began to move, steaming for the shore. 'How proud we felt as we watched,' declared Davis – his trousers still minus their seat – knowing that it was 'only by our achieve-ments that they were now able to come . . . so close to the land'. Unbeknown to Mayne and his men, theirs was the only success signal that would be received from any Allied forces on Sicily that morning. It was as if the entire airborne contingent had been blasted into Armageddon by the storm.

'The great fleet started to move in as the first light streaked the distant horizon,' noted Harrison. 'We were back in Europe,' he reminded himself, proudly. He and his section had been responsible for the entire demolitions. Now, they headed off to take up defensive positions, in readiness for the counter-attack. Nearby there would be German officers, with a force under their command that vastly outnumbered the SAS. Less than 500 yards inland lay a fortified farmstead – one that they'd codenamed 'Damiero' in mission briefings – with a series of similar strong points stretching beyond that. From what they could tell from the airborne troops they'd rescued, very few gliders had reached their objectives. They had to assume that they were largely on their own.

As if to underscore such fears, the growing light revealed a horrifying scene stretching in all directions out to sea. Harrison was aghast. Offshore lay 'sinister black shapes drifting heavily and listlessly in the morning swell' – gliders that had ditched at sea. From that mass of doomed aircraft the SAS had managed to save barely half-a-dozen souls. 'How many more had we passed by unheeding,' Harrison would write, 'as we made for the shore? How many of them had watched our LCAs approach, with new hope in their hearts? Who can measure the despair with which they saw us glide by to be swallowed up again by the night?' Surveying the empty wreckage, he could only imagine the 'hungry sea, so peaceful now, had sucked them from their flimsy rafts'.

Davis, likewise, was numb with shock. He reckoned twenty gliders had ditched, just within sight of their promontory. If each had carried an average of fifteen troops, that equated to some 300 elite warriors who had not even got the chance to serve and to fight. As with Harrison, it was now that his 'cheerfulness died away on the spot'. He realised suddenly that the 'action' he had so hungered for was a 'grim and ghastly business, a matter of pitting one's wits and one's strengths, not only against the enemy but also against tricks of fate'. Turning inland, he ran his eyes across a bare, barren, rock-strewn and largely treeless landscape, criss-crossed by dry-stone walls. Parched, dusty and sun-scorched, the grass was tall and brown and offered precious little cover. Not great for combat, but at least they would be able to see the enemy coming.

Then, with a start, he noticed something far more shocking – a glider, its nose embedded within one of the dry-stone walls, which it had clearly struck at high speed and with catastrophic force. Beyond that, another, its back broken in two. As his gaze wandered further afield, he realised there were more. 'Heavens they were all over the place! What a massacre!' The very sight of it, and what it signified for the fate of the 'glider boys', sent a cold shiver down his spine.

Another thing was crystal clear to Davis. If Mayne had not retained an iron grip on their own mission – insisting on keeping absolute control over how they were to be deployed, and how exactly he was to train them – they might well have suffered a similar fate. Someone, somewhere, had got the entire airborne picture so very, very wrong. The terrain all around was just so totally unsuited to glider-borne operations. There were no viable landing grounds – no large, flat expanses of grass. Everywhere was rock: either rock-strewn beaches, solid cliffs, boulder-studded grassland or stretches of dry-stone walling.

At the crest of the nearest ridge lay one such wall. Harrison ranged his forces along it, Tommy guns poking aggressively inland, menacing the route by which the enemy would have to come. The body of an Italian soldier lay across a nearby track, his face assuming the blotchy, 'grey-green' hue of his drab uniform.

In the distance, aircraft 'wheeled and dived like birds'. The sound of their guns drifted across the terrain. Even now, a few dozen miles down the coast, the main body of the invasion force would be steaming in to hit the beaches, their intention to push towards the SAS positions and to Syracuse beyond.

Mayne's 287-strong party of raiders had landed at 3.15 a.m. By 5 a.m. the battery had been taken. They had seized fifty to sixty enemy POWs, as the SAS War Diary noted, plus fifty more were listed as 'Killed or Wounded'. They'd also destroyed four heavy guns, two light anti-aircraft guns, plus several light and heavy machineguns, and they had yet to lose a man. 'Own casualties none,' the War Diary declared, elatedly.

Even so, no one doubted that this was the calm before the coming storm.

Chapter Six

COLD STEEL

As Harrison, Wiseman, Fraser et al. held the defensive perimeter, others of Mayne's raiders got busy clearing the caves that dotted the shoreline. While they went about their work, Private Jack Nixon – the man who'd landed some forty-eight hours earlier, with the COPP, to prove the landing beaches – remembered something. The lone Italian standing sentry at the clifftops who'd seemed dumbstruck with fear – no one had gone to check on him. Retracing his steps, Nixon was amazed to find him in the gathering light of dawn still rooted to the exact same spot.

Nixon fetched the Italian sentry in, and he was added to the mass of POWs. More Red Berets were also converging on their redoubt – more airborne survivors, brought to them in dribs and drabs. Soon, there were twenty or more. They were drawn to Brigadier Hicks, who was deep in conversation with Mayne. It hadn't escaped anyone's notice that some at least of the Italian troops had treated their captives appallingly. There were tales of wounded 'glider boys' being stripped of their clothing and left to die of exposure. Others had been beaten and robbed of all their possessions.

Mayne had an idea as to how they might turn the tables. If

the surviving airborne troops would serve as a stand-in guard force, it would relieve him of an impossible burden, for he knew in his bones that the time was fast approaching when he would need all of his men to fight. It would also be poetic justice. Hicks – hugely impressed with the SAS commander and his men – agreed wholeheartedly. Then, with incredible fortitude and resilience, he declared: 'Well, I suppose I had better look for my bloody brigade.' With that the brigadier set out to track down whatever survivors he could find.

Davis got into conversation with some of those glider boys. They were 'loud and angry', pointing out what a debacle the whole airborne side of operations had been. In contrast to the SAS's exhaustive preparations, their briefings had been wafer-thin. They hadn't been shown any recce photos – not even of the kind of terrain that Capo Murro di Porco offered – and thus had no idea that the isthmus was 'honeycombed' by those stone walls. They were aghast at how their gliders had been let loose so far from target at the first hint of any anti-aircraft fire, and into the teeth of the howling storm. In short, it was clear that an 'enormous and unnecessary' loss of life had occurred, almost exclusively due to 'inexperience and bad planning'.

With his defences sorted, Mayne turned his mind to other matters. It was around 6 a.m., and it was a testament to the sheer humanity of their warrior-leader that he saw fit to remind his men to bring the enemy soldiers in alive, if at all possible.

'Don't shoot at them,' he instructed. 'Send one of the prisoners over to tell them to give themselves up, or we will shoot.'

During the long months of the desert war, Mayne had taken any number of enemy troops captive. Invariably, he'd chosen to appeal to the basic humanity that all shared – Irish, English,

Scots, Welsh, Italians and Germans. With the SAS based in their deep desert camps, such as Bir El Quseir, a shallow escarpment that cut through the dry terrain, the Italian POWs had doubled as their cooks and bottle-washers. And both Italian and German captives had been obliged to join in the SAS's wild, rum-fuelled singalongs, offering up renditions of their own national – martial – tunes.

Indeed, in recent months the de facto anthem of the Afrika Korps – 'Lili Marlene', a love song written by a German soldier to his sweetheart of that name – had been co-opted by the SAS as their own marching song. It was Mayne who'd composed the lyrics, for in addition to being immensely well-read, he fancied himself as something of a scribe.

> There was a song we always used to hear,
> Out in the desert, romantic, soft and clear,
> Over the ether, came the strain,
> That soft refrain, each night again,
> To you, Lili Marlene, to you, Lili Marlene.

> Check you're in position; see your guns are right,
> Wait until the convoy comes creeping through the night,
> Now you can pull the trigger, son,
> And blow the Hun to Kingdom come,
> And Lili Marlene's boyfriend will never see Marlene.

And so the strikingly warlike verses continued. Those stanzas reflected Mayne's view of how to treat the enemy in combat. But it was a different matter entirely when an adversary sought to lay down his arms.

In time Mayne would draft a report for the Psychological Warfare Branch of Allied Forces, which laid out his views on the dividing line between soldiers in the full flood of battle and those seeking to give themselves up. 'Before they surrender, the Germans must be subjected to every known trick, stratagem and explosive which will kill, threaten, frighten and unsettle them,' he wrote, 'but they must know that they will be safe and unharmed if they surrender.' He added that it was crucial to get the message to the enemy that 'there are armed British soldiers behind their lines and if they [the Germans] surrender . . . they will be taken to a safe place and unharmed'. What held good for the Germans held good for the Italians, disregarding their at times appalling treatment of Allied soldiers who had fallen into their hands.

A powerful demonstration was about to take place regarding Mayne's views – about showing compassion to those seeking to give themselves up. A few hundred yards to the east of the gun battery, together with its high range-finding tower, there lay another, taller structure – the Faro di Capo Murro di Porco. Perched on the very clifftops, that hexagonal white lighthouse topped with its lantern of glass had been one of the guiding features for the LCA fleet as they had crept in to land. Right beside it, Alex Muirhead spotted what looked like a gun pit. Thanks to his binoculars, he could tell there were enemy troops busying themselves in and around it.

Zeroing in with his mortar, he sent over just the one bomb. It burst adjacent to the gun pit in an open field. Immediately, three Italian soldiers darted up from the emplacement and made a run for it, one pedalling furiously on his bicycle. Muirhead sent up another bomb. As the Italians heard it whistling through the air, they hared back to the cover of their gun pit. There they remained, 'peeping over the sandbags', without the slightest idea where the fire was coming from. Once again they set out, creeping ahead, glancing around furtively, before Muirhead sent over a third bomb. This time when they fled back to the gun emplacement, the one with the bicycle left it behind, 'wheels spinning gaily'.

Not long after that, all three walked out with their hands in the air, and they were duly taken prisoner. Realising what a key role the mortar platoon had played in the entire attack, Mayne beckoned Muirhead over for a quiet word. Never one to beat about the bush, he got straight to it. Muirhead was to be congratulated on a fine morning's work.

'Do you want a medal or a promotion?' Mayne demanded.

Muirhead pondered the question for a long moment, before replying, quite calmly: 'I'll take the promotion, sir, if you don't mind, as I am sure my widow could do with the extra money.'

Muirhead, born in Calcutta in 1919, and not yet twenty-four years old, had had his first untimely brush with death back at Azzib, when training his mortar platoon. From a hidden observation post, he'd sent through an order for his team to fire 'five bombs rapid' onto a point set 500 yards to their front, little realising that was exactly where he was positioned. As soon as the first round was airborne, Muirhead had realised his mistake, but by then it was too late to stop the barrage. The terrible realisation that five rounds were inbound, any one of which might score a direct hit, was enough to freeze the blood. As it was, Muirhead was extremely lucky to walk away with only a cut to the back of his head from flying shrapnel.

Mayne knew full well that men followed courage and example, as opposed to rank, and he took Muirhead's wry comment in the spirit it was intended. The man had more than proved his mettle that morning. Equally, he knew that Muirhead didn't seek the acclaim of having medals pinned to his chest. Indeed, that was the foremost filter that Mayne put his recruits through – the glory-seekers were binned at the first opportunity. The chief honour these men hungered for was to wear the prized SAS wings – displaying a parachute, over the stylised wings of an ibis bird, as shown in representations of the ancient Egyptian god Isis – on their left breast. That accolade was reserved for those who'd completed several operations behind enemy lines, as Muirhead hoped to do, at least if he lived that long, as the comment about his widow reflected.

As if to underscore Muirhead's sentiments, the comparative calm of that July morning was shattered by a sudden ear-splitting shriek. From somewhere, a first massive shell cut through the skies, and moments later a fountain of blasted water shot high into the air, in the direction of the nearest flank of the Allied warships. As the ground shook, the crump of a large-calibre gun was clearly audible. From a good mile or so inland, what had to be a second battery had started lobbing in rounds. The enemy gunners were being forced to fire across the breadth of the Pig's Snout peninsula, in an effort to hit the invasion fleet, but they were still capable of causing immense damage among the Allied fleet.

Mayne's orders had been crystal clear. After seizing the first battery, it was a case of 'subsequent action at discretion of O.C. [officer commanding] Squadron'. That left him the leeway to do exactly as he chose to do now – instantly transforming his mission from a defensive to an offensive one. It was time to seize the moment and silence the new threat. 'Major R. B. Mayne,

DSO decided to push North-westwards and attack C.D. [coastal defence] Battery 165267 which had opened fire ,' noted the War Diary.

On his word, the lead sections set off, seizing the Casa Damiero, the nearest of the series of fortified farmsteads. But even as they got there, the first salvoes of answering fire from the warships thundered overhead, as the Royal Naval gunners sought to silence their adversaries. Mayne and his raiders were sandwiched in the middle.

In the cover of the Casa Damiero, Harry Poat – the former Guernsey tomato farmer – gathered his men, Harrison and Davis included. 'The battery seems to be there,' he indicated, 'just the other side of those trees. Get down to those trees and I'll give you further orders . . .' He turned to Lieutenant Harrison. 'Harry, you'll lead with your section.' Harrison had earned the nickname 'Harry' back at Azzib. He would lead the charge.

Poat pointed out what resembled a giant T-shaped structure, set atop a high tower. 'That is obviously their rangefinder. And we are now going to show them a thing or two.' The 'stereoscopic rangefinder', to give its full name, was a device that resembled a length of drainpipe laid on its side, and attached to a tall pillar. Via a combination of optics and scales, it enabled the distance to a target to be calculated, relying on the user's binocular vision to do so. It gave the enemy the ability to zero in their fire on a target, as they were doing now with the Allied war fleet. Harrison's patrol would lead, Poat continued, with Davis in support, while he would take his own section and attack from the flank, so hitting the enemy from all sides.

Harrison set forth, his men spread out behind him, and with a Bren gunner on either flank to give covering fire. The ground sloped away gently from Casa Damiero, but it was horribly open, just the odd stone wall offering any kind of cover. Within minutes, they'd stumbled into the first signs of trouble – part of a cordon of enemy defences that had been flung around their second battery of big guns.

Harrison felt a hand on his shoulder. 'Careful, sir. Someone's shooting at us.'

Looking where was indicated, Harrison spied a gun barrel slide over the lip of a nearby wall, followed by a helmet. In seconds, he and his men slipped behind some cover and began 'slinging shots at that tin hat'. Breaking out, Harrison led his men after the enemy. One dashed away, but a well-aimed grenade brought him down. He was captured, hands in the air, and sent to join the mass of prisoners they'd left at their first objective. Numbering well over 200 by now, the captives had been left in the very capable hands of Brigadier Hicks and his glider boys – former prisoners now turned guards.

As Harrison got his men on the move again, the Brens began to open fire, pumping in tracer rounds. From a small wooden building a group of enemy soldiers were putting up stiff resistance, but the fiery streams of Bren rounds tore into that hut, setting it alight. Out they ran, a handful of Italians, hands in the air, before turning back towards the inferno and dashing inside again. Harrison just didn't know what to make of it. Maybe it was the sheer sight of the raiders with their fixed bayonets that made them about-turn. In any case, Harrison had his own troubles to deal with. From a farmstead to their left came volleys of accurate fire. Harrison and his men were moving up an open farm track, which offered zero cover, and there was little option but to launch a full-frontal assault.

Jumping to his feet, Harrison led the charge. As he thundered across the barren terrain, the hostile fire died away. Instead, a white handkerchief tied on the end of a rifle began to wave to and fro. The rifle looked suspiciously British. So too did the figures who emerged. Harrison's 'prisoners' turned out to be yet more of the glider boys who'd been dropped in the wrong place, but had decided to 'try to hold the farm'. With Harrison and his men wearing their blue-grey shirts and khaki berets, the occupants of the farmhouse had, 'not unnaturally, taken us for Italians'. No other Allied troops dressed that way at the time, and it did lend the SAS 'a rather foreign appearance'. The commander of the airborne troops sought out Harry Poat, offering profuse apologies for having killed one of the SAS troopers. But shortly, the fallen man was identified as a 'very dead Italian', so there were no hard feelings on either side.

From across what seemed like the entire breadth of the peninsula there came the fierce rattle of gunfire. A second fortified farmstead began to pour in tracers, in an effort to prevent Harrison and his men from reaching the guns. In response, he split his section in two. One group of ten would follow Harrison, to take out that farmstead. The remaining ten, under his sergeant, would dash ahead to take the battery. Advancing, and hosing down the enemy position as they went, Harrison and his men had covered no more than fifty yards, when half-a-dozen figures emerged from the cover of the farm buildings. While they didn't have their hands raised, theirs was an obvious gesture of surrender, for all had laid down their arms.

'Holding our fire, we advanced in open formation across the dry, sun-scorched fields,' Harrison wrote. They'd closed the gap by a hundred yards, when, with zero warning, the enemy soldiers dropped out of sight, diving behind a low bank. At that very instant a light machinegun opened up, tracer rounds cutting through the ranks of Harrison's patrol. Yelling at those behind to take cover, Harrison hurled a couple of grenades. The first one exploded, even as a pair of Italian grenades came sailing back in the opposite direction. As if in slow motion, Harrison watched the nearest land a couple of yards away, before the blast blew him – plus one of his fellow soldiers – 'off our feet'.

Incredibly, neither man was badly hurt. But as Harrison realised, this was now a 'deadlock'. They could neither try to fall back nor advance, for the machinegunner had them pinned down, nor could they stay where they were, for more grenades were bound to follow. 'I cursed myself for falling into such a trap,' noted Harrison, for they'd swallowed the vilest trick of war – the mock surrender. In desperation, he felt around for some kind of weapon to break the impasse. His hand came to rest upon a German signal pistol that he was carrying, one that he'd scavenged earlier. He pulled it out and, 'as a last resort', took aim at the bank behind which the Italians troops were sheltering, and fired.

'It was a forlorn hope, but successful in a way I had not dreamed.' The flare round landed in the long, dry grass, and within moments it had transformed the entire area into a sea of flames. Faced with being burned to death, the enemy soldiers broke cover, and shielded by the thick smoke they dashed back into the farmstead. As rapidly as he could Harrison sent three more flare rounds in their direction, as tendrils of smoke began to writhe forth from the building's cracked windows. Within five minutes the entire place was a blazing inferno. Harrison and his men watched with eagle eyes for anyone who might try to flee, but no one did. It seemed as if the enemy 'preferred to take their chances with the flames'.

After their mock surrender, it was perhaps not surprising.

Breaking cover, Harrison led his men on the final dash towards the guns, but as they neared the target the first of the mortar bombs began to fall, exploding in and around the battery. Either the enemy were unleashing hell on their own position, or Muirhead must have got his mortar patrol into action. Spying what looked to be an enemy mortar unit preparing to open fire, Harrison changed course. They charged in like berserkers with steel to the fore, driven on by the rage they felt about the false surrender, and the enemy soldiers crouching in that mortar pit 'fell to our bayonets'.

As Harrison's men had been dodging fake surrenders, Johnny Wiseman's section had been at the forefront of the fight. Sadly, they were to be subjected to the same kind of subterfuge as Harrison's patrol, only with far darker consequences. Advancing through similar terrain, it was Jack Nixon who'd spied the first enemy. A crack shot with the Bren, Nixon had opened up, taking out that first enemy soldier with a deadly accurate burst to the head. 'Jack was incredible with that thing [the Bren] and I was just glad that he was on our side,' remarked Private Douggie Monteith, a fellow Bren gunner in their section.

Further fortified farms fell to Wiseman's advance: 'mopped up several bunches of enemy snipers and defended farms: C [Casa] Vacche ... C Massa ... etc', recorded the SAS War Diary. The rural nature of their origins was clear: House of the Cows, House of the Rocky Mass ... But those farmsteads had been modified for war, having watchtowers and machinegun posts built into them. At one, the garrison seemed decidedly unwilling to put up a fight. They emerged, white flags to the fore, waving them back and forth frantically. Recognising the universal signal of surrender, Wiseman and his men had moved forward to accept their capitulation.

But all of a sudden a figure emerged from behind the white flags, brandishing a submachine gun, and opened fire. As none of Wiseman's section had yet been exposed to this kind of trick, they were taken completely off guard. Two men were hit in the onslaught, one, Corporal Geoff Caton, suffering terrible injuries. Taking the full brunt, he collapsed where he stood, bullets having torn into his groin area. Though stunned at such duplicity, and the fact that such a popular and iconic figure as Caton had been cut down, the rest of the patrol reacted with brute ferocity. Storming forward, they made sure that none of those enemy soldiers would ever replicate such an act of bloody duplicity again.

Caton was clearly in a bad way. A Lancashire lad, the twenty-two-year-old former woodworker had served under Mayne for as long as just about anyone. An army reservist prior to the war, and a hugely talented boxer – he'd been a regular sparring partner for the pre-war heavyweight Jack Stanner – Caton had volunteered for Special Service in August 1940. He was posted to No. 11 (Scottish) Commando, along with Mayne, Fraser, McGonigal et al. He'd gone on to fight alongside them at the Litani River, where he'd been badly wounded, spending several weeks in hospital. Just as soon as he was discharged, Caton had volunteered for the SAS, going on to serve under Mayne across the length and breadth of the North African desert.

Recently, Caton had penned his application for that ultimate of SAS accolades – to wear his wings on his left breast. It read:

Benghazi operation – front gunner in jeep in the late Capt. Chambers' party.

Howards Cairn – went out from Sand Sea . . . mined the road and blew the railway line.

Bir Zelten . . . Went out five times . . . 1). Set out for coastal road and returned owing to trouble with Jeeps stuck in slit trenches etc. 2). Captured and destroyed four (ten-ton) lorries and trailers loaded with arms and ammunition (& Italians). 3). Went out to mine roads but chased by armoured cars. 4). Strafed vehicles moving along coast road. 5). Mined a secondary road, laid booby traps . . .

During one of those operations, Caton's jeep had driven into an enemy trench by accident, Caton being thrown clear. Though he was uninjured, the jeep's tyres were damaged and they had to be bodged up with a temporary repair using Elastoplast. During his long months at war, Caton had earned a reputation for always being right in the heat of battle, winning praise from all for his 'coolness and courage'. Yet right now, he'd been cut down in a hail of fire from a party of treacherous enemy. Despite the terrible pain he was in, Caton remained upbeat. He wasn't about to die here, to an act of cowardly subterfuge, especially as there was so much more to be done.

The grinding advance continued, as the raiders found themselves facing 'strong opposition'. Enemy snipers became the single greatest threat. Recognising this, Alex Skinner, a former railway clerk who shouldn't even have been in the fight anymore decided to go hunting. Skinner – a sandy-haired, fresh-faced twenty-three-year-old – was known to all as 'Blondie' or 'Jesus', the latter due to the thick beard he'd grown during desert operations.

In the spring of 1945 columns of heavily armed SAS jeeps fought their way into Germany, facing die-hard resistance from the SS, Hitler Youth and Volkssturm 'home guard' units. Under the command of Colonel Blair 'Paddy' Mayne, and advancing far ahead of the lead Allied forces, at one stage the SAS overran and captured a train loaded with V2 rockets (pictured right), while at every turn they hunted down key Nazi war criminals.

Barackenlager der I. M.-G.-K. in Schneeren.

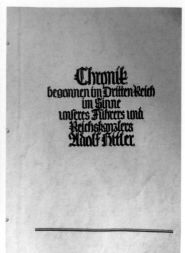

Chronik
begonnen im Dritten Reich
im Sinne
unseres Führers und
Reichskanzlers
Adolf Hitler

One of the bloodiest battles took place at Schneeren (above left), in Northwest Germany, a place steeped in martial tradition. There the SAS seized the Chronik, Hitler's gift to his chosen townsfolk. Removing the massive pages of the leather-bound tome (pictured above, right), they replaced them with what became known as the 'Paddy Mayne/SAS War Diary', a trove of letters, reports, photos and maps recording five years of operations behind enemy lines.

Mayne commandeered a Mercedes saloon car, getting Sergeant Bill Deakins, his demolitions and safe-breaking expert, to stencil the SAS's iconic 'winged dagger' badge onto the vehicle. With the war over, much of the 'booty' was brought back to the UK, including the Chronik-turned-SAS War Diary. But by October 1945 the SAS had been summarily disbanded. As veteran Alec 'Boy' Borrie (above right) put it: 'They couldn't get shot of us quick enough.'

Two years earlier, in summer 1943, Sergeant Deakins had been tasked by Mayne to craft a giant wooden 'winged dagger' badge (above, left) to grace the prow of the warship that would carry the SAS into war. Steaming aboard that vessel, the *Ulster Monarch*, Mayne's raiders formed the tip of the spear for Operation HUSKY, the Allied invasion of Fascist Italy. Upon their shoulders rested the fate of the largest invasion fleet ever assembled, as they bludgeoned open Nazi-occupied shores.

Aware of the incredibly high stakes, Mayne had spent months honing his 250-strong force. Inspired by Commando training, he instigated ferocious endurance marches, fierce cliff-climbing, plus assault courses menaced by hails of live bullets, in what amounted to the forerunner of modern-day SAS selection.

In February 1943, David Stirling, the SAS's founder (above left, shown in his last photo prior to capture) was ambushed while undertaking a daring patrol in North Africa. Taken prisoner, it was left to Mayne (above right), to save the SAS from those who wished it harm and to hone the unit for the challenges to come.

The sixth of seven siblings, Robert Blair 'Paddy' Mayne (above, in pram), was an acclaimed sportsman prior to the war, being the Irish Universities heavyweight boxing champion. Hailing from Ulster, Mayne (right, in rugby shirt) was a proud Irishman, and had been capped numerous times for both the Irish rugby team, plus the British and Irish Lions.

With his battle-hardened desert raiders to the fore – including decorated First World War veteran Captain Bob Melot (above left), irrepressible warrior-joker Sergeant Bill Cumper (above, centre), iconic Scottish berserker Jim McDiarmid (above right), plus Sergeant Ernest 'Buttercup Joe' Goldsmith, (below, second from left), Richard Lea (below, in sunglasses) and Captain John Tonkin (below, standing, in cap) – Mayne launched a daring night-raid on Sicily. Their top-secret mission was to take out the enemy's powerful shore guns, which threatened to blow the Allied invasion fleet out of the water.

Facing the threat of the Allied landings, Hitler vowed that Italy would not fall, dispatching some of his finest combat forces – including elite Alpine troops (above right) – to bolster his defences. More worryingly for the SAS, the Fuhrer had also issued his notorious 'Commando Order', in which he decreed that all captured Allied special forces were to be shown no mercy and shot out of hand.

★ Troops of the S.A.S. aboard a landing craft during training for their attack on Sicily. This photograph was taken by Blair Mayne.

The key commanders for the HUSKY landings – Winston Churchill, Generals Miles Dempsey (centre, in cap) and Bernard Montgomery (right, in beret) – had placed their faith in the SAS. They were not to be disappointed. Despite being outnumbered some fifty to one, and facing fearsome defences, Mayne's raiders took the heavy shore guns by storm. Dempsey would praise 'a brilliant operation, brilliantly planned and brilliantly carried out.'

In a real-life *Guns of Navarone* assault, the first of the heavy batteries were blown to pieces by Sergeant Bill Deakins and his team. Subsequent gun emplacements were given over to Allied troops, who by then were streaming ashore, so they could be turned on the enemy.

Against all odds, the storm-lashed weather included, the SAS delivered, with hundreds of POWs being captured (pictured, above right). But Mayne's battle-worn troops were given scant respite, being forced to re-arm and re-group right away for the next mission.

Sergeant Joe Goldsmith (above, in foreground), gathers his men in the Sicilian port town of Syracuse, as they prepare for another landing in the teeth of enemy fire. At the nearby enemy naval base of Augusta – which boasted warships, a fleet of U-boats, plus a squadron of CANT Z.506 Airone (Heron) seaplanes – a white flag had supposedly been spotted, suggesting the enemy was poised to surrender.

Along with Caton, Skinner was another veteran of Operation Bigamy – the SAS raid on Benghazi. Here on Sicily, Skinner had been at the forefront of 'one of the few bayonet charges of the war', as they'd taken the first gun battery. But in the process an S-mine – a 'Bouncing Betty' to British troops – had been triggered, the explosion of the spring-loaded device raking Skinner with shrapnel. Though injured in the legs and hips, Skinner had refused to step away from the fight.

As sniper bullets whined and cut through the air, it was clear that the Italians had a far greater range than did the raiders. Skinner decided to set out through the open terrain to track the snipers, plagued though he was by his injuries. Through careful observation, he figured he'd spied the hidden positions they were using as their firing points. With the effective range of his rifle being around 500 yards, he had to get close enough to engage the enemy. Moving 'very slowly and cautiously', he slipped through the land, which was rocky and bare of vegetation. Despite this, Skinner managed to get within range. Once there, he settled down to wait, watching for the slightest hint of movement, or the flash from a sniper's muzzle, or a puff of tell-tale smoke. With infinite patience, and with the fine marksmanship skills honed during their Azzib training, Skinner pinned them, one by one, in his sights, and each of the snipers was silenced.

The further the SAS pushed inland, in an attempt to get to that second gun battery, the worse the threat of snipers became. Following Skinner's example, Nobby Noble – the man in Fraser's troop who'd wielded the Bren to such good effect during the first battles – went into action. Spotting some of the sniper's hidden positions, Noble got moving with his Bren – accurate up to a thousand yards – creeping into a position from where he could fire. Noble's courageous actions proved decisive, for he took out a further eight snipers, clearing the way to advance on the guns.

By now, Harrison and Davis's sections had fought their way past the battery, seeking to encircle the entire position. In the process of doing so, they'd moved through a sparse village, at which each building had to be cleared. Finally, they'd reached a small church. The priest was striding about outside, his face a picture of anxiety. Spying the two British lieutenants, he approached them and in workable English began to make his case. Would they possibly spare his church, he asked, for the women and children had come to it, seeking refuge. Of course they would, Davis and Harrison told him. The priest seemed overcome with gratitude. Mussolini's propaganda had rammed home the message that Allied troops would 'act like monsters', leaving 'no man, woman or child alive'.

Moving on, all forces converged on the gun battery. Mayne himself was 'in the thick of it', driving the advance. But as one man, former No. 8 Commando man Douggie Monteith, sought to find a better position to lay down covering fire with his Bren, he heard a very familiar voice bark out an urgent command.

'Get down!'

Monteith had had no idea that Mayne was anywhere thereabouts. Yet there was the tall Irishman, striding about in full view, his pistol still firmly holstered and with one arm 'waving about his officer's cane as if conducting some kind of an orchestra'. From where he'd taken cover, Monteith – a relatively new recruit to the squadron – glanced up at Mayne.

'Be careful, and keep your head down, laddie,' Mayne admonished, matter-of-factly, 'for you'll be no good to me with a hole in it.'

Reg Seekings, in the vanguard as always, found his section

pinned down by concentrated fire. It was coming from an enemy 'pillbox' – a dug-in concrete machinegun post, with slits to fire through, forming part of the battery's network of defences. While getting hammered from that direction, they were also taking horribly accurate mortar fire. If they stayed put, they were finished, of that much Seekings was certain. In the spirit of their earlier actions, Seekings led his men on a suicidal-seeming dash towards that pillbox, racing through 'a storm of machinegun rounds and mortar bombs'. Incredibly, they managed to overrun that enemy position, killing all who were stationed there. Not content with that, Seekings led a second berserker charge, this time taking out the enemy mortar team and silencing their guns.

With that done, the way to the battery was clear. Together – Poat leading his No. 2 Troop, and Fraser leading No. 1 – a phalanx of SAS fighters thundered into the enemy position. Overwhelming their adversaries with the sheer speed and ferocity of their assault, they killed or captured the sixty-strong garrison, the guns promptly falling silent. In the rush, Mayne had been in action, once again using his lightning-quick reflexes in defence of one of his men. Sergeant Major Graham 'Johnny' Rose – a former manager of a Woolworths department store, and one of Mayne's stalwarts – had been moving in to take the guns. Suddenly, Mayne had spun around and fired from the hip, his Colt .45 pistol spitting out two rounds and shooting dead an Italian soldier. That man had been poised to 'drill Rose in the back', but Mayne had been too quick for him.

'Mr Rose, be more careful,' Mayne was heard to mutter, before they went back to the task in hand.

Even as Mayne and his men overran the second gun battery on Capo Murro di Porco, so Bill Fraser's force surged onwards, to the far shore of the headland. There a third battery would fall to their bayonets. 'No. 1 Troop went forward . . . and captured gun position 165287,' noted the SAS War Diary. 'Prisoners: Battery commander and personnel.' All together, three coastal defence guns, eight anti-aircraft guns, numerous machineguns, plus four 4-inch mortars had been captured. They'd also seized '1 Large Rangefinder', the target that Harry Poat had set his section to deal with at the outset of that morning's battle.

In quick order, Bill Deakins was called in to get to work on the big guns, some of which still had shells in their breeches, as they'd been primed to fire another salvo. After blowing the first battery he didn't have enough explosives left, so Deakins had to content himself with wrecking the guns' 'traversing and elevating gear', which left the barrels pointing almost vertically skywards. While they were still usable, the 'shells would be fired straight up into the air', which wasn't something that any sane person would be keen to try, for obvious reasons: what goes up must come down.

Of far more concern was the discovery Deakins made in the battery's underground magazines. Warned that there were heaps of shells that appeared to have been booby-trapped, he made his way below ground with great caution. Deakins had been trained to 'check and disarm' but this would be a true test of his skills. With infinite care, he began to search through the 'racks of shells and charges', bit by bit realising that the entire magazine had been to take out any force that might try to seize the battery. As Deakins went about making those charges safe, he realised how fortunate all had been. If the device had been triggered, 'the resulting explosion would have just about wiped out all in the area'.

Anyone detonating those charges would very likely have been killed in the process, so presumably none of the gun's garrison had nurtured that much of a death wish. But it underlined how close Mayne and his men had come to getting blown to smithereens. It was yet another incredible escape, in a day defined by them. Indeed, Deakins's demolitions squad had experienced their own similarly incredible brush with death.

One of Deakins's team had been carrying a bulky mine-detector in his backpack. They'd come under mortar fire, one of the shells landing in among the mine-detecting kit. Taking the full force of the explosion, the equipment was a 'complete wreck'. But 'in a strange way, the detector probably saved his life,' Deakins noted of his operator. He'd ended up suffering shrapnel wounds to his buttocks, but the heavy and bulky detecting kit had shielded him from the worst of the blast.

It was around midday by now, and, settling into the shade of a grove of mixed olive and walnut trees, the men of the SAS paused to eat their first meal since going into action some twelve hours earlier. The doors to the food store were wrenched open, as the SAS, plus the glider boys that they'd rescued, proceeded to treat themselves to a late breakfast. For Lieutenant Davis, there was a big bonus to capturing this second battery. To his utter delight, it boasted an Italian officer's mess, inside which he found a replacement pair of trousers. Speaking to an Italian priest while having no seat to his pants had reminded Davis just how inappropriately he was dressed.

Mayne's force of 287 men had by now taken possession of the length and breadth of Capo Murro di Porco – the headland being some five kilometres long by two wide. In doing so, they'd seized hundreds of prisoners; at one stage Mayne resorted to

117

disarming them and ordering them to sit and wait in a field, so that the main Allied force might collect them. In seizing the entire isthmus, and all of its defensive positions, Mayne had demonstrated a crucial grasp of 'battle tactics . . . flexibility and the flare for swift assault', plus his ability to lead a battalion-sized force of men at arms. More to the point, this was a very different form of fighting from the kind of hit-and-run operations that he had excelled in during the desert war, when operating in small, highly mobile patrols. It was also a powerful testament to his abilities as a leader of men.

Yet as Mayne fully appreciated, the fight was far from over. With his force strung out across the entire expanse of terrain, his lines were vulnerable to counter-attack. He had no idea when the main Allied force might appear, or even if they had managed to take the port of Syracuse, which now lay within their sight to the north. Accordingly, he 'wheeled the squadron around', gathering all at one of the former Italian military fortified farmsteads. By now fatigue was beginning to set in, as the adrenaline rush of the battle drained from the men's systems.

But it was crucial to keep alert and watchful for whatever fate might hold in store.

Chapter Seven

A BRIDGE TOO FAR

It was mid-afternoon by the time Mayne ordered his force to move out. They formed up their prisoners into a massive column some 500-strong, and set off to march towards Syracuse. One way or another they would discover what fate had befallen that vital port. Their route would take them almost due west, heading inland, before hooking north along the main road leading into Syracuse. The column of men and prisoners tramped down the narrow Sicilians lanes, churning up clouds of fine dust. It enveloped the soldiers – British and Italian alike – in a chalky-white coating, 'mingling with the sweat on our arms and faces, blinding and nearly choking us', noted Harrison.

They passed by the church once again, the priest offering his thanks for sparing all who were inside. Harrison paused for a few brief words, as the holy man explained that they had only finished building this place of worship in recent months. 'I hope later you may come back, so I may show you my church,' the priest added, wistfully. 'Tell me, when will the *biscotti* [biscuits] arrive? Our women and children are so hungry. No food, you realise. The Germans . . . all . . .' He shrugged his shoulders. The Germans had confiscated so much of the locals' produce, and few seemed sad to see the back of them, at least not here on Capo Murro di Porco.

Here and there the column of marchers stumbled into the odd pocket of resistance, but these were soon silenced. 'Proceeding towards main road,' ran a note in the War Diary, 'mopping up on our way . . . several defended farms and a bunch of snipers.' By sundown, there had still been no contact with the main Allied force, the British 5th Division, part of Montgomery's Eighth Army. There was nothing for it but to occupy an area adjacent to a cluster of farm buildings. 'After a wash at the well, and a brew of tea, we settled down to sleep along the edge of the track,' Harrison noted. The men grabbed armfuls of dry grass to create makeshift beds and for the warmth. Then, as the 'fires flickered and died', all bar the sentries fell into an exhausted sleep.

Before bedding down for the night, Bill Deakins paused to have words with Geoff Caton, the man who'd been shot in the mock surrender ruse. He had been laid beside a hedge and seemed in decent enough spirits, all things considered. The SAS's medics had tended to his wounds, but without getting him to a hospital could do no more. Caton was a hugely popular member of the squadron, and he and Deakins were close friends. Deakins asked for the details about what had happened. With a wry smile Caton explained that he'd just got unlucky. Deakins wished him a swift recovery, and they promised to see each other when Caton returned from hospital.

Not an hour later, Caton would pass away, dying of his wounds. He'd been carried into one of the farm buildings, with both Mayne and the squadron padre, Captain Lunt, at his side. Mayne had held Caton's hand, even as he had breathed his last. Typically, the dying man's final words to his commanding officer were 'I'm ever so sorry to be such a nuisance, sir.' That evening Caton was buried a short distance from the farmstead, beneath a spreading olive tree, the padre reading the last rites as a small group of his comrades paid silent homage.

Each such death hit Mayne hard. It was a side of him that few would ever see, but that those who had served with him for long enough had come to understand. Indeed, it was one reason why he earned the trust and devotion of his men. Mayne had this deep-seated sensitivity to death – or at least to the loss of those in his charge whom he had failed to save. Shortly, he would write a letter home describing Caton's passing, mentioning how 'he, poor chap, had been with me right since the time we started the Commando in Galashiels [No. 11 Scottish Commando]. I was very fond of him.' Losses like Caton's – and all of those who had gone before, and were to come – constituted a heavy burden that Mayne would have to carry.

Others were equally troubled. Johnny Wiseman, Caton's section commander, would write to his family, describing how their son 'took part in the first landing on European soil and was one of those who made the original bridgehead through which our armies are advancing. He fought extremely well all day, until an unexpected burst of fire caught him. We did all we could to make him comfortable, and he suffered his wounds bravely, before passing peacefully away.'

Corporal Bill McNinch – the man whose rousing songs had stiffened all of their spirits during the Azzib forced marches – felt the loss most personally. He would write to his mother: 'I lost my best friend in this lot. We've been together now for three years, and have been the greatest of friends, and I'll miss him more than I can say.' Johnny Rose, the squadron sergeant major, also wrote to Caton's parents, telling them how he 'knew Geoff well and felt his passing very keenly. He leaves a gap in our ranks that can never be filled. I shall forward his wings to you along with his badge, on which is inscribed "Who Dares Wins". We salute the memory of a great and gallant soldier.'

The SAS War Diary recorded Caton's death thus: 'Own Casualties. Killed in Action: Cpl. G. Caton, 10th July 1943, buried at farm ALACONA, on left side of lane leading to farm, 50 yds from latter.' There were also two men listed as wounded in action, one of whom, Private A. Allen, had been injured alongside Caton during that singular act of treachery. While Allen would survive, his injuries were so serious he would never return to the field of battle. Oddly, neither man who was listed as 'wounded' was Blondie Skinner, the man who'd been injured with shrapnel from the S-mine; the 'Bouncing Betty'. As an incredible testament to the spirit that had been forged within this unit, Skinner would opt to keep his injuries quiet and to treat them himself, so as not to be removed from the squadron or their coming battles.

Strangely, Mayne seemed to bear no ill-will for Caton's death. As his men dropped off to sleep, wrapped in blankets beside that track, he found himself under scrutiny from a thousand eyes clouded with worry. They'd brought with them their hundreds of captives, and as Mayne went about the final business of the day their eyes followed his every move. Being the commanding officer of the unit, the immediate fate of the prisoners did rest in his hands. But Mayne was dog-tired and burdened by Caton's loss; all he wanted was a bottle of Italian red wine, before turning in. Yet he felt horribly self-conscious before that sea of humanity, from whom the self-pity and need cried out relentlessly.

Finally, he turned to Bob Bennett and remarked: 'I'm fed up

with this lot, Bob. Take them away and plank them somewhere.' Mayne figured they were 'harmless enough', and either way he didn't have the rations to be able to feed them all.

Doing Mayne's bidding, Bennett herded the prisoners into a nearby field. Using sign language, he tried to indicate that they should lie down where he indicated, but the reaction was not what he'd expected at all. A horrible 'unearthly wailing' rose up from the ranks of prisoners. Aware of the kind of atrocities some among their German comrades – the SS in particular – were accustomed to visiting on vanquished enemies, the POWs expected a similar kind of treatment here. Nothing Bennett could say or do would set their minds at ease. Eventually he dashed off, leaving them to stew 'in their misery'.

Some time in the depths of the night, Davis felt himself jerked awake. It was bitingly cold, the chill cutting through his single blanket. Getting to his feet, he tried to stamp some life back into his frozen limbs. The night was eerily quiet. Above stretched a wide swathe of deep dark blue ribbed with skeins of light – the Mediterranean's star-spangled heavens. Barely a sound was audible from the hundreds of men – British and Italians – sleeping by the roadside, save for the occasional cough of a sentry or the rustle of a man in his straw. 'What a day it had been,' Davis reflected, as groups of men bedded down in that roadside ditch, just as if they were on one of Mayne's Azzib training schemes. It struck him as being incredible that only the previous night 'this island had been invaded by the largest force history had ever seen'.

The following morning, after an hour's further march, the raiders reached the main road leading into Syracuse. They were overjoyed to find it clogged with convoys of Allied armour, speeding inland. Clearly, the invasion was going great guns. Finally, Mayne was able to hand over his massed ranks of POWs to the 5th Division forces, and to be shot of that burden. Together with those killed and wounded, his small force had accounted for some 700 enemy troops, not to mention all the crucial war materiel that had been captured or put out of action.

All were eager to make it into Syracuse, to rejoin the *Ulster Monarch*, but the route ahead would take them into a very dark place indeed. The main road to Syracuse crossed over the key bridge that the glider boys had been sent in to seize and hold. As Mayne and his men approached the area, the terrain told its own terrible and tragic story.

The first signs were more wrecked gliders. At least two aircraft had suffered catastrophic landings in and around the bridge – the Ponte Grande – that led into Syracuse. The 'joke of gliders being "flying coffins" was seen here as a grim reality', noted Bill Deakins of the horrific scene. The signs of fierce and bloody battle were everywhere, including the bodies of the dead. While Mayne and his men knew few details of the epic struggle that had unfolded here, one thing was crystal clear: the bridge was still standing, but of the 'deeds of heroism' it had taken to hold it the SAS was yet to learn.

In truth, only one glider had made it to the Ponte Grande intact. The force riding aboard her were commanded by Lieutenant Leonard Withers of C Company, 2nd South Staffordshires, and at the glider's controls was Staff Sergeant Denis Galpin. Fortunately, they had been towed to target by an experienced pilot who'd had the good sense to bring them in closer to the landing zone (LZ), to try to get them through the storm and the flak. Still, Lieutenant Withers was shocked to discover there were no other aircraft at the LZ. One lone Horsa appeared above, was hit by flak and fell like a flaming comet to land. There were only three survivors and all were badly injured.

Withers realised then that they were alone. The force of 254 men that was supposed to take and hold the Ponte Grande had been reduced to just thirty. He'd also hurt his ankle during the landing. Regardless, he split his force into two. He would lead five men to swim the river and attack from the north shore, while the main force would steal onto the bridge from the south and rush its defenders. And that was exactly what they proceeded to do – incredibly, seizing the bridge without a man among them being injured. Having taken it, they then had to hold it until the main Allied forces arrived. Withers got his demolitions experts to check the bridge for explosive charges, and to remove any that were found, and to cut the telephone wires. Then the wait began.

As the minutes ticked by, figures stumbled out of the darkness – all with horror stories of gliders crash-landing way off target. By shortly after dawn – just as Mayne and his men were storming the second gun battery on the Pig's Snout headland – there were some eighty men dug in around the Ponte Grande, awaiting whatever the day might bring. The enemy counterattack had started with an artillery bombardment, and then mortars, machinegun units and snipers began to hammer in fire, as the glider boys began taking casualties. By midday, when the enemy launched its big push to retake the bridge, there were barely fifteen men who remained uninjured. Had Mayne been alerted to their plight, his force might have been able to come to their aid, but he was not, of course.

By mid-afternoon, amid fierce fighting, the enemy had seized the far, northern end of the bridge. By 3.30 p.m. the few surviving glider boys were overrun, their ammunition exhausted. But the enemy victory came too late for them to bring down the Ponte Grande. The first Allied troops had been landed, and they proceeded to launch a blistering counter-attack, taking the bridge in short order and freeing those who had been taken captive. With the road to Syracuse then open, the city had quickly fallen, leaving its superb Grand Harbour open to the invasion fleet, from where the advance into Sicily would be reinforced and resupplied, as originally intended.

Lieutenant Withers survived and would be awarded an MC for his heroism, the citation reading: 'his resourcefulness and courage contributed largely to the early capture of Syracuse.' But of the 2,500 glider-borne troops who were supposed to have been dropped over Sicily, 600 had been killed or wounded, some 300 of whom were drowned at sea. Very few reached their intended targets. Lieutenant Colonel Chatterton, the glider force commander, had tried to warn those on high that the plan was almost doomed to fail, due to the lack of proper experience and training of the aircrew and the wholly unsuitable nature of the terrain. He was threatened with the sack for doing so.

In the weeks leading up to the landings, General Kurt Student, the chief of the Germans' airborne forces, had written a study of Allied options regarding Sicily. The detailed report acknowledged the calibre of Britain's airborne forces: 'From experience of our troops during the fighting [they] are of a high morale and most formidable opponents.' Student predicted that the Allies would aim to capture a port at the earliest opportunity, landing airborne troops nearby. He also predicted that a 'night attack' using gliders was 'most likely', in conjunction with seaborne raiders 'being landed in darkness before dawn'. Syracuse as a potential target got high billing. But Student also made the same mistake as the Allied commanders, presuming that in 'June, July and August the weather is settled and . . . there is little likelihood of airborne operations being affected'.

While Student's predictions were startlingly accurate in all other aspects, one glaring absence from his report was any suggestion that the landing zones chosen by the British were in any way suitable. In short, the British airborne operation had been a triumph of wishful thinking over reality. That in turn only served to underline the pragmatism and good sense of the means of attack employed by the SAS. With a force barely a tenth of the size of the airborne contingent, they had achieved so very much, with just one man, Geoff Caton, being killed. So it was that with their heads held deservedly high, the SAS marched into Syracuse, three abreast, with the tall figure of Mayne at their fore.

From the battle-scarred town they were ferried back to the *Ulster Monarch*, which was anchored offshore amid a larger fleet of warships. To one side, the 'hulk of an ammunition ship, hit squarely by a German dive bomber, burned fiercely', noted Harrison, but despite a series of fierce air attacks their mothership remained unscathed. Every now and then the 'crackle of exploding ammunition' drifted across the water, accompanied by the occasional larger blast, 'as cases of high explosives went sky-high'. Aboard ship, everyone seemed to be talking all at once, as everyone tried to make a beeline for the showers. After that first night sleeping beside the track, almost everyone had ended up infested with 'sheep ticks' – *Ixodes ricinus* – and all were desperate for a good delousing and a proper scrub clean.

A queue formed in the steamy air below decks, as wafts of soap and singing drifted out of the ship's showers. On all sides figures were busy removing detonators from explosives, cleaning their weapons and sorting their gear. Everyone was longing to hear the order to 'stand down', at which point they could hit their hammocks and get that 'long, long sleep' all craved. Word of 'congratulations from the top brass' had already done the rounds, for theirs was a mission brilliantly executed. Mayne had also said a few words to his men, stressing that it was mission accomplished, with a large number of prisoners taken and so very few casualties. But with typical wry humour, he'd also added a note of caution. If the squadron used 'as much ammunition in future operations', they were to be 'sent ashore with five rounds apiece'.

Between crossing the Ponte Grande – the site of the heroic stand by those few dozen airborne warriors – and boarding the *Ulster Monarch*, there had been a twenty-four-hour delay, during which Mayne's squadron had billeted themselves in a grand house and grounds that had, until recently, been occupied by some Fascist dignitary. There, they'd manage to purloin ample stocks of chickens and ducks, to keep hunger at bay. Of this episode, Mayne would include a tongue-in-cheek entry in his typed mission report, filed in the War Diary: '11/7/43: Squadron moved up to Farms which we occupied capturing 50 Gallini and normal complement.' *Gallini* was Italian for 'chickens', and the 'normal complement' was of course their eggs. There is an added, handwritten note, as if in afterthought: 'estimated enemy killed or wounded – 200.'

For sure, the past seventy-two hours had been fraught with surprise, shock, heroic endeavour and glory, not to mention subterfuge, treachery and dismay. What all hungered for now was a decent meal and a good sleep. But it was not to be. Even as men took to their bunks, so a rumour started doing the rounds. It was late afternoon, and the SAS was to be called upon to undertake another mission *that very evening*. Mayne had just received a new set of urgent orders from General Dempsey, their overall commander. With precious little time to prepare or to plan, this was all very different from their first mission. In truth, it would be far more akin to the kind of desert raids the old hands were used to – moving fast, seizing the moment and hitting the target on the fly.

Mayne pulled his officers into a hurried briefing. Some fifteen miles north of Syracuse lay a second port city, Augusta. It sat across a similar-sized promontory as Capo Murro di Porco, this one resembling the head, front paws and body of a running dog, one that appeared to be dashing south-east, away from the land and out to sea. Apparently, Augusta was a major naval base, which played host to dozens of enemy seaplanes, E-boats and submarines. But apparently, the white flag of surrender had been spotted flying above the base. The *Ulster Monarch* was going to steam into the harbour to put the SAS ashore, so they could take the town. They were to hold it until relieved by the 'main army'. Their forces were only five miles distant, so they should be there shortly after nightfall.

That at least was the brief from on high. After their recent experiences of white flags and so-called surrenders, 'this was not an enviable position to be in,' noted Davis, to be charged to 'verify a rumour'. If it proved to be false, or worse still a deliberate ruse, then the prospects looked dire and especially with the number of gun emplacements that menaced the port. Many others harboured similar reservations, Mayne first and foremost. Augusta was a veritable fortress, reputedly boasting the best harbour defences in all of Sicily. The town was steeped in two millennia of war-torn history, having been founded by the

Greeks as the colony of Megara Hyblaea in the eighth century BC. Right then, in the summer of 1943, it was a honeycomb of shore batteries, anti-aircraft bunkers and machinegun posts, linked by subterranean walkways.

Reports indicated both Italian and German troops were based there. A fleet of Italian Airforce CANT Z.506 Airone seaplanes were anchored in the harbour, the graceful aircraft being one of the most potent floatplanes of the war. It certainly didn't look like the kind of a place that would have been left undefended, or whose garrisons would have thrown in the towel. No matter how they studied the terrain and the means of approach, there was no way to sugar-coat this. They were about to steam into a 'strongly fortified harbour' riding in a converted 'cross-channel steamer', which boasted one 12-pounder gun as its most potent form of firepower. No amount of lateral thinking could get them around those simple facts, and as Davis had surmised, 'there would certainly be no future in it' if the white flag of surrender turned out to be a lie.

Mayne thrilled to the 'bubbling light-heartedness' of this unit, the ability to fight like devils in the face of death and to win through, and to celebrate with wild wine and song thereafter. That was one of the universal threads that bound them all as one. So too was the ferocious pace of training, which almost never slackened. Through Mayne's leadership, all were coming to realise that the better-honed their skills, the greater the chances of survival. As he had emphasised time and again, he'd much rather have them alive as long-experienced elite forces soldiers, than dead as heroes. But this raid – these orders – had him flummoxed.

Indeed, this had all the hallmarks of the SAS's disastrous September 1942 raid on Benghazi, an ill-fated mission that had been foisted on the regiment. Despite all the signs that the enemy had known they were coming, and were forewarned and forearmed, they had been ordered to go in and attack anyway. The aim was supposedly to seize that coastal city, and to comprehensively wreck the port. They had never even got close and had lost many good men in the process and afterwards, as they were hounded across the desert by a vengeful enemy. As David Stirling had remarked at the time, to high command the SAS were little more than pieces on a chessboard.

Mayne harboured similar reservations right now. He feared they were pretty much expendable if the higher powers demanded it. While he believed absolutely that the Nazi and Fascist enemy had to be fought relentlessly and defeated, he also believed the risk should be justified by the ends. He hated throwing his men – this unit that he had selected, shaped and honed so intensively – into the fray, if they were to be little short of cannon fodder. In fact, it was due to their faith in their commander not to risk them needlessly in battle that so many felt such an intense loyalty to him.

But orders were orders. In short, while Mayne's reservations remained compelling, he kept them to himself. When he had been a young schoolboy studying at Regent House, a grammar school in his hometown of Newtownards, Mayne had memorised the immortal lines of Alfred Tennyson's poem 'The Charge of the Light Brigade'. The present predicament was redolent of a certain unforgettable stanza:

> Theirs not to reason why,
> Theirs but to do and die.
> Into the valley of death
> Rode the six hundred.

Reminding himself that 'I cannot live for ever', he shrugged off the malaise that had gripped him, even as the *Ulster Monarch* shivered along her entire length, her engines throbbing into life as she prepared to set sail for war.

'It was a perfect summer evening,' wrote Derrick Harrison of their steaming out of Syracuse harbour. 'The sun was dipping towards the land ... there was nothing to disturb the tranquillity. The *Ulster Monarch* sailed on like a cruise liner. As we turned towards Augusta the enchantment faded.' From the ship's deck, Harrison scanned the harbour side with his binoculars. It was 'strangely deserted. It was like a town that had died.' As he studied the spot where they planned to land, he knew in his bones that it just didn't feel right. Certainly, no white flags of surrender could be spied anywhere. 'The place might be deserted, or it might be a trap.'

Aboard ship, all had been chaos, as the men shook themselves from their bunks, grabbed weapons and ammo and stuffed their pockets with food, for many had yet to sit down to a proper meal. Bill Deakins found that he and his party of Royal Engineers were being issued with American M1 carbines, for they would need to carry no heavy loads of explosives on this mission. With its folding butt, single shot or semi-automatic fire and light weight, it was a fine gun for 'close range action', as Deakins well appreciated. And thanks to Mayne's rigorous training, there was barely any weapon that they hadn't learned to fire. The plan was for the SAS to be spirited onto the landing beach in two waves, with Deakins and his men riding in the second party.

Such was the speed with which this mission had been foisted upon the men, many being dragged out of the first moments of precious sleep, that accidents were almost bound to happen. Below decks, the ship's crew had been forced to abandon laying out a sumptuous feast, one fit to welcome back the winged-dagger raiders, in order to get the vessel battle-ready, with another amphibious landing looming. The forward mess deck had been transformed into a makeshift war room, where Mayne's warriors were busy stuffing magazines with ammo and priming grenades.

Suddenly, a wild yell went up: *'Grenade!'*

One of the men had fumbled in his task, and let the safety pin of a grenade spring free. In such cramped quarters, the explosion threatened to be devastating, but by a stroke of good fortune a hatch above had been opened to let in fresh air. In an instant the grenade was lobbed up through it, caught by a fellow raider and hurled into the sea. There it promptly exploded, showering the onlookers with nothing more lethal than a burst of sea spray. But even *in extremis* – thrown into action at the least expected moment, and facing the unknown – this body of men remained a fearsome apparition . . . Eyeing their preparations and their demeanour, the ship's paymaster, Lieutenant St. John Coates, remarked: 'When those boys hit the beaches you were glad they were not heading in your direction.'

Catching the mood of the moment – the wild, devil-may-care spirit – the ship's commander, Captain 'Cheery' Kingscote, was poised to earn his second nickname, *Captain Crash*. The hastily concocted plan was to hove-to about two miles offshore, and to launch the LCAs from there. But a pair of eagle eyes on the bridge noticed something unexpected about the port's defences. The protective boom – a floating barrier, attached to a series of buoys, that would normally safeguard a harbour entrance – had been dragged aside. Inside, over a dozen of the graceful CANT

Airone seaplanes could be seen riding at their anchors, plus numerous other warships.

Seizing the moment, and entirely in keeping with the motto gracing his bows, Commander Kingscote – 'our intrepid Captain' – turned his vessel towards shore, and began to steam at top speed for the harbour entrance. No sooner had his intentions become clear than an urgent message arrived by telegraph from a very perplexed commander of their main escort ship, the cruiser HMS *Norfolk*.

'Where on earth do you think you are going?'

'Am going in.'

'Proceed south immediately.' (In other words, execute an about-turn.)

'Am going in to land my troops.'

A pause. 'In that case, what support do you want?'

'All that you've got.'

By way of response, HMS *Norfolk* promised all the fire support Kingscote might wish for. As he read that last message, Kingscote was heard to mutter under his breath that he would 'ram this tub onto the beach if needed'. Hence – *Captain Crash*. In him, his ship and his crew, the SAS had found their perfect brothers-in-arms.

As the *Ulster Monarch*'s gunners readied their weapons – one 12-pounder, two 2-pounder guns, plus four 20mm cannons – the plucky vessel beat a path through the harbour entrance and ploughed onwards, coming to rest just 300 yards from the shore. But even while figures dashed about, lowering LCAs and preparing to board the landing craft, so the first 'Wumff-wumff, wumff' cut the air, as 'just beyond the *Monarch*'s masthead three puffs of black smoke blossomed in the air'. Having found their range, the enemy gunners began to pump 'shells over as fast as they could', noted Harrison, who had begun to feel 'very naked standing on that deck'.

If anyone had ever doubted whether the harbour's defenders had truly surrendered, now they knew for sure.

Chapter Eight

THEIRS NOT TO REASON WHY

I cannot live for ever, Mayne had reminded himself. Now, he crouched in the bows of the lead LCA as it surged across Augusta harbour, poised to be first off the ramp into whatever might await. If the staccato beat of machinegun bullets hammering against their thinly armoured front and flanks was anything to go by, it was going to be sheer hell. Spouts of seawater erupted on all sides, the spray drifting across those hunched in the shelter of the craft, as fresh bursts of fire reached out to find their target.

Through a spyhole in the raised ramp, he ran an eye across the harbourside. The heavy shore guns were blasting away, but it was now that Commander Kingscote's daredevil dash with the *Monarch* would truly pay dividends: already, they were in too close for the shore batteries to depress their guns low enough to be able to fire on the little craft. Mayne allowed himself a grim smile. Right now, he was thankful for small mercies. Then he noticed a puff of white smoke, plus the crash of an explosion that echoed across the bay, as the *Norfolk*'s guns scored a direct hit, one of the batteries falling silent.

The Royal Navy were once again proving their worth. Then, one of the cruiser's diminutive-seeming destroyer escorts dashed into the harbour, making directly for the surviving batteries at full speed. Though she was asking to get blown out of the water, she 'kept right on, guns still firing until she was close inshore'. There, she turned to deliver a murderously accurate broadside, a gun emplacement getting 'blasted off the face of the earth', one of the raiders noted. As all the SAS appreciated, 'the God of brave men' sailed with all aboard those Royal Navy ship that day.

Still, an 'invisible hand' seemed to reach out and scoop 'cigar-shaped' clefts from the water to either side of the LCA – the effects of long bursts of machinegun fire raking the seas. In response, the *Ulster Monarch*'s guns spat fire. From her decks, Commander Kingscote's crew threw out a storm of rounds from their 20mm cannons, seeking to silence the machinegun pits that were hosing down the landing craft flotilla. On the beach up ahead streams of red tracer could be seen cascading into the rocks, 'to whine and sing' as they ricocheted high into the sky.

To those men in the second wave, waiting at the *Monarch*'s open hatches, it seemed impossible that any of the landing craft could run the gauntlet. As Davis noted, though they'd long been suspicious of the white-flag-over-Augusta reports, the sheer scale of the opposition they were facing hit them with a 'numbing shock'. Another figure, Bob Lowson, one of Davis's men, was equally aghast, his mind a churn of conflicting thoughts. How many would they lose during the landings, he wondered. Would any of the craft even survive to make it back to the *Monarch*? And just what could he and the rest expect, as they tried to battle their way to shore?

Those crouched in the lead LCA's bows were living such fears at close quarters. As they neared shore, a figure in the prow hunched ever lower over the mounted twin Vickers-K machineguns, poised to let rip. As soon as the ramp slammed down, he would be hammering out the fire from their hundred-round magazines. Anything to give those aboard a little backup; to aid their dash across the exposed shoreline, as they tried to make some precious cover. Originally designed as a fighter aircraft armament, the Vickers-K had an extremely high rate of fire. Those mounted in the LCA could deliver up to 1,200 tracer, ball, phosphorus and armour-piercing rounds per minute.

The SAS had a long and very special relationship with the Vickers-K. Facing ever stiffer defences from Rommel's troops in North Africa, in a flash of genius the unit had experimented with mounting scavenged Vickers-K guns onto a bunch of US-made Willys jeeps. Melding the toughness, reliability, fantastic off-road performance and versatility of the 4x4 vehicle with the Vickers's raw firepower was truly inspired. It had enabled the raiders to punch their way through Rommel's heavily defended airbase perimeters and to rip his aircraft to shreds, disappearing just as quickly.

Right now, as Mayne counted down the seconds before their LCA hit the shore, all aboard were relying on the Vickers-K gunner to clear a swathe, so they could dash across the sands. As the seconds ran out, there was a 'shudder and a crunch' and the LCA beached, the ramp slamming down. Instantly, the Vickers spat fire, the pair of drum magazines blasting out a funnel of leaden death, a thick drift of muzzle smoke rolling across the bows. With the Vickers 'belching ammunition at the beaches ahead and the houses behind', Mayne gave the order.

'Let's go!' he roared, his tall figure leading the charge.

Thundering up the sand, those men crammed into the lead LCA seemed to take the enemy by surprise, the sheer speed and aggression of their assault winning through. All made the shelter of the sea wall, at which point Mayne vaulted over it and dashed for the streets beyond, calling for his men to follow. To their rear, others were not to be so fortunate. With no time to survey or study the landing beaches, some of the LCAs were caught short. Men were forced to leap out and struggle to shore, fighting their way through bullet-whipped seas. Alf Dignum found himself swimming under 'very heavy fire'. He reached the shore to find one of the 'lads was laying across a dead trooper and was also dead'. He had no chance to stop, for the fire proved murderous, and in any case he 'had a job to do' clearing Augusta town.

Showing incredible bravery, one figure had halted to give aid to the fallen. Eight months earlier, Captain Philip McLean Gunn had taken over as the SAS's medical officer (MO). He'd replaced Captain Malcolm James Pleydell, who had recruited Gunn into the unit. Pleydell – an iconic and hugely trusted figure; 'the lads would go anywhere' knowing he was there to patch them up – had resigned from the SAS due to a bout of the 'cafard'. Physically and mentally exhausted from repeated back-to-back operations, and from the cumulative stress of trying to save so many, Pleydell would never return to active duty. Hospitalised, he would be 'invalided home', only to find England to be an alien country after so many years at war, and to feel 'totally out of place'.

Upon recruiting Gunn, Pleydell had said of him that he was 'perhaps the best MO I have ever met'. Today in Augusta, that remark was to be proved a hundred times over.

The first man to be hit in the storm of fire at Augusta was Corporal John William Bentley, a twenty-six-year-old former textile worker hailing from Stockport in the north-west of England. In 1939, Bentley had signed up to the Royal Army

Medical Corps (RAMC), volunteering for the SAS on 23 May 1943, to become one of Gunn's team of medics. Having been with the unit for less than two months, Bentley was hit and wounded, even as he'd dashed down the LCA's open ramp. He was dragged to the beach by his comrades, where Gunn – known to all as 'Phil' – set about trying to save him. As the bullets flew and whined, Gunn tried to stem the worst of the bleeding. But within minutes he was seen to fling down a bandage in frustration, shaking his head in despair. Despite his best efforts, Bentley had breathed his last.

As he stormed off another LCA into the maelstrom of fire, Syd Payne – the SBS warrior who'd jumped ship to join the SAS – had a second RAMC man, Private George Shaw, at his side. Striking out for shore, they were surging towards the beach when Payne saw Shaw hit by a burst of rounds. Payne was struck by a terrible thought: if Shaw's body hadn't taken the full brunt of the fire, he felt sure the barrage would have done for him. Despite the huge danger he was in, Payne grabbed Shaw's body and dragged it from the water and laid it on a nearby rock. By now, he knew well the look of death, and he was pretty certain Shaw had been killed outright.

Reaching the beach, Payne alerted Gunn to Shaw's plight. The SAS medic got to work on Shaw right away, but was unable to revive him. Shaw, twenty-two years of age, was a former Rolls-Royce worker hailing from Derby, in the English midlands. Married, with two young daughters, Betty and Margaret, in 1936 he'd signed up as a territorial in the RAMC. He'd volunteered for the SAS in March 1943, so was another relatively fresh recruit. In the short time that he'd been with the unit, he'd distinguished himself as a man with a huge heart, doing all he could to 'help the local population with their medical problems', remarked one of his comrades.

Gunn remained resolute and implacable, as he tried to save the lives of those men on that bullet-torn beach. The fact that both were, by chance, from his own medical unit was immaterial. Gunn would have done the same for any of the fallen. He had very particular reasons to stand firm in the face of the enemy. Hailing from the Wirral, in Cheshire, he was one of four brothers, who, at Sedbergh School, where they were boarders, became known as 'the Gunn Battery'. After studying medicine at university, Phil Gunn had signed up to the RAMC in 1940, volunteering for the SAS on 16 November 1942. His three brothers were serving with Allied forces, two with the Royal Artillery, and one likewise as a medic, in Burma, with the Special Operations Executive (SOE), otherwise known as Churchill's 'Ministry of Ungentlemanly Warfare'.

Several months back, his eldest brother, Lieutenant George Ward Gunn, had been awarded a posthumous Victoria Cross in Libya, for manning the last surviving anti-tank gun in his battery, when attacked by dozens of enemy Panzers. Lieutenant Gunn had gone down keeping the gun firing to the last. With the Gunn family, soldiering ran deep, but so too did the tradition of saving lives amid the horrors of war. As with Malcolm Pleydell, the former SAS medic, Mayne would forge an iron bond with Phil Gunn. He would write to his own mother, Margaret Mayne, describing Gunn as 'a charming person, very brave & extremely talented'. Mayne would go on to say of Gunn that his popularity 'was founded not only on his cheerful and courageous conduct under all conditions, but on the admiration which one could not but feel for his great talents both as a doctor and a soldier'.

Right then, as the evening light faded across Augusta town, Phil Gunn's selfless work with the dying and the wounded had only just begun.

With Shaw and Bentley killed in action, two had fallen within the first minutes of the assault. There were others with injuries, but many more had surged ashore. All things considered, under the superb cover provided by the Navy's guns and their own Vickers-Ks, the landings had been executed in the face of ferocious fire with remarkably few casualties. But of course, the garrison at Augusta – which included crack troops of the Panzer-Division Hermann Göring – had more than shown its true colours, and no one doubted that every inch of territory was going to be fiercely and bloodily contested. As the lead group edged into Augusta town – the narrow, twisting streets of white-walled houses offering a labyrinthine killing ground – the eerie silence was cut by the whine of sniper rounds.

As those first into action flitted into the cover of the nearest walls, Mayne spared a thought for Lieutenant Pratt, the iron-willed commander of the LCA fleet. Amazingly, Pratt had not only navigated them through the hell-storm of the landings, but he'd been first out, to hold the boat firm 'while we were disembarking', as Mayne would note of his actions. Then, with steely fortitude, Pratt had kept his craft rock-steady, 'although still under fire', as he waited to re-embark the SAS's wounded. No wonder Mayne would conclude of Pratt, 'I would very much like to have him and his flotilla for any future operations.' But before any of that could happen, there was a battle to be fought and won.

As Bill Deakins, brandishing his American M1 carbine, edged into the narrow confines of Augusta, a striking sight met his eyes. Up ahead he caught sight of Mayne, striding along, 'slightly pigeon-toed, the cuffs of his battledress as always turned back, one hand in his pocket, his signaller following'. As Deakins appreciated, rather than this being done for any kind of bravado effect, Mayne's singular style of leadership was all about imbuing confidence and calm, even while immersed in the heat of combat. A born leader, he understood instinctively what those new to combat would read in his dress and his bearing. It served to put confidence – much-needed steel – in their souls. And for sure, fighting their way into the narrow confines of Augusta, they had need of it.

Creeping along the streets that stretched ahead, small-arms fire crackled through the evening shadows, bullets whining off walls. On all sides, windows were broken and gaping – sightless doors and window frames splintered with bullet strikes. Heavier fire began to rain down, shell-bursts tearing through the air, as the thud of shrapnel echoed through 'the narrow streets, falling roof slates adding to the confusion'. Dashing from doorway to doorway and taking cover 'lying in the gutters among the glass and debris', inch-by-inch Mayne's raiders fought their way into the town. To many, this was their first taste of urban combat. As a file of men crept up both sides of a narrow road, each group covering the other, a pair of tail-end Charlies would walk back-wards to cover their rear. As the fighting worsened, patrols put more men in the tail-end position, alert for a 'hidden enemy to rise up behind us'.

Typically, Bob Bennett was in the thick of it. 'If a building was occupied we used grenades. You threw a couple in, then smashed through the door spraying the room with fire as you went. We killed quite a few that way and there weren't many pris-oners.' Eagle-eyed attention had to be paid to high windows and rooftops – the enemy's favoured sniping positions. Moving house by house, this proved slow and agonising work. In the process, Mayne's unit took 'casualties from all hazards', a growing body of injured men being gathered at a makeshift dressing station, where Phil Gunn was frantically busy giving aid.

One of the first to have been hit was Sergeant Douglas 'Douggie' Eccles, who 'went down wounded in the thigh'. He was rushed back to Gunn's Aid Post for treatment. Even among the worst of the wounded, there would be stunning acts of bravery, as the battle for Augusta raged. One man, Sergeant Andrew Frame, was caught in a heavy burst of machinegun fire. Bleeding profusely from the neck, Frame refused to be led away to Gunn's medical station. Instead, taking a grip on his pain, Frame ordered his section to consolidate the ground they had seized, while he executed a lone recce. An enemy pillbox blocked one route of advance. Frame wanted to get a sense of its defences, and how they might defeat them. Though getting weaker with every step, still he slipped into the half-light, checked out that position, and made it back again, his blue shirt soaked in his own blood.

Derrick Harrison had landed in the second wave. He found himself leading his patrol through a town that 'seemed like a cemetery. It jangled the nerves. Every window, every doorway held a possible enemy.' As he quickly realised, 'the Germans were either watching and waiting, or had left booby-traps behind.' With dusk setting in, the streets rang to the harsh chatter of fire. Any number of Mayne's men had begun to wonder if the 'white flag of Syracuse' had actually been a come-on; a deliberate ruse. Had they been drawn into Augusta, simply to meet a bloody and brutal end?

If that was the intention, Mayne's raiders had one unexpected factor in their favour right then: the gathering night. No other unit had trained to own the darkness so thoroughly, of that they felt certain. If, as seemed likely, a long night of combat lay ahead, all believed that they would prove the finest fighting unit in town. Harrison's patrol pressed on. Up ahead, a fierce red glow drove back the darkness. Harrison pulled a compass from his pocket. That was the direction in which they needed to head. Orders were for the patrols to regroup in Augusta's main square, while they tried to assess just what was what. Thirty minutes later Harrison's patrol arrived there.

Apart from the one building that was blazing furiously, all was wreathed in darkness. All units were accounted for, barring No. 3 Troop. On Mayne's orders they had pushed northwards, advancing towards the railway line that cut east–west through the town, and moving towards their chief objective, the cross-roads beyond. There, the Viale Italia intersected with the Viale America, and whoever held that junction held the key to Augusta and its harbour. Inland from there ran the main highway – linking Augusta to Syracuse in the south, and Catania to the north, the island's second city. But the enemy clearly had the same idea – to hold that crucial crossroads – for No. 3 Troop were about to stumble into serious trouble.

At their positions in the town's green and leafy Giardini Pubblici – the main park, complete with its statues, monuments and ornate churches – Harrison and Davis watched the twi-light deepen, as shells whined menacingly overhead. From the north, the gathering darkness was ripped apart by fiery bursts of machinegun fire and the blasts of mortar rounds. Every now and again a 'stream of green tracer' came lancing down the Viale Italia, the road by which No. 3 Troop were making their advance, so they had to be taking enemy fire. Harrison and Davis's section had been tasked to hold the square, so there was little that they could do to help. Mayne's force was spread painfully thinly across Augusta, as they waited for what night might bring.

'Everywhere, the atmosphere was sultry, oppressive and filled with suspense,' Davis noted. Longing to be up front in the thick of it, they had no option but to stay put, mired in 'uncertainty and doubt'. Mayne had established his headquarters adjacent to the burning building. Right then, he had no idea how the men of No. 3 Troop were faring. Not for the first time, all of the SAS's radios had gone down. It was the dousing in seawater that had done for them, during the unexpectedly fraught and bloody landings. Bereft of radios, there was no way Mayne could make contact with those of his men who'd fought their way forward. Equally, he had no means of speaking to either the Royal Navy ships lying offshore, to call for support from their guns, or to headquarters, to get an update on when the main Allied forces might roll into town.

As the night thickened, the air became chill. Every now and then, the clatter of what sounded like tank tracks could be heard, echoing across the town from the north. Somewhere out there, armour was on the move, and it could only be that of the enemy. A mission that they'd been led to believe would be a walkover was morphing into something very different indeed.

Thinking on his feet, Mayne did the only thing that seemed practicable. He and his men held the port, which sat on one side of the two-headed promontory. Only a thin strip of road, or a narrow bridge, linked their isthmus to what lay beyond. They'd cleared the harbour area of enemy troops, of that he felt certain. He'd push out his men to the limits of that territory, so they could menace all approaches. If it came to a siege, they had water

146

on all sides, and could command fire over that, as well as the two narrow routes of approach from inland.

Harrison, together with Muirhead's mortar platoon, were pushed out 200 yards towards the road and the bridge – those perilous links to the main landmass. There, they hunkered down in their positions, eyeing the darkened terrain that lay just across the thin stretch of water. If the tanks were to come, it would have to be via this route – the thin line of raised tarmac that snaked across the intervening sea – for in every other direction the isthmus was surrounded by open water. A long, cold night lay ahead, 'and a dawn which we knew we might never see if the enemy attacked in strength'.

Writing in the SAS War Diary, Mayne summed up their situation succinctly: 'No possible contact with any ship, because nearly all wireless sets ... out of action due to landings conditions ... Shortage of ammunition of all kinds ... Enemy A.F.Vs. [armoured fighting vehicles] ... Total ignorance of 17 Bde [brigade] Position and movements ... any offensive movement on our part ... unduly risky ... impossibility to hold any new gain against enemy's probable counter attack ... took up defensive position on the outskirts of the town behind the two bridges leading into it.' As for No. 3 Troop – some eighty fighting men – they remained unaccounted for, and at that moment they were as good as missing.

For a man of Mayne's martial calibre and offensive mindset, that grim War Diary entry reflected the dire state of play. As the siege mentality set in, little of this was lost on his men. At Harrison's position, figures did their best to keep their spirits up, but they'd come to Augusta woefully unprepared Most had brought only what little food they'd been able to stuff in their pockets. Worse still, they'd taken barely half a standard allocation of combat ammo, for they'd been told to expect little resistance. Yet from the sounds of the fighting up ahead, their comrades had to be running desperately short of rounds. When giving his orders to hold the isthmus, Mayne admonished that rigid fire discipline was absolutely critical now: one shot had to equal one kill, if they were to eke out their ammo.

All around Harrison's position 'huddled figures . . . stirred restlessly' as they tried to snatch some sleep, before their turn on watch. 'Even the stars were frozen into the dark blue sky.' His men had gathered around a 'a small ornamental fountain', but that too had 'died when we landed', he noted. No water sprang forth, and the stone seemed to glitter 'coldly in the starlight'. Harrison tried his radio. Nothing. It was stone-cold dead. In the intense chill of the night, what little juice remained in the radio's batteries had died.

From his position nearby, Bill Deakins tried to get comfortable, lying as he was in a flowerbed. He heard a man strike up the soft humming notes of the song 'What a Friend We Have in Jesus'. But as he started to fill in the words, Deakins realised it was a very different, quintessentially soldierly version that he was offering up tonight.

When this fucking war is over,
Oh how happy I will be;
When I get my civvie clothes on
No more soldiering for me.
No more Church parades on Sunday,
No more putting in for leave
How I'll miss the sergeant major
How his poor old heart will grieve . . .

As the lone figure sang, so voices joined in from left and right, mostly humming along. Right then, it felt incredibly uplifting. Now and then a voice cried out for all to quieten it, as sound seemed to carry for ever in the quiet stillness, but those singing proved resolute. Once that first song was done, someone else took up the baton, with a rendition of 'We're Here Because We're Here' sung to the tune of 'Auld Lang Syne'. Right then, in the depths of that cold Augusta night, those words felt so peculiarly apposite. It was as if they summed up the entire moment far better than anything else ever could, for no one could quite determine why they were there, isolated, outnumbered and outgunned, having expected to meet an enemy keen to surrender.

Eventually, sometime after midnight, Harrison and Davis were called into Mayne's HQ at the 'burning house'. There, they found their commander ensconced with Harry Poat, and the 'rock-like coolness' of the commanders had the immediate effect of calming both men's fears and their doubts. Set at ease by the 'calm of their manner', Davis found his 'confidence . . . immediately restored'. Steadily and patiently, Mayne explained what was on his mind. He had decided to send out a probing patrol, he explained, to try to make contact with the missing troop. Harrison and Davis were to lead it.

'Keep right to the edge of the road,' they were warned, 'as they are sending occasional bursts down it, and when you get to a small stone bridge crossing the road, wait there for further orders.'

Waking their men, Harrison and Davis gathered up what little ammo they could and set out, creeping ahead into the darkness. Soon, the light of the burning building had been left behind them, as they led their men into the thick darkness.

It never ceased to amaze Davis how Mayne seemed to treat all of his men as equals, regardless of rank or combat experience. His first meeting with the SAS commander – 'one of the most outstanding characters that this war brought to light' – had proved unforgettable. He was first struck by the pure physical prowess of the man, whose 'wrists were twice the size of a normal man, with fists . . . as large as a polo ball'. Davis figured he had to weigh close to 17 stone, but 'his powers of endurance were unlimited'. The impression of raw warrior potency was under-lined by the massive reddish beard that Mayne was even then in the act of shaving off, for he'd been away on desert operations. Once Mayne had finished his ablutions, Davis was skewered by his 'piercing blue eyes', which studied him for long seconds, 'betraying his remarkable talent of being able to sum up a person within a minute of meeting him'.

The scrutiny over – seemingly, Davis had passed that first test – Mayne introduced himself. Davis was struck by his 'shy manner . . . his voice low and halting, with a musical sing-song quality and the . . . tinge of an Irish brogue'. A while later Mayne had sought Davis out in his tent, to ask if he might borrow one of his patrol members for a forthcoming mission. What had struck Davis most powerfully was that the 'great man' had deemed to come to him and ask, rather than summoning his junior officer and giving orders. Later, Davis would observe Mayne at his hap-piest, at the mess, drink in hand, 'watching in silence with those sharp, penetrating eyes of his . . . making a mental picture for future reference of the private individual character of everyone he observed'. In that way, he would know how to steer each of his men in the full flood of battle, just as he was doing now at Augusta.

Even as Davis and Harrison set off on the mission Mayne had given them, so a lone figure was flitting back in the opposite direction – seeking to find his way to Mayne's headquarters. It was none other than John 'Jack' Sillito, the man who in October 1942 had executed an incredible 180-mile solo escape across the Sahara on foot. If anything, tonight's solo journey had been equally death-defying. As No. 3 Troop had advanced into heavy enemy fire, braving repeated counter-attacks, it had become critical to make contact with headquarters. The men needed ammo, reinforcements, better weaponry, and they needed fire support, if they were to have a chance of holding out. With their radios out of service, only a runner could make it through.

Typically, Sillito had volunteered to go. A little more than a thousand yards separated No. 3 Troop's bruised and bloodied frontline positions from Mayne's HQ. It was but a snip, compared to Sillito's epic, trans-Sahara getaway, but there would be one major difference. Here in Augusta, he would be facing the threat of snipers all the way, and would consistently find himself under very heavy enemy fire. Sillito's desert escape had proved to be an eight-day survival marathon, during which he'd been forced to resort to drinking his own urine to survive. His dash across Augusta would take a fraction of that time, but repeatedly he was forced to run the gauntlet of the enemy's guns.

When Sillito had stumbled out of the sun-blasted desert, back in October '42, he'd been passed into Malcom Pleydell's expert care. The SAS medic noted the 'dazed vacant look in his eyes', reflecting the 'harrowing experience' he had endured. Reaching Mayne's HQ after his death-defying foray through the streets of Augusta, Sillito looked similarly harried. By reaching it alive, he'd proved an age-old adage of warfare, one that Mayne and his stalwarts had learned well: one man could often make it through, where a larger force was bound to get seen by the enemy.

Upon arrival, Sillito delivered a hurried report on all that had transpired with No. 3 Troop. As they'd pushed north from the isthmus, the force had split into three sections – one heading straight down the guts of the Viale Italia, while on either flank the others flitted along more minor roads. In that manner they'd passed over the railway line, which bisected the Viale Italia, with Augusta's main train station lying just to the left of their line of march. As they'd pushed ahead, all eyes and ears were on alert for any signs of 17 Brigade, the Allied troops supposedly moving in to relieve them. They had a brief engagement with an enemy patrol, but those troops had melted away swiftly, showing little apparent stomach for the fight.

Encouraged, they had pressed on. Up ahead lay the crossroads, some 600 yards beyond the railroad. According to the hastily set plan aboard the *Ulster Monarch*, 17 Brigade were supposed to rendezvous with them at that spot. But as the raiders neared it, all hell let loose. The first hint of trouble was the signature whistle of inbound 4-inch mortars, as the lead elements of the troop had come under intense and concentrated fire. Worse still was the accompanying onslaught from the enemy's machinegun nests – their belt-fed MG34s, nicknamed the 'Spandau' by British troops, and capable of belting out 900 rounds a minute – hammering out accurate and deadly fire.

As bullets and mortar shrapnel tore into the buildings all around, ricocheting into the night sky, it was clear that 'the enemy were there in force' holding the crossroads. 'Fire came towards us on fixed lines, tracer ricocheting off the buildings and down the streets . . . mechanical vehicles could be heard.' There came the grunt of heavy engines and the whine of gearboxes, as three Panzers rumbled into view, the noise of their tracks clattering eerily along the Viale Italia. Armed as the raiders were with only light weapons, and with no radio contact possible with Mayne, there was no way to call for any heavy fire support, and of course, they were desperately low on ammo.

As the German troops pressed home their attack, the lead tank swung in their direction. The heaviest piece of weaponry carried by the troop was also one of its least-loved – a PIAT (Projector, Infantry, Anti-Tank). A British-designed man-portable anti-tank weapon, the PIAT was hampered by its limited range – claimed to be around a hundred yards, but in reality around half that distance – and the notorious unreliability of its 2.5-pound warhead. Launched from the prone position resting on a monopod, the charge was fired by a massive spring, the savage recoil from which was to be taken by the operator's shoulder. Regardless, it was the only piece of weaponry with which the troop might stop the armour now bearing down upon them.

Lying prone on the street, the PIAT's operator took aim, waiting for the moment when the Panzer came within range. As it loomed ever closer, he forced himself to hold his fire. Finally, there was a blast of smoke from the PIAT's muzzle, and the rocket-like warhead streaked towards the Panzer's sloped armour, bounced off without detonating, before careering into the roof of a nearby house and blasting that asunder. Inside the tank, they must have believed they were up against something far more substantial than a PIAT, for the armoured beast ground to a halt. Sensing the tank crew's uncertainty, the troop's Bren gunners began to hammer in fire, hosing down its armoured flanks.

Moments later, the Panzer had gone into reverse and started to inch its way back up the Viale Italia. Such an unexpected victory over the enemy's armour had provided only a temporary respite. In the vicinity of Augusta's railway station a telephone started to ring. Without thinking, one of the SAS men picked it up and answered. Moments later, the first of a salvo of heavy shells slammed into that position. The enemy must have had their weapons zeroed in on that very spot, and were just waiting for a British voice to answer. The shelling continued, and it was about to usher in the enemy's first concerted counter-attack.

Under the cover of that barrage, a force of two dozen enemy troops began to push forward, in an attempt to outflank the raiders. Creeping ahead, they made for a series of large petrol storage tanks that were positioned near the railway line. Hit in the crossfire, they had started burning fiercely, hungry flames throwing the surrounding streets into harsh light and shadow. As the German troops flitted through one patch of ghostly illumination, they were spotted. The troops holding that position kept an eagle-eyed watch, eyes straining in the half-light, as they let the enemy advance towards the crossroads around fifty yards away. There, they would be exposed to fire from all sides.

Taking the apparent lack of opposition as a green light to advance, the enemy hurried ahead, bunching together ever more closely. As they hit the a crossroads, the word was given to open up. Caught in a savage hail of Bren gun fire, the ranks of the enemy were torn apart, those not cut down instantly turning tail to flee. Many were 'killed outright', while the wounded were left where they lay. Neither their German comrades, nor the men of No. 3 Troop, could risk going to their aid. 'The enemy wounded were crying out, but we could do nothing for them,' one of Mayne's raiders remarked; 'the cries became moans and some must have died.'

That was the first of a series of fierce counter-attacks, yet each was beaten back by spirited and diehard resistance. But as Sillito reported, they were desperately short of ammunition, plus they'd taken casualties. They needed to get their wounded to the harbourside, so that a boat could be brought in to evacuate them to the *Ulster Monarch*'s sickbay. Having heard Sillito's report, Mayne asked him to return the way he had come carrying an urgent order: No. 3 Troop were to pull back into the relative safety of the isthmus. Heading back into the enemy fire, Sillito retraced his steps and delivered that message. Executing a fighting withdrawal, the men of No. 3 Troop began to sneak back the way they had come, to reunite with the main force.

Their pulling back became largely a question of 'every man for himself', as they tried to slip past the enemy in dribs and drabs. All went well until they reached the narrow strip of water, barring entry to the isthmus. There, the bridge proved to be so menaced by the enemy, it would have been 'suicidal' to attempt to cross it. Instead, they were forced to swim for it. Incredibly, moving in ones and twos, most made it back alive. There were several missing, and they'd taken casualties on the way, but no one had been killed, as far as anyone could tell.

By now it was around 2 a.m. on the morning of 13 July. Mayne's raiders had taken and held Augusta and its port for fully eight hours. As No. 3 Troop had been ordered to withdraw, so Davis and Harrison's sections were reeled back in. Returning to his position, Davis found himself chatting about this and that with his corporal, Bill Mitchell, a man whose counsel he valued hugely. Mitchell, a 'shrewd leader and excellent soldier', was very experienced, and Davis had found him loyal to a fault. As they awaited whatever first light might bring, the two men did their best to keep each other awake, while the quiet of night 'reigned unchallenged'.

At around 4 a.m. a distant noise echoed across the water. It got Davis and Mitchell bolt upright and instantly alert. The sound drifted across to them – 'tracked vehicles moving along the road'. As they strained their ears, trying to work out in which direction the armour was headed, they caught the sounds of what had to be wheeled transport. Across the water, a significant military force was getting on the move. 'Was this the expected counter-attack?' Davis wondered.

First light was the classic time to launch an assault. What else could it be?

Chapter Nine

EAT, DRINK AND BE MERRY

A few streets away from where Davis was keeping watch, Harrison found that 'heavy boots' were tramping 'through his dreams'. He awoke with a start. Exhausted, he'd drifted off. A man stood beside him. One of his sentries.

'Patrol of six men from 17 Brigade,' he announced. 'They've reached the crossroads.'

Harrison tried to shake the cobwebs from his head. 'Reached the crossroads? I didn't hear any fighting.'

'They say the Germans had pulled out before they got there.'

'OK. Tell the chaps to stand-to while I nip back to the Troop HQ and tell them.'

Harrison hurried over towards Mayne's headquarters, seeking to deliver the news. By now, the 'bleak light of dawn' was chasing night's shadows from the town. A harsh noise broke the stillness. 'Wumff wumff' – two puffs of black smoke erupted in the air not a hundred yards ahead of him. Airburst shells. Lethal fragments of shrapnel 'whined and zinged down through the trees'. Everyone dived flat on their faces, Harrison included.

'Anybody hit?' he yelled out.

A chorus of voices reported in: all were unhurt.

Three more airbursts cut through the skies, closer still to Harrison's position. Clearly, not all of the enemy had pulled out. Somewhere on the high ground they clearly had a lookout post with commanding views over the isthmus, from where they were calling in the fire now that it was light enough to see. Harrison arrived at the main square. A couple more shells burst above, causing a deluge of shrapnel and shattered masonry, before the firing petered out. The enemy spotters must have lost sight of their prey.

Harrison reached Mayne's HQ, to be joined by Davis. All were eager to discover if the news was true. There, they got absolute confirmation: 'Yes, the army had made contact . . . and Jerry had pulled out.'

By sunrise, all of the missing No. 3 Troop men had been accounted for and while there were scores of injuries, serious casualties proved to be miraculously few. As recorded in the War Diary, the battle for Augusta had cost the unit 'Wounded . . . 8. Killed . . . 2.' None of the forces – not even No. 3 Troop – had suffered anything like as badly as feared during that long night's fraught uncertainty and the bitter street fighting. Under their commander's guiding hand, somehow they had emerged largely unscathed.

Many would claim of Mayne that he was blessed with 'the luck of the Irish', and he did seem to have a habit of calling on good fortune when *in extremis*. At one stage in North Africa, he and his small patrol had faced being abandoned in the desert, deep behind enemy lines. But by a stroke of sheer chance, they had been found and rescued. Mayne had written to his younger brother, Douglas – who was serving with the Royal Artillery – about the remarkable incident, urging him: 'never disbelieve in luck again or coincidence, or whatever you like to call it.' Likewise, luck had been with them in Augusta, and across their earlier Sicily battles.

At one stage, Mayne had been gathered with five of his men, during a break in the fighting, so they could brew some tea. They had been standing around chatting, when there was the shriek of an incoming mortar round. With no time to take cover, the 4-inch shell had landed right in the midst of them. Or, more precisely, it had ploughed into the earth 'right between the slightly splayed feet of Paddy Mayne'. Remaining upright for a few instants, the shell had emitted a few feeble puffs of smoke, before toppling over harmlessly. It was a dud.

In less than a week of fighting, Mayne and his men had stormed Fortress Europe's steel shores, bludgeoned a way through, seized the mighty shore guns of the Pig's Snout peninsula, taken hundreds of enemy prisoners, safeguarded an invasion fleet, run the gauntlet of false surrender – repeatedly – and to cap it all they had routed a crack unit of the Panzer-Division Hermann Göring, here in Augusta. Equally importantly, they had seized a key port at Augusta, with its complement of E-boat pens, seaplanes and ships – including an enemy submarine complete with her crew, which would be forced to surrender – and with its harbour facilities, oil tanks and hangars intact. They had faced down enemy armour with little more than sheer bluff and courage, and at every stage of the battle they had never once broken or faltered.

At heart, much of this was down to their *esprit de corps*, their discipline and their training. Of course, all were volunteers, but when they had stepped into their Azzib base and had been flayed and hounded over the sun-blasted plains and hills, many had resented it; resented their merciless taskmaster – Mayne. Many of Mayne's men – originals and newbies alike – had felt him too strict, too hard, too unyielding, as he'd pushed them to their limits, both physically and mentally. Many felt he'd held them to too high a standard, as he'd forced them to work and labour and endure the seemingly unendurable, when in their minds they deserved to rest and take it easy. But now, Mayne had been vindicated. It was their fortitude and above all their spirit, imbued in their training, that had held them firm when many would have faltered.

Having seen Mayne in action, they knew too that he would never ask them to do anything that he would not do himself. For Mayne, that one recognition – that bond – was greater than any accolade from any senior commander; that he could stand tall in the eyes of those he commanded meant all. Over the days just gone his men had been plagued by lack of sleep, proper food, shelter, and in many cases beset by trauma and injury, yet they had pulled through. Key to that had been their sheer physical fitness and stamina – attributes, as Mayne knew from long experience, that were crucial to this kind of war-fighting. That, coupled with their ability to own the night, had enabled them to keep a grip on their nerves long after the breaking point of many would have been reached.

That they had been moulded into single-minded, dauntless, physically superlative, Spartan soldiers had almost passed them by at Azzib; or perhaps the reasons had escaped them. But not anymore. Now, Mayne's raiders understood. Over the days just gone they had displayed the full majesty of their mettle and their martial spirit, and the results spoke for themselves. *This* is what it had all been for. *This* is what justified the seemingly pitiless and punishing regime at Azzib, and the rejections of those who had not made the grade.

Many of these warriors had always looked on Mayne as the greatest leader imaginable. But there had been some who had griped and grumbled as he had striven to keep them at the absolute zenith of physical and mental toughness, in preparation for what they were to endure. Not anymore After they had seen Mayne in action during six days of battle – his sheer calm and coolness under pressure; his laser focus; his instant decision making; his fine animal instincts and innate sense of the fight – he had earned the enduring respect of those he commanded, and their loyalty beyond measure.

Right now, in Augusta, as the gentle hues of a new dawn lit the town, Mayne's warriors felt pretty good. They had run the gauntlet and they had endured. But it had a very close-run thing. Mayne's raiders had been 'pitchforked into a suicidal operation', and once the white flag of surrender had proven false, by rights this should not have gone well for them. If all the heavy gun batteries in Augusta had been properly brought to bear, if the enemy had used their armour to press home their attack, the battle for Augusta could have – should have – constituted 'another Dieppe and annihilation'. Many more would have been killed, wounded, maimed for life, blinded or taken prisoner.

The SAS had just captured the first major enemy naval base in all of Europe. It had done so via a daylight raid, facing ferocious and unexpected resistance. As an indication of what a telling blow it had struck against the enemy, a German military spokesperson would remark that the battle for Augusta had been a 'night of terror the Germans will never forget'. News reports would appear in Germany, describing how it was 'the last straw when in daylight a British Parachute Regiment [sic] landed at Augusta. We were helpless – machine-guns, artillery and mortars were turned on them but still they came on, nothing could stop them.' For those facing Mayne's raiders in the full flood of combat, it had been a night of 'horrors and suspense', one 'they would always remember, among their most uncomfortable experiences'.

As 17 Brigade moved into Augusta, and the SAS wound down from the night's tumult, it was time to do that most special of things – to let the maverick, 'bubbling light-heartedness' of the unit shine through. Having come ashore without rations, 'we set about foraging for food,' Harrison noted. Soon, scores of fires were lit on the pavements, and the 'smell of cooking set our nostrils quivering and our mouths watering . . . The strain on our nerves released, everyone was now in high good humour.' As the tension of the long night ebbed away, spirits soared. Against all odds, they had survived. Apart from the few sad losses, they had lived to fight another day.

Quietly, Mayne drew his senior officers in for a private chat. 'Gentlemen,' he announced, 'I've asked you here to give you what you will take if I don't – a licence to loot.' But he warned them there was one condition: they had two hours to go about their business, no more. 'Anyone who flouts this order will be punished . . . Understood?'

They understood, but many were flummoxed, especially those officers relatively new to the unit. While they realised that their commander was somewhat unorthodox, to give a licence to loot risked a court-martial if it were found out. Mayne, who'd qualified as a lawyer before the war and was working as a solicitor with an Ulster law firm, had a fine grasp of the law. He would have understood exactly the legal ramifications of his actions here. But of course, the men had that very thing in mind anyway – they had already filched whatever food they could find, and had 'booty' on their thoughts – so Mayne was simply giving them the nod.

Still, Bob Bennett felt the need to ask for a private word. 'What about the lads up front, sir? Are they to get nothing?' It was a good point. Some of the units were still holding the perimeter.

'You had better shop for them, Bob,' Mayne replied.

So the die was cast.

Shortly, Bennett found himself quietly passing on that message – the grant of a formal licence to loot – to his men, though of course many were already secretly doing what their commanding officer had seen fit to permit. In a sense, it was almost a let-down to discover that what they'd thought they were taking clandestinely was actually now theirs by right. As Oscar Wilde had once said, 'I love drinking Bovril in secret. It seems almost like a vice.' Or perhaps better still, for where Mayne's men now found themselves: 'I can resist anything except temptation.'

After four years of war, and now the Allied invasion, there was little left in Augusta of great value to filch. But there was a great deal of abandoned Italian and German weaponry, plus an abundance of good Italian wine, and there were the dead to drink to, and not just those of Augusta town. As Bill Deakins noted, seared into his mind from earlier in the war was the image of a 'friend, who, during an advance under shellfire had his head blown off, his body still standing in the erect position'. Those kinds of memories – those horrific images of ordinary men 'making the supreme sacrifice' – haunted the living, especially as they knew it could be them next time around, and that 'there would always be the next time'. The next Tobruk. The next Capo Murro di Porco. The next Augusta.

While food was scarce, Davis, like everyone, discovered there was plenty of liquor 'and soon everyone was feeling pretty merry'. The local Fascist headquarters was tracked down and it was found to be stuffed with propaganda leaflets – now fit only to feed the cooking fires. Syd Payne managed to grab a handful of pens, which he promptly handed around to the men, with the admonition, 'Now be sure and write some letters home, lads.' As he was about to enter one building, Private F. 'Killer' Casey, another of the unit's Irish recruits, found the padre had got there ahead of him.

'What, looting?' Padre Lunt had admonished, being a man of the cloth.

Ignoring the rebuke, Casey and a pal had slid around the back and proceeded to force the rear entrance. Upon stepping inside, they discovered the padre was there already, rummaging around in a cupboard. As the padre spied Casey and his friend, he snatched up a Bible and brandished it, exclaiming, 'I was looking to see if I could find some prayer books for the boys.' Later, all such pretence fell away when the padre turned up in the main square pushing a wheelbarrow heaped with wine – a far more welcome gift for 'the boys' than any holy books.

Padre Lunt – know to all as 'Ronnie' – claimed that he'd collected the vino for the libations, as there was the sorry task of laying the dead to rest. A burial party was detailed to carry out the sombre duty. The padre argued, rightly, that some of his barrowload of bottles should be held in reserve for those tasked to bury the dead – Corporal Bentley and Private Shaw. Phil Gunn was also busy tending to the wounded, and he could surely also do with a stiffener. The padre's points were well made.

Somewhere, someone discovered a pianola – a self-playing piano – and dragged it out onto the streets. Seated on its stool and miming the part to perfection, Corporal Bill Mitchell, Lieutenant Davis's 'shrewd and excellent soldier', acted for all the world as if he were a virtuoso. When someone asked in amazement where he'd learned to play the piano like that, Mitchell turned away from the keyboard and lifted a glass of champagne, as the music continued to play uninterrupted – look, no hands! – to uproarious laughter.

The pianola spawned a spontaneous street party. Shortly, the iconic strains of 'Lili Marlene' – the SAS's own version, penned by Mayne's hand – were ringing out across Augusta town. Oddly, though Mayne himself loved nothing more than a good sing-along, he could barely hold a note, and was generally to be seen mumbling along tunelessly to the words. It did little to dampen his enjoyment. One of the men snapped a photo. It showed a group of merry figures gathered around the pianola, while others sat at kitchen chairs and tables, or lounged in the shade of trees on rugs and blankets.

Though the street cuisine proved basic, the 'unspecified contents' of billies were welcome, especially since 'various bottles of wine had been found to wash down the concoctions'. The carnival atmosphere was redoubled once a now-deserted brothel was discovered. It was well-known among Allied troops that the Axis provided official 'female comforts' to their soldiers. Bereft of its womenfolk and their clientele, the brothel drew the more thespian-minded among Mayne's raiders. Shortly, figures waltzed into the square dressed in all kinds of purloined lingerie. They were bedecked in 'bras, French knickers, petticoats, suspenders, stockings', noted Bill Deakins, and some had managed to squeeze their feet into high-heeled shoes. 'Some of the bolder participants even applied lipstick, rouge and powder to great effect.'

A master of ceremonies stepped forward, and complete with a 'tall, black top hat' he began to direct the 'ladies' in a dance, beating out the rhythm with a cane. As more musical instruments were retrieved from the nearby houses, a makeshift band took up the beat, wielding trumpets, cymbals and tambourines. From somewhere, one of Mayne's men managed to retrieve a three-wheeled Italian ice-cream cart, and he got busy cycling it to and fro. After all, what kind of Italian Carnevale was complete without *gelato*?

A pair of news reporters turned up, complete with their cine cameras. They had been dispatched to Augusta to capture the momentous events – the heroic and daring capture of this major enemy naval base by Allied forces. They had arrived to be met by a scene such as this. Neither reporter seemed the least bit discombobulated – they 'delightedly recorded the scene', before being 'carried off to do a little celebrating of their own'. As for Bill Deakins, he was about to be spirited off on a mystery assignation of a very different nature.

Mayne, together with his trusted corporal, Tommy 'Geordie' Corps, had been scouring the town. Together, they'd discovered an Italian Army barracks and the safe it contained. They'd managed to crowbar it open, only to discover it was full of nothing more than a collection of military stamps. They'd taken them anyway. Who knew – they might come in handy for future operations. From there they'd graduated to the main bank in Augusta's square. The stately building, with its high white façade and ornate iron balconies, had yielded to their demands for entry, but not the bank's safe. The crowbar had done little more than 'break through the outer casing into the fire resistant blue powder' within.

It would require more than a gemmy to bust open, and so Bill Deakins was summoned. He was sitting in the square at the time, enjoying the sun and the 'carnival atmosphere', when Tommy Corps, a good friend, came to find him. The CO wanted him at the town's bank, Corps explained. Deakins made his way over there, to find Mayne busy examining a 'free-standing safe, about four feet by three feet by three'.

Mayne glanced at Deakins. 'Sergeant, I want you to open this safe.'

Who was Deakins to argue? After all, he was 'a Royal Engineer, and they were reputed to do anything, well almost'. Deakins's main problem was that he'd been told their Augusta mission was going to be 'a piece of cake' – no specialist explosives called for – so he'd brought nothing with him. But as he quickly realised, 'this was no excuse.' He asked Mayne and Corps if they might gather together 'six hand grenades . . . some envelopes and a bit of string'. Once the requested items had been fetched, Deakins set to work.

First and foremost, he removed the detonators from the grenades. Just in case. That done, he opened each by removing the 'screw filler caps'. Then, he emptied out their black powder onto a sheet of paper, after which he bodged up some sausage-shaped charges, by stuffing a little of the explosives into each of the envelopes and binding them tight with string. That done, he proceeded to stuff the sausage-charges into the lining of the safe door, wedging them tight against its steel casing. He'd kept one grenade back, and making sure the safety pin was loose in its socket, he wedged it against the nearest of the sausage-shaped charges. Finally, he took the string, tied one end onto the grenade's pin, and looped the length of it up and over a light fitting, around the corner of a nearby staircase and onto the stairs themselves.

When all were gathered 'safely' on the staircase, Deakins gave a sharp tug on the string. Nothing happened. He glanced around the edge of the staircase, only to spy the grenade hanging by its pin and suspended on the end of the string at the level of the light fitting. If the pin popped out, they would have four seconds to dash for cover, before it all went kaboom. With infinite care Deakins stepped across to the grenade, reached up, lowered it and put it back in place, before wiggling the pin into a position from which it could not fail to spring free. All this time, Mayne had been waiting patiently, Deakins noticed, 'knowing a golden rule is that one should not hurry in the use of explosives'.

Back in cover, Deakins tugged again. 'This time, success. A tremendous crash and flash, the whole room was filled with a cloud of choking blue smoke from the fire-resistant materials.' A pall of dust drifted down, covering the three safe-breakers with a fine blue powder. This being Deakins's first experience of acting as a safe-breaker, he was relieved to discover the target had been 'successfully split'. Inside, it was mostly empty. There was a thick sheaf of documents, although as none could read Italian they couldn't quite assess their importance or value. There were also 'six silver spoons tied in a bundle, a gold ring made up of two twined together and a cameo brooch [a brooch showing a figure carved of gemstone]'.

Mayne pulled out the valuables and placed them atop the safe. He turned to Deakins. 'Sergeant, these are for you.' His reward for a job well done.

Then Mayne grabbed the bundle of papers, and he and Tommy Corps left the bank.

In a sense it was inevitable that, sooner or later, news of the freelance larceny and partying in Augusta would reach the ears of the authorities. An Army provost marshal – a military police commander – had arrived in town, intent on getting the area under proper military rule. The entire place was deserted of locals – not a soul was to be seen anywhere – and few Allied ships had yet docked at the port, for there were reports of active gun emplacements sited in the hills, and there had been the odd crash of gunfire. The provost marshal dispatched one of his team – a 'rather pompous' captain – to investigate the rumours of looting and other wild misdemeanours.

He arrived at the town square, surveyed the riotous and chaotic scenes, and ill-advisedly decided to go and tackle whoever the commander of this unit might be. Bustling about self-importantly, he sought out Major Mayne, acting like some sort of 'avenging angel'. In the past, Mayne had had more than his fair share of run-ins with MPs – otherwise known as 'Redcaps', due to their distinctive berets. While he understood they had a job to do, when they muscled in on a scene like this, where brave young men had just experienced some of the toughest fighting of the Sicily campaign, and were now deservedly letting their hair down, he had little sympathy with them.

'Major Mayne,' the Redcap officer began, stiffly, 'I observe that there has been considerable pilfering by your men in this area and I would like to have your explanation . . . Do I make myself clear?'

'You certainly do.' In a flash, Mayne's blue-grey eyes had turned icy, but the young officer failed to detect the tell-tale danger signs.

In a few short strides Mayne crossed the room, grabbed the MP by the scuff of his neck, lifted him up and propelled him through the door. 'Get out, you mongrel dog! And stay out, if you don't want your mongrel neck broken!'

In truth, the captain was fortunate to have left the building by the door and not the window. Deciding discretion was the better part of valour, he beat a hasty retreat. But either way, the spell was broken. For a few short hours Mayne and his men had rested their martial spirits, dropping their guard and letting off steam in Augusta, a key enemy naval base that they had seized by dint of their courage, their verve and their audacity in action. But all good things come to an end.

A destroyer steamed into view. It was there to ferry the raiders back to their winged-dagger warship – the *Ulster Monarch* – before any more harm could be done. It was mid-afternoon when a procession formed up heading for the docks, one that Deakins described as surpassing 'any gathering at the finish of a jumble sale'. One man loaded his booty into a pram. Several others followed suit. There were typewriters, purloined from the odd shop or office, and armfuls of bottles, 'those not used in the celebrations'. Fittingly, the padre clutched several, one joker suggesting he was bringing home the 'communion wine'.

With all loaded aboard, the destroyer made a fast dash for the *Monarch*, zigzagging as she went and throwing up 'tremendous bow waves' as a result of her evasive manoeuvres. Apparently, there was still a threat of submarine attacks or shelling from the distant shore guns, although Deakins suspected the skipper's real motive was to 'shake overboard the piles of souvenirs on his ship's deck'. Arriving at the mothership, the raiders were welcomed home as returning heroes, despite their somewhat odd attire and their eclectic souvenirs. Hot showers and piles of food were the order of the day.

Once he was fed, watered and scrubbed, Deakins made his way to his cabin. A couple of the ship's crew paid him a visit. They asked, jokingly, what souvenirs he had brought them. Deakins figured they deserved something special, bearing in mind how the *Monarch* and her crew had safeguarded and cosseted the ranks of the raiders. To one he gave the gold ring from the bank in Augusta, and to the other the silver spoons. The cameo brooch he kept for himself, or rather for his mother, 'in the hopes I would eventually return home with my present'.

The ship's purser got a typewriter, something he'd long been after. Incredibly, a team would also manage to manhandle the pianola from port to transit ship, and from there onto the *Monarch*, where it would be presented to the vessel's commander, Captain Crash. It would remain with the *Monarch*, playing away merrily, until the end of her service. As for the men of the SAS, they would in time get one of their greatest rewards of all, in the form of the very highest praise from General Dempsey himself, a commander whom they were learning to admire and respect.

'No one . . . could have foretold that things would have turned out as they have,' Dempsey would tell them, with reference to their Augusta mission. Thrust into it with 'no time for careful planning . . . still you were highly successful.' Their Augusta triumph crowned their previous achievements at Capo Murro di Porco, which constituted 'a brilliant operation, brilliantly planned and brilliantly carried out', as Dempsey would describe it. 'Your orders were to capture and destroy a coastal battery, but you did more.'

An extraordinary haul of honours and decorations would

follow for the actions of Mayne and his men during both the Augusta mission and the Capo Murro di Porco raid. For David Sillito, in recognition of his outstanding bravery in executing his two solo dashes through the Augusta streets at the height of the fighting, there was a second bar to his existing Military Medal (MM), the MM first being granted for his solo escape across the desert. For Sergeant Frame – the man who'd carried on leading his patrol through Augusta town, despite being shot in the neck – there was also an MM.

Harry Poat was awarded the MC, while Reg Seekings's actions were honoured with an MM, to add to his Distinguished Conduct Medal (DCM), Britain's oldest award for gallantry (though now discontinued), and which he'd earned for a dozen daring desert raids. Lance-Corporals Dalziel and Jones, and Privates Noble and 'Blondie' Skinner – the man who'd continued fighting on the Pig's Snout peninsula, despite being injured by the 'Bouncing Betty' S-mine – were also awarded the MM.

Johnny Wiseman was awarded a Military Cross (MC), for leading his patrol into the heart of the Pig's Snout gun batteries, bayonets to the fore. 'While the battery was under fire from our mortars, by clever use of ground he led his section to the outskirts of the position without being detected and made his way through the wire,' read Wiseman's citation. Fittingly, it was personally signed off by Mayne. 'Immediately the mortar fire finished, he went straight in, achieving complete surprise, killing, capturing and wounding forty of the enemy. By his good leadership and courage he achieved this without sustaining a single casualty.' The citation further lauded Wiseman's 'determination, initiative, leadership and personal bravery'.

For commanding the Capo Murro di Porco and Augusta

missions, Mayne himself would earn a bar to his existing DSO, an honour given to officers for acts of gallantry just short of deserving the Victoria Cross. The citation praised the 'capture and destruction of a C.D. battery on Capo-Murro-di-Porco, the outcome of which was vital to safe landing of XIII corps. By nightfall . . . had captured 3 additional batteries, 450 prisoners, as well as killing 2–300 Italians.' It also lauded the 'audacity displayed' in the 'capture and holding of town of Augusta. Landing was carried out in daylight, a most hazardous combined operation . . . In both these operations it was Major Mayne's courage, determination and superb leadership, which proved the key to success. He personally led his men from the landing craft, in the face of heavy machine gun fire . . .'

When the Allied commanders had first game-planned the invasion of Sicily, it had been expected to take some ninety days for the seizure of the island to be complete. In fact, it took just thirty-eight. A huge number of Italians were taken prisoner, some 200,000, but their casualties were correspondingly light with some 7,000–8,000 being killed. By contrast, the German forces had fought with far more tenacity and dogged determination, with some 23,000 killed or wounded in action. By dint of courage and tenacity, and by weathering any number of incredibly hard-fought battles, the Allies had won their springboard into the soft underbelly of Europe.

But in mid-July 1943 there was more – much more – to be done.

Chapter Ten

NO ROOM FOR PASSENGERS

In the coming months the *Daily Express* heralded the SAS's outstanding achievements, with a headline running 'The Story of Britain's Most Romantic, Most Daring, and Most Secret Army'. Under a photo of Stirling, captioned 'Colonel David Stirling D.S.O., founder . . . of the S.A.S. He is a prisoner in Germany', the report lauded the Capo Murro di Porco raids especially. 'The SAS were . . . given the honour of starting the invasion of Sicily. Their task was to make an assault landing to eliminate the coastal batteries. They destroyed four batteries and took 500 prisoners.'

It continued:

One day when the war is over it will be possible to do justice to the exploits and personalities of the S.A.S. One Squadron alone . . . has already earned six mentions in dispatches and 45 decorations. Because of the intimate contact between men and officers and the nature of their work, there is enormous camaraderie between all ranks. They seem unconventional and to those that do not know them very free and easy. But like the successful pirates of the 17th Century they are ruthlessly efficient about their work. There is no room for passengers.

As the *Express* article made clear, much of this had been achieved after 'Mayne took over command'.

Yet in truth Mayne had only secured his position of command by default. On 14 February 1943, David Stirling's capture had been reported in the SAS War Diary: 'Lt. Co. A. [Archibald] D. Stirling D.S.O. (Scots Gds) the Commanding Officer of this unit was officially reported as missing, believed prisoner of war.' The very next day there is an entry which reads: 'Major V. W. Street O.B.E. M.C. (DEVONS) returned from convalescence and assumed command of this unit.' From then onwards 'Major V W Street O.B.E. M.C.' is listed as 'Commanding Officer, 1st S.A.S. Regiment'.

Major Street – Wellington School-educated and Royal Military College, Sandhurst-trained – had earned his MC in 1938 for his 'untiring energy and devotion to duty' while combatting 'Arab insurgents' in Palestine. Recruited by Stirling, he was a courageous and experienced officer, but had joined the SAS only relatively recently, being given command of B Squadron, a unit of mostly fresh recruits, in October 1942. He lacked the longevity, the experience and the talismanic status within the unit that Mayne possessed. A matter of weeks after being appointed as the SAS's commander, Street was himself captured while leading a patrol to harass Rommel's lines. 'Reached his area and believed to have attacked enemy column of vehicles,' noted a report in the SAS War Diary. 'Later was forced to leave jeeps. He marched a considerable distance for several days, but was eventually captured.'

After Street had been taken prisoner, on 8 March 1943 'Lt. Col H. J. Cator M.C.' assumed command of the SAS. Henry 'Kid' Cator, Royal Scots Greys, was the former commander of No. 51 Commando, which had done sterling work in the East Africa campaign, fighting the Italians in what was then Abyssinia and in Eritrea. As much as anything, Cator's appointment reflected the desire from on high to do away with this troublesome unit – these 'raiders of the thug variety' – and to shoehorn them into the Commandos. As the exploits of Mayne's raiders in Italy had proven so resoundingly, in this they had failed. Yet it certainly wasn't for want of trying.

In due course Vivien Street would execute a daring escape from a torpedoed Italian submarine, returning to the SAS base camp in the spring of 1943. But by then the die was cast. As Stirling realised, his own capture had presented the perfect opportunity for 'reeling in the troublesome SAS'. Stirling viewed Middle East Headquarters (MEHQ) as a bunch of 'mediocrities from the First World War who were opposed to the methods of the SAS'. They longed to put the unit back in its box.

From captivity in Campo No. 5, in Gavi, Italy – a forbidding medieval fortress known to all as the 'hell camp' – Stirling had intervened, sending word on whom his successor should be. As far as he was concerned, Mayne had a 'marvellous battle nostril. He could really sense precisely what he had to do in a situation.' He was also the man who would fight tooth and nail to stop the SAS from being snuffed out, of that Stirling felt certain. 'Paddy was hugely brave,' he would declare, and 'he was exactly the man I wanted to succeed me in command of 1 SAS.'

Amateurs rather than career soldiers – Mayne was a solicitor, Stirling an adventurer and an artist – both were unconstrained by regimented, parade-ground thinking. Neither had been moulded by traditional military instruction. Indeed, prior to the war, at Queen's University Officer Training Corps (OTC), Mayne had been assessed as 'unpromising material for a combat regiment, undisciplined, unruly and generally unreliable'. In the SAS, both he and Stirling had striven for something far more elusive: the alchemy of 'transformational command'. They had sought to lead not by dint of rank, privilege or diktat, but by sheer example, and inspired by the need to defeat a great evil – Nazism. Being bound together in a 'superior adventure' – a moral crusade – lent 'immense value to our striving', as one recruit would put it. Cliché though it might sound, they were 'all for one, and one for all', united in the one overarching cause.

A proud Irishman and Ulsterman, hailing from a well-to-do Protestant mercantile and landowning family, Mayne was neither public school-educated nor of the titled aristocracy. Stirling was both, as were so many who had joined No. 8 Guards Commando and had been subsequently recruited into the SAS. But that had done nothing to detract from their union of equals, Stirling and Mayne, as they had honed and shaped and nurtured this unit. Yet it did much to account for the official reticence about appointing Mayne – the maverick and the outsider – to a position of command.

In addition to his sheer physical presence and martial repute, Mayne had a manner that tended to unsettle people. The sixth of seven siblings, he'd been raised in a busy, convivial family, at Mount Pleasant, a fine Georgian house surrounded by 40 acres of woodland, perfect for hunting and fishing, some of his favourite childhood pastimes. Schooled at the local Newtownards grammar – he'd proved a shy, awkward type, with his head forever stuck in a book; a 'gentle giant', as his schoolmates referred to him. But then he'd discovered sport, and rugby in particular, and the future warrior-leader began to emerge. By age eighteen he had been made captain of the local Ards Rugby Club First XV, a team that boasted any number of grizzled veterans of the game, Mayne being viewed as 'an ideal leader'.

While studying law at Queen's University, Belfast, he'd taken up boxing, and by 1936, aged twenty-one, had been crowned the Irish Universities heavyweight champion. The following year he'd won the first of his six caps for Ireland at rugby, against Wales, before being selected for the Lions tour. But his sporting record was peppered with his maverick, leftfield mindset. Modest to a fault, he'd found the praise heaped upon him intensely embarrassing. Hugely loyal, he would do whatever it took to protect and safeguard his teammates. Yet with his strict moral code and compass, a legacy of his upbringing, those two things often pulled in opposite directions.

One story demonstrates this most powerfully. In Mayne's last appearance for Ireland, before war was declared, they'd played Wales in Belfast, Ireland losing 7-0. At one stage Mayne had seen his diminutive Queen's University and Lions room-mate and friend, George Cromey, floored by a massive Welsh forward. After Mayne had appealed to the referee, who took no action, he wrought his own form of justice. At the next breakdown, he 'knocked out four Welsh forwards, with one of them left bleeding profusely'.

Some of Mayne's family were watching the match, and his mother sent one of his sisters down to the touchline, bearing a handkerchief and a note. It read: 'That was very unsportsmanlike Blair. Use the hanky to tidy up that young man's face.'

Mayne approached his bloodied victim. 'My mother says I've to clean your nose and if you don't stand still and play along while I do I'll break every bone in your face.'

During the Lions tour of South Africa he'd torn it up with the best of them. Two of Mayne's singularly rambunctious exploits would come to define his behaviour off the field. In the first, growing bored at an official black-tie function, he'd wandered off, gone hunting with some Afrikaners, bagged a springbok – an African antelope – and returned to the squad's hotel in a bloodied tuxedo, bearing 'fresh meat' for the team. In the second, which epitomised his fierce association with the underdog, he and a Welsh teammate, Bill Travers, had freed a black 'convict' – serving seven years for stealing a chicken – cutting his chains, and giving him their clothes in which to make good his getaway. When 'Rooster', as they'd nicknamed him, was finally recaptured, he was found to be wearing a blazer with Mayne's name sewn into the collar.

Mayne's tendency to do what he believed was right – taking the law into his own hands, if necessary – as opposed to what was diplomatic or in his own best interests, would come to define him. It made him beloved by those he commanded, yet loathed by many in high command. In his lightning assessment of others, he found it impossible to hide his dislike of those he took against; those who managed to 'get his goat'. His quiet, faltering, shy manner – especially in front of crowds – did little to finesse his outspoken ways. He seemed pathologically incapable of not telling the truth, or of not saying exactly what he thought. As just one example, many of the blue-blood types tended to refer to SAS operations, somewhat euphemistically, as 'good sport'. Mayne termed them simply 'good killing'.

When he'd first used that phrase before Malcolm Pleydell, the SAS's newly recruited medic had been shocked. But in time he came to understand that it epitomised Mayne's clarity of vision. Mayne knew and accepted exactly what they were there for, and he didn't beat about the bush. He understood what he and his men had to do, and he faced it head-on. That was the kind of mindset that lay behind the decision to go in at Capo Murro di Porco with fixed bayonets, to break the Italians' resolve and their nerve. It wasn't nice and it wasn't pretty – it certainly wasn't 'good sport' – but it was what was needed to turn the Allies' fortunes in this war.

Over time Mayne's attitude drew those that he led into a steely alliance; an unbreakable bond. In time, Mayne and the well-read, cultured Pleydell would become the best of friends, the doctor ending up being Mayne's unlikely champion. As Pleydell had confessed in his diary, he was nervous of showing a lack of fortitude and bravery. 'Courage with me was flickering and evanescent, present one second, absent the next. Just a matter of trying to control fear, let alone panic and cowardice.' By contrast, and as Pleydell had appreciated, fighting was in Mayne's blood. More often than not, it was his sharply honed instincts that had kept them alive. Even after Pleydell had left the SAS, plagued by the 'cafard', he and Mayne would remain close friends. Mayne would write to Pleydell from Italy, as the doctor languished in hospital finding it 'difficult not to day-dream' about his time in the desert with his friends. While Pleydell had resigned from the unit, his nerve having gone, he missed them all – 'those moments of good fellowship' – terribly.

Describing in his letters their seaborne landings on Sicily, Mayne regaled Pleydell with how 'the Unit has done smashingly well. General Dempsey, the Corps commander, paid us what, I imagine, were the highest compliments of any unit. Amongst other things he said we were the best crowd he had ever had under his command. I think he is right, too; the lads have done well!' Languishing in his hospital bed, Pleydell comforted himself with the thought that the SAS's hard-won 'desert reputation' looked set to be 'more than justified by its deeds in Europe'.

To many, Mayne was an oddball. To those he commanded, he was little short of a god. As Seekings would remark, 'Paddy Mayne was the man by now – Paddy was Paddy in no uncertain terms.' Mayne despised humbug and hypocrisy, yet in no way did he despise authority itself; rather, he abhorred 'the abuse of it; those who were proud and conceited'. With the SAS being a classless, egalitarian outfit, Mayne epitomised that spirit. He was happy to spend time talking to anyone, no matter their rank or social status. While he would forge a healthy rapport with senior commanders like Dempsey and Montgomery, he could not abide grandstanding. As Syd Payne noted, when Mayne introduced General Montgomery to Johnny Rose, their regimental sergeant major, during a troop inspection, Monty seemed minded to ignore Rose. Mayne's response was to grab hold of Monty and reiterate, pointedly, 'And this is my RSM!'

Some had feared that Mayne, their superlative frontline warrior, would fail to win the backroom battles to safeguard their unit from ruin. That had been David Stirling's forte. As Mayne fully appreciated, Stirling had the gift of the gab and of persuasion, and he knew absolutely how to play the game. Stirling had recruited Churchill's son, Randolph, for a raid on Benghazi. He and Randolph had served together in No. 8 Commando, and once Randolph had related his SAS experiences to his father, it had won them Churchill's undying support. Canny, when facing so many powerful detractors. As Mayne recognised, Stirling was a master of 'making you think you are the most important person . . . Stirling was a master of that art and it got him good results.' Mayne was not blessed with the gift of the gab or of an easy charm. Instead, he inspired by pure example.

Having saved the SAS from ruin, Mayne felt a driving need to prove that the unit still had a purpose. When he had mustered his men at Azzib in March 1943, prior to starting their long months of training, he'd talked to them plainly about the challenges that lay ahead. His words, simply and forthrightly offered, and spoken in that 'shy, halting' manner of his, tinged with a strong Irish brogue, spoke volumes. 'As some of you no doubt know, I have been up in Cairo during the past week at G.H.Q. The war in the desert is over. When I first went to G.H.Q. I was told there was no more useful work for the S.A.S. I did not agree. I said as much. It has been a hard fight and a long one.'

Mayne had won them a reprieve, but they were very much on probation. The upside, as Peter Davis noted, was that 'Paddy was the boss and took no orders from anyone'. Four months later, they had proved their worth, and by mid-July 1943 Mayne and his men had been fully vindicated. As the SAS War Diary concluded of this time, Mayne 'resisted successfully all attempts' to eviscerate the SAS, ensuring that 'the Regiment lived on. His untiring efforts, his insistence upon proper discipline, and his instinctive realisation of the really important things, soon welded the Special Raiding Squadron into a formidable fighting unit . . .'

After their wild partying in Augusta was done – that momentary upsurge of 'bubbling light-heartedness' – Mayne reverted to his unyielding strictures and rigid regimen. In the direct aftermath of Augusta, seven officers and men were returned to their units, for they had abandoned their positions guarding the approaches to the isthmus at the height of that long night's fighting. No censure – no dishonour – accrued to those who had 'crapped out'. There was no public shaming. It was purely in the cause of safeguarding the lives of *all* of those he commanded – those who remained, and those that he was obliged to reject – that Mayne sent them on their way.

Likewise, a few days after pulling out of Augusta, he and his men were back at it, training. Augusta had been no more than a blip. Fleetingly, Mayne had given his men a licence to loot and to party and to let off steam. Just as quickly, it was back to business, as the entries in the War Diary made clear. 'General training (Cliff work, PT, etc), nothing to note.' 'General training. Nothing to note.' 'General training. Nothing to note.' 'Nothing to note. 2 ORs returned to unit for disciplinary reasons.'

At the same time as he honed his unit for impending action, Mayne was determined that all should know exactly what risks they faced. The horrific treatment of some of the captured 'glider boys' on Sicily had set the tone for what they all should expect. The intimations of Hitler's Commando Order cast a darker shadow, especially as they would increasingly face German forces once the thrust into mainland Italy began. In due course Mayne would issue a directive, stating that anyone taking part in 'SAS operations should be fully informed of the risks they are running and be given the opportunity of refusing'. Likewise, 'any person concerned with the planning of any such operations must be fully aware of the risks the men . . . are running.'

For Mayne, keeping such things secret was unconscionable.

Only those who knew the risks and accepted them wholeheartedly should be there. Otherwise, it would sow division and disunity. Whether Mayne knew it or not – and he must have suspected – he was personally at the top of the enemy's hit list. With Stirling's capture, a stool pigeon – the nastiest species of traitor and turncoat – had been inserted into the erstwhile SAS commander's prison cell. Shrewd, cunning, devious, Theodore Schurch was a former British soldier turned Italian agent who had chosen to betray his country due to a perceived slight, but mostly in pursuit of status and money.

Schurch had been given a special duty – to penetrate the SAS and winkle out its secrets. Already, intelligence he had provided had resulted in the capture of a number of SAS patrols, as he would confess after the war. 'I mixed with three officers and also other ranks . . . and from information received in this manner and from documents captured we found where other patrols were located, and also their strength. From this information . . . we were able to capture two other patrols and acquired information as to the operations of other patrols in the area . . .'

Unsurprisingly, Stirling had proven a restless prisoner, and his characteristic defiance had resulted in his being 'struck . . . in the face' when 'attempting to escape' in April 1943. His attacker, Colonel Giuseppe Moscatelli, an 'ardent Fascist', was notorious for his 'harsh and unjust sentences'. But no amount of beatings, solitary confinement or being chained in his cell had any great effect on Stirling. Thus it was that subterfuge was resorted to, in an effort to break his resilience . . . and in the form of Theodore Schurch.

As Schurch would subsequently confess, he had felt a bizarre kind of thrill upon coming face to face with David Stirling, 'the commanding officer of the men and officers with whom he had spent all his time obtaining information'. He spent two weeks in and out of Stirling's company, posing as 'Captain John Richards', a British officer captured during the fall of Tobruk. Though each man would recall their time together quite differently, Schurch was adamant that he had achieved his mission – to discover Stirling's successor. 'This I found out to be a Captain Paddy Mayne,' he noted, simply.

If not from Schurch, then Mayne's role and identity were bound to be known from an even more odious traitor, one who had served at the heart of the SAS itself. A serial fantasist, fraudster, philanderer and bigamist, the self-declared 'Honourable Douglas Webster St Aubyn Berneville-Claye, Lord Charlesworth' was in truth plain Douglas Claye. Somehow, at the outbreak of war he had used his fake aristocratic identity to talk his way into Sandhurst, earning an officer's commission, and in the autumn of 1942 he had volunteered for the SAS. With his 'film star looks' and his bloated pomposity – 'an intelligent and vain man who always brags' – Claye proved deeply unpopular, rapidly earning the nickname 'Lord Chuff', a polite word for backside.

Shortly before Christmas Day 1942, Claye was captured while on operations. An entry in the SAS War Diary reflected how completely Claye's deception had been swallowed by the unit: '2/ Lt. D.W. St. A. Berneville-Claye (Lord Charlesworth) . . . reported missing on operations in W. Desert, 23-12-42.' A future member of the SS (*Schutzstaffel*) who would go on to lead a patrol of the British Free Corps – a Waffen-SS unit made up of British volunteers – Claye would be questioned in depth by his captors about his time with the SAS. Becoming in turn a stool pigeon, a German informant and an agent spreading pro-Nazi propaganda, Claye had served on Operation Bigamy, the SAS's disastrous September '43 Benghazi raid. Worse still, he'd soldiered for a short period under Mayne.

A few weeks prior to his capture, Claye had joined Mayne's A Squadron on its 440-mile trans-Saharan sojourn, forty jeeps covering that distance in a record thirty-six hours, to reach a new operational base at Bir Zelten. With Rommel on the retreat, this had become the place from which to harry the enemy's supply lines. During that epic drive, Claye had shared a jeep with none other than Johnny Wiseman – the man whose bayonet charge at the Pig's Snout peninsula would earn him an MC. 'The jeep driven by 2/Lt. Lord Charlesworth and 2/Lt. Wiseman had nine punctures,' the SAS War Diary noted of that long drive, most of which Claye spent behind the wheel. Taken captive not a month later, Claye knew the operations of the SAS from the inside out, and, as his future actions would betray, he had every reason to talk.

So hungry had Rommel been to destroy the SAS – this cause of 'considerable havoc', who 'seriously disquieted' his troops – that he had set up a special unit tasked to hunt down their patrols. The *Fallschirmjäger* z.b.V. 250 battalion – several hundred elite German paratroopers – had trained with captured SAS jeeps, to better understand what exactly they were up against. Sure enough, it was that unit that had captured David Stirling in February '43. Knowing that Mayne was Stirling's successor, and that the SAS would be at the forefront of the push into Europe, the enemy would be vigilant. Mayne was right to be wary of their predations, and to seek to alert his men. Forewarned was forearmed.

*

Two days after being pulled out of Augusta, the SAS was put ashore again, for the *Ulster Monarch* – like most Allied warships then anchored off Sicily – had come under sustained attack from enemy warplanes. As the fleet of LCAs ferried them to shore, all had presumed this was only a temporary parting, so no proper farewells were necessary. But as matters transpired, fate was taking the captain and crew of the *Monarch* – complete with her winged-dagger badges – and the SAS in very different directions. The ship boasted a 'very gallant and big-hearted' crew, as Davis described them, who would be sorely missed.

The SAS pitched camp among some olive trees. For a few days life reverted to a mixture of R&R – mainly swimming in the sea – and training, with a good dash of local colour and the odd air raid thrown in. Padre Lunt tried reinstating Sunday church service: a diving, strafing German fighter – a Messerschmitt Me 109 – put paid to all that. Someone stole a local pig to supplement their monotonous diet – mostly bully beef and hardtack biscuit. The farmer came and complained to Mayne. His response was to fine all of those who had feasted on the meat to compensate the farmer for his loss. On the shoreline they discovered an abandoned Italian military dinghy, complete with heaps of kit. Italian soldiers were simply downing guns, donning civilian clothing and returning to their villages.

There were fallouts between individuals, but as Deakins pointed out, in a unit such as theirs 'men with difficult personalities' did not last. Ever resourceful, Deakins, realising they could no longer make use of the *Ulster Monarch*'s laundry facilities, noticed some Sicilian women washing clothes in a stream. He cut a deal for them to do the same for him. When he returned with a bundle of clothing plus some bars of soap, the Italian women 'broke out into excited chatter'. They'd not seen real soap for an age. They asked if they could use it to wash their hair. It seemed more than fair. At that they stripped to their waists and began to lather up, excitedly. It made Deakins realise 'how much female company meant in our lives'. He ended up giving them all the soap he had, it 'meaning so much to them'.

Their diet being so dull, Deakins – along with the rest of the men – tried a little barter with the locals. Their cigarettes and chocolate were the most sought-after items. At one farm, an elderly man exchanged some beef for cigarettes. A young lady was breastfeeding an infant, with another child clutching her skirts. Deakins gave her some chocolate. She disappeared into the farmhouse and returned with a cup of milk. Taking it gratefully, Deakins began to drink, before realising that it was the woman's 'own milk'. Growing up in the Devon countryside, he knew the taste of cow's milk, and with four younger sisters, he knew the smell of breast milk too. The elderly farmer laughed. Deakins, he gestured, had just 'made a friend for life'.

There was a mail delivery. As the men used to joke, serving in Middle East Forces (the MEF) signified that they were the 'Men England Forgot'. Mail was invariably late. Of course, there were some letters that would never be read by the intended recipients – the fallen of the squadron. 'Perhaps this is where the expression "dead letter" comes from,' observed Deakins, bleakly. But it also meant a chance to dispatch letters home, and for Mayne to write – as he did religiously – to the families of those they had lost. Mayne also wrote extensively to his own family, especially his mother, and to Barbara – 'Babs' – the third eldest sibling, with whom he'd always had close, big-sisterly kind of relations.

'Before we came on this op, we were inspected and spoken to

by all the generals and, I believe, impressed them with our looks and turnout,' Mayne wrote to her. 'I was pleased with that, but I was more pleased by how we impressed the Jerrys and Ities, and we did that to no mean tune. We went at them like terriers after rats . . .' Writing of the 'attack on Augusta', he remarked: 'I wonder if you heard anything about it on the wireless or in the papers. Probably didn't – we never have had much publicity.'

Mayne's pride in the reconstituted SAS jumps off the pages, as does his regret that his men – 'Britain's Most Secret Army' as the *Daily Express* would hail them – rarely got any public recognition. 'I would like to bring this unit home and swagger about Great Britain with them. They would make the home troops look pretty pallid. They look damned smart. We wear blue shirts with our parachute wings on the left breast if they have done three successful operations behind the line, and on the right arm if they haven't. We have a very snappy beret, beige and our own badge. I'll send you one sometime. Altogether we look pretty nifty . . . Absolutely beautiful day. Blue Mediterranean. A pleasant cool wind blowing. I hope Douggie got the watch I sent him. Be good. B.' 'B' was for Blair, of course, and Douggie was Mayne's younger brother.

Mayne was full of pride that so many Irishmen served in the SAS. There was Sergeant Christie O'Dowd, with his wild mop of curly dark hair, one of eleven siblings of Galway farming stock. There was Lieutenant Bill McDermott, a wild raider cut from the same cloth as Mayne. In North Africa, McDermott and O'Dowd had taken an SAS patrol deep into the desert, to seize and lay waste to an enemy railway station. For that mission, O'Dowd would earn an MM, his citation stressing his 'consistent bravery and steadiness'. (Sadly, McDermott would get captured, alongside David Stirling.) There had been Eoin McGonigal, of course, Mayne's best friend, who hailed from Donegal and who'd perished on the SAS's first, ill-fated mission. Then there was Sergeant Charles 'Pat' Riley, a giant of an Irish-American who had inveigled his way into the British military, and was an SAS original and another standout warrior. And there were many more.

Mayne and his siblings had grown up in a house full of Irish music, invariably the folk songs of Percy French, with their roguishly rebellious lyrics. Likewise, when operating from their base in the Great Sand Sea, Mayne's A Squadron had taken on a markedly Celtic hue. They'd painted lucky shamrocks on their jeeps, Mayne's deputies wheeling out their range of Irish renegade songs around the fire of an evening. 'Paddy was Irish all right,' Pleydell would remark of that time, 'Irish from top to toe; from the lazy eyes that could light into anger so quickly, to the quiet voice and its intonation.'

The Mayne family home was always full of animals – chickens, ducks and dogs. Mayne would nurture a lifelong love of them, but especially of dogs. His favourite, a St Bernard-Collie cross, would know instinctively when his master was about to come home and would go outside and wait for him. Mayne would write to his eldest sister, Mary (known to all as 'Mollie' in the family), about a new puppy she was looking after while he was away waging war. 'I am sorry the pup has given you so much trouble, it is very good of you to look after it for me.' Mayne added that he 'hoped to manage some leave' – he was now twenty-eight years old and had not been home for well over two years – so he could get to see the pup. 'He sounds quite pleasant.'

Mayne also wrote extensively to 'Funnyface' – his nickname

for his niece, Margaret – his letters full of a playful, offbeat sense of humour. From the Lions tour of South Africa, he'd described how 'You would certainly enjoy yourself out here, there are hundreds of animals – stags, antelopes, elephants; in fact everything that runs on four legs.' He'd signed off the missive, 'I sent your young brother a card ... Tell him I expect a reply in his own writing. My address is: British Rugby Football Team, c/o South African Rugby Football Board, PO 2336, Capetown.' As Margaret was only nine years old, it was a typical Mayne tease about her younger brother, whom he'd nicknamed 'String', writing a reply to his 'uncle Blair'. He also warned her that if she got 'her Daddy' to read his letter, 'I will tie your ears together when I come home.' He signed off by reminding her, tongue in cheek, 'Don't forget to put your curls in at night.'

The solicitous, playful 'Uncle Blair' was a side of the SAS commander that those who served with him for long enough got to see, in the care and concern he showed for his men, and in the boisterous partying that bubbled up every now and again. But with his niece, it came to the fore chiefly in his letters. 'I am surprised to hear you are getting a band in your mouth,' he wrote to Funnyface. By band he meant a molar band, a type of a braces. 'You must have grown a lot since I last saw you, but still I can't see how you can possibly get more than one or two instruments in. If you want ... music, I would have thought a small wireless set would have been better ... Must finish, don't forget to let me know how the band plays & give my best wishes to all your family.'

Those few short days of downtime – letter-writing, sea-swimming, bartering food – camped out above Augusta couldn't last. As Mussolini himself had admitted, when writing in his diary,

Sicily looked set to fail to emulate Stalingrad in a quite spectacular fashion. In his 14 July diary entry, Il Duce described the situation as both delicate and disquieting. In identifying the factors that had led to such runaway Allied gains, he listed the fall of Syracuse and Augusta as being two of the greatest concern. Among other aspects, Mussolini noted that the battle for Sicily had reached a critical point, due to the Allies using 'special service troops'.

Just as Il Duce stressed the crucial role of 'special service troops', so Allied commanders were fully aware what a potent force they constituted. They were a game-changer. Within forty-eight hours of setting camp above Augusta, the SAS was warned off for the first of several do-or-die missions. Catania – the island's second city and a key Allied objective – was stubbornly holding out. The SAS was to lead a spearhead assault to try to 'break the deadlock'. As Derrick Harrison remarked, the men sensed that this was it – that 'the Special Raiding Squadron was about to go out in a blaze of glory'.

While his men readied themselves, grimly, for whatever might lie before them, Mayne was whisked aboard a Royal Navy ship for a planning conference. His return was watched closely for some sign, for his 'expression was an accurate barometer of the difficulties ahead', remarked Harrison. 'He smiled, and the tenseness fell away.' The relieved cry went up: 'Job off!'

A second mission was announced. The SAS was to be dropped behind the lines, at Capo d'Alì, lying some 150 kilometres north of Augusta, to sabotage a key road and railway tunnel, so barring the enemy's route of retreat. Deakins began to practise with whatever explosives he could muster, scavenging some barrel-like depth charges from the Italian naval base at Augusta. He reckoned those, attached to a length of detonating cord, plus a 'twenty-five pound tin of ammonal' – a budget version of TNT – would do the trick. The resulting blast on an 'elevated section of virtually unused country road' sent 'masonry and debris whistling through the air', and caused 'considerable damage to the roadway'. Unfortunately, the eruption had been so massive that it had also served to blow in most of the nearby doors and windows.

A delegation of officers was sent around, offering apologies to the locals. One was a Royal Engineers captain who'd been foisted upon the squadron by headquarters, to oversee the demolitions side of things. Mayne had accepted this imposition, but only on one condition – that Deakins remained fully in charge on the ground. Despite the success of Deakin's DIY charges, the mission was called off. The Royal Engineers captain was sent on his way, but not before he'd offered Sergeant Deakins – with whom he had been mightily impressed – immediate promotion if he would join his own unit. Deakins – 'extremely gratified in the confidence' Mayne had shown in his abilities – declined.

Apparently, their mission was cancelled because Allied commanders feared the tunnel, once blown, would hold up any Allied advance, as much as it might hinder the enemy in retreat. One moment, the men had been stiffening their nerves, as they faced a mission deep behind enemy lines. The next, they had been stood down. Twice now. Chafing at the bit, the mood worsened. From somewhere, Padre Lunt procured a barrel of red wine. 'Instead of fighting for our lives we spent the night drinking from a cask,' Davis noted, as the men did their best to bury their frustrations. As all hungered for action, this did not sit well with the men at all.

The air raids intensified. Dawn showed where chunks of shrapnel had rained down all night long. No matter the pace of training – the early-morning route marches were back with a vengeance – frustration due to the lack of action and a sense of purpose kept mounting. Sensing this, Mayne set his men a new challenge. All barring those temporarily disabled due to injury or sickness were to scale the 11,000-foot peak of Mount Etna. This they did, only to realise that Mayne intended several such training climbs.

Even so, discipline frayed. In ones and twos, 'loot crazy' men sneaked off for a spree of covert larceny. Augusta town had been declared 'off-limits' by the Redcaps, due to the 'disgraceful amount of looting' that had gone on before. Mayne's response – the lawyer in him to the fore – was to pass a series of anti-looting laws. But not everyone paid heed. 'Some ass in No. 3 Troop' decided to ignore the orders, Davis noted. Mayne found out, and was immediately on the warpath. He paraded the entire troop, going down the line and emptying out 'the kit of each man, throwing onto a fire . . . any article which had not been in the man's possession' before reaching Sicily. It stopped the looting in its tracks, but it also caused a degree of bitterness among the men. Yet, as Davis noted, 'bitterness could not last long in a regiment such as ours,' and especially bearing in mind what was coming.

As Mayne had become their Leonidas at the Pass of Thermopylae, so they were the Spartans. An elite bond had been forged. As with the Spartans, there was a strong sense of fatalism – that they were doomed to die in battle, but gloriously. As much as Mayne welded them into a brotherhood, he epitomised all that they longed to be, and this strengthened their bond. His sporting renown, his martial repute, his leading from the front – but also his sense of what was right, of the righteousness of their fight, and his fairness to all – forged the brotherhood more closely. As the future padre of the SAS, Fraser McLuskey, would remark: 'he had a natural sensitivity . . . with the men he commanded. If they were in trouble . . . if they suffered from a raid, he would suffer with them . . . More than that, he was both loved and trusted by them in a unique degree.'

The squadron decamped and loaded aboard a slow and lumbering Italian train, which steamed north towards Catania. That vital objective had recently fallen to Allied forces, after a fearsome artillery bombardment had finally broken the enemy's resolve. Sadly, in the interim, the *Ulster Monarch* had been in the thick of the action, being set upon by enemy warplanes. Three bombs had targeted the ship, the first two being near-misses, straddling her midships, while the third had hit her 12-pounder stern gun and torn through the deck below, the blast ripping through the hull just above the waterline. The explosion had triggered a fire, threatening to ignite the ship's stores of fuel and, worse still, the magazines of ammunition. Heroic actions from the crew had saved the day, for if the ammo had exploded, the ship would have been lost.

The *Monarch* had steamed to Tripoli for repairs, and to offload her dead and wounded. In her place, at Catania a fleet of US-made Landing Craft Infantry (LCI) vessels awaited the SAS. Far larger than the diminutive craft that the *Monarch* had carried, each LCI was approaching 160 feet in length, and could carry around 180 men. With a top speed of 16 knots and a crew of twenty-four, these were self-sufficient ships designed to spirit troops and their kit across oceans and to land them ashore. A far meatier kind of craft, boasting four Oerlikon 20mm cannons and armour, the LCIs were in theory a big step up from the *Monarch*'s boats. But how they would compare when the bullets started to fly remained to be seen.

Shell-scarred and depopulated, Catania appeared 'dark, black and cold; all very eerie', Deakins noted. On arrival, he was sadly to be grounded, or at least taken off combat operations. Plagued by an old wartime injury – back trouble – he was to wait there for the arrival of the squadron's transport section, which was being shipped over from North Africa. It came complete with a fleet of 15cwt Bedford trucks, a powerful and versatile vehicle perfect for carrying the SAS's stores. Equally important, as far as Deakins was concerned, they were bringing with them Tiny, a terrier bitch who was 'very much a friend once again' when she was reunited with the men.

In theory, Tiny belonged to Corporal Tommy 'Geordie' Corps, Mayne's sometime batman, and Deakins's erstwhile partner in blowing up the safe in the Augusta bank. In practice, Tiny was beloved of all the men, and was the squadron's de facto mascot. Somehow, Mayne didn't feel a military camp was ever complete without a dog. Tiny filled that vacuum. But for now, she would arrive too late to sail from Catania with the main force. Once again, the role set the SAS, at General Dempsey's behest, was to crowbar open the enemy's defences, spearheading the move into mainland Italy itself. Perhaps Tiny – and Deakins – were blessed with good fortune not to be setting sail, considering all that was to follow.

For the coming landings, the SAS was charged to 'capture, occupy and hold Bagnara Calabra' – a coastal town set on the south-western tip of Italy – before thrusting on to seize the vital road and bridges leading inland. As the incredibly detailed RAF reconnaissance photos revealed, that road snaked inland from the shore, climbing steeply through dramatic hills, being channelled through a series of hairpin bends, rock-hewn chasms and tunnels. It was intended to be the vital artery to speed the Allied advance. Under Montgomery, the Eighth Army was to follow in the SAS's wake, landing nearby before advancing through Bagnara, using its road to link up with the US Fifth Army, which would be putting ashore at Salerno, further north along the coast.

The SAS had sailed from North Africa for Sicily with 288 men. They would set out for the landings on the Italian mainland with seventeen officers and 227 men – so 244 all told. The rest had fallen by the wayside, killed or wounded in action, or – like Deakins – beset by illness or plagued by old injuries. The distance by sea from the northern tip of Allied-held Sicily to Bagnara Calabra – enemy territory – was less than 20 kilometres.

Yet the challenges the coming mission posed to Mayne's raiders would prove legion.

Chapter Eleven

HIT THE BEACHES

The September night was icy-black and bitterly cold on the exposed LCI's deck. Harrison awoke, cold and cramped. He'd tried to find some shelter in the lee of one of the guns, but still he was frozen stiff. Unused to operating from the LCIs, he felt confused and disoriented. This was no *Ulster Monarch*, that was for certain. Up ahead lay the Italian coastline, 'like a long black cloud low on the horizon'. Slowly, 'alone with the white wash of our propellers', the ship crept closer towards shore, the two banks of powerful Detroit diesel engines gradually quietening, until forward progress was at a dead slow.

Two tiny shapes detached themselves from the LCI and flitted like shadows towards land – a pair of assault craft bearing the beach-proving party. All there was to do on the mothership now was wait. 'We strained our eyes,' remarked Harrison, 'watching for the winking light that was to be our signal to close in . . .' The minutes seemed like hours. 'Then it came. Two long flashes and one short.' The signal that all seemed clear. The LCI's engines revved, as this and her sister ship – the SAS was riding aboard two LCIs – closed for the shore.

The ship's invasion lighting, casting a dull red or blue glow, 'gave a sinister and grotesque twist to our faces', Davis noted, as ghostly figures hurried forward to gather, tensely, at the landing ramps. Hunched in the half-light, poised for the 'Go!', a 'resounding boom' echoed across from the shoreline. A whisper ran around the ship: 'Demolitions!' Did that mean their force had been spotted? No way of knowing. No turning back now.

Davis noticed Harry Poat, his section commander, looking decidedly unsettled. In fact, he seemed to be in a steaming temper, which wasn't like the former Guernsey tomato farmer at all. Something had to be wrong.

'God knows what the Navy think they are doing,' Poat barked, gruffly. 'I've never come across a more clueless lot in all my life! Look! There's the riverbed and the bloody fools have gone right past it!'

Davis glanced where Poat indicated. A thin white ribbon could be seen, cutting the dark shoreline. That riverbed was supposed to be the landmark to guide the force into their chosen place of landing. No doubt about it, it was slipping astern.

'Tell your section that in all probability we are being landed in the wrong place,' Poat continued, 'and that we have not a minute to waste, as it will be light in less than an hour.' With that he stomped off to spread the word.

As the ships glided in towards their mystery landing point, a pair of 'giant antennae' – two heavy steel walkways – were run out by the Royal Navy crew on either side of the prow, clattering down with a rattle of chains, making a noise 'fit to waken the dead'. The lead vessel 'grounded gently'. Rubber-soled feet flitted down the ramps, as the first of the 244 raiders hurried ashore. A lone figure was perched on the ramp, silhouetted against the gathering light. It was Mayne. Stopping a man here and there, he whispered a few last words of encouragement or instruction, before they darted ashore.

Neither the whine of a sniper's bullet nor the squirt of fiery tracer cut the night as the landing progressed in total silence, 'save the sighing of the wind and the lapping of the water'. But the beach seemed decidedly odd. Lumpy. As if it might be mined. 'We hopped across like scalded cats,' noted Harrison, '. . . waiting for that first orange flash and the crash of a mine going up.' Nothing. All seemed to make it across safely.

As Davis had passed by, Mayne had whispered a hurried instruction, for they were trying to make the best of the botched landing. They'd been dropped two miles out of position, and several hours late. They were supposed to have landed beside the riverbed, where the road snaked through a narrow cutting, so as to advance and seize it under cover of darkness. Instead, they'd been deposited on the very fringes of Bagnara Calabra itself, just before dawn. The only thing shielding them from the view of the town was a narrow spur, which jutted into the water's edge. Accordingly, Mayne had switched plans. With no time to lose, they would advance directly into the town, thrust through it, and seize the road from there, advancing along its length.

Davis marvelled at the speed with which Mayne had changed tack. At moments such as these he proved himself to be not only a 'born leader, but the born soldier as well'. His few words, muttered closely in the darkness, had worked wonders for Davis's nerves. That ability to make 'split-second decisions . . . is certainly not common to many people, but it was a marked characteristic of the real genius of Paddy . . . so completely inscrutable himself, and yet so astute in his unfailing ability to anticipate the decisions of the commander opposing him, and to act accordingly.'

The first raiders moved off, creeping through the gloom, even as the stars began to dwindle and the 'first chill rays of dawn came to throw their unwelcome light on our activities,' noted Davis. He and Harrison pushed ahead, leading their sections past the houses that clustered along the shoreline, moving stealthily in their rubber-soled boots. With every step, buildings seemed to etch themselves ever more clearly in the gathering light. Within minutes, the white walls and red-tiled roofs of ancient houses were visible, seemingly carved into the very hillside. Of Roman origins, the labyrinthine streets of this ancient fishing village would have offered perfect cover for a force moving through under the cloak of darkness. But not anymore

On the hillside ahead rose a 'long flight of broad stone steps' leading to an ancient and ornate church, appearing 'like a picture of an Aztec temple'. Not a sniff of the enemy anywhere. Not yet. To their right, the wooden shutters of a window were flung wide. An old Italian woman was framed in the opening. For several seconds she stared down in dumbstruck amazement, before crying out excitedly: *'Inglesi! Inglesi!'*

As her cries echoed down the streets, more doors and windows were thrown open, sleep-befuddled Italians stumbling into wakefulness to the surprise news of the dawn. 'Fingers on triggers, we waited for the first German to show himself,' remarked Harrison. Instead, the street became thronged with crowds of Italians – 'women, children and old men, shouting and gesticulating wildly. *"Inglesi! Inglesi! Mussolini finito! Inglesi!"*'

'Get them back into the houses!' Harrison yelled. 'And make them shut up.' His sixth sense was screaming at him that danger lurked somewhere nearby.

Unceremoniously, his men bundled the townsfolk back into

their homes. One figure paused, as a fat Italian woman came forth bearing gifts of grapes. 'Here, just a minute, ma,' he gestured, grabbing a bunch. 'O.K. Thanks. Now, in you go.'

Still not a hint of any enemy anywhere.

They climbed higher, reaching a dark, shadowed passageway leading into the upper section of the town. On the far side shattered chunks of masonry blocked the way, and a 'thick white dust' drifted over everything. All that remained of the town's main bridge was a series of jagged, shattered pillars, which had once cradled graceful stone arches. The massive form of the Ponte di Caravila – the bridge that enabled the main highway to climb into the hill above – had been blown asunder. 'This must have been the explosion we had heard before we landed,' Harrison mused. If the enemy were no longer here, they had left very recently. Vigilance was redoubled.

One section of troops had already taken up position around the ruins of the bridge. Davis took his men forward to guard the far side. As Harrison went to follow, he glanced behind, checking on his patrol. In the distance he spied a column of troops marching into view, 'rifles at the trail', so gripped horizontally at their sides and ready for immediate use. By their smart bearing and demeanour, Harrison figured they had to be Americans. But 'what the devil are Americans doing here?' he wondered. An instant later, it clicked.

'*Germans!*' he yelled.

Instantly, his two Bren gunners pivoted with their weapons and opened fire, unleashing from the hip. Taken by complete surprise – they must have mistaken the British raiders for Italian troops – the enemy patrol was engulfed in a cloud of dust, as concentrated blasts of fire tore into them. Those not hit tried to fall back, but a bend in the road exposed them again, and further bursts of Bren fire ripped into their ranks. Those not killed outright ran for it, blundering into another section of Mayne's men, this one led by the redoubtable Irish-American Pat Riley. 'We had a bit of a scuffle,' Riley related, 'but we took them – twenty-one prisoners': those who had survived the initial onslaught.

As Mayne noted in the War Diary, those German troops had been completely blindsided. 'Prisoners questioned stated that they were completely . . . unaware of the landings until we engaged them. It can therefore be presumed that had our landings taken place at 0200 hrs [hours] as intended, the whole position would have been cleared with far fewer casualties.' Under questioning, the captives also revealed that they were engineers, and that they'd been sent into the town to carry out further demolition work. Notably, they were the 'first German prisoners taken in [mainland] Italy' by Allied forces. First strike to the SAS. The captives also revealed the wider enemy intentions. While the town was to be made impassable, the heights above were to be held as the new defensive line.

Contact with the enemy made, Harrison and his men skirted around the ruined bridge and into the heights beyond. A series of dramatic bends threaded into the mountains – this being the vital terrain that Mayne and his men had been ordered to seize and to hold. Around a series of those swingeing hairpins Harrison and his men marched, before coming across a familiar figure squatting on a doorstep beside the road. It was Mayne, and he was bent over an aerial photo, studying it intently.

Spotting Harrison, he called him over.

'Sir?' Harrison queried.

'Look. We've found the Germans are holding a hastily pre-pared line just south of town, more or less where we should have landed.'

'Lucky we didn't.' If they had landed where they had intended, it looked as if they'd have done so in full view of the enemy's guns.

'Yes. But they know we are here now – and if they are going to counter-attack it will be down this road. See this bend? I want you to take your section up there. If they attack, hold them off for as long as you can, then fall back slowly down the road . . . we cannot hope to do more than that.' Mayne paused. 'Quite clear? Right. Get off with you now.'

Harrison led his men on the stiff climb. They reached the bend Mayne had indicated, only to find that Fraser's troop had got there ahead of them. Typically, the veteran raider was squatted by the roadside, seemingly without a care in the world, frying some bacon for breakfast. Above, the road rose in a wild switch-back fashion, until it reached what seemed to be a wall of sheer cliffs. There it disappeared into a tunnel carved through the rock. But one glance was enough to convince Harrison of the terrible defensive position they faced, overlooked on all sides by those towering hills.

He pushed on to the next bend, and was just allocating his men to their positions when the 'sharp angry whine of a sniper's bullet' cut through the dawn stillness. Next moment, there was the spine-chilling whine of a salvo of mortars, bearing down on them fast. 'Wummp-wummp-wummp-wummp.' Four bombs in quick succession ploughed into the highway right where Fraser's troop had been brewing up. Moments later, a cry went up.

'Medic!'

Fraser's troop must have taken casualties.

From the heights, a bigger gun – perhaps an 88mm – barked defiance, a shell whining overhead to fall with a crash in the town. Another sniper's round whipped past Harrison, as he threw himself into cover. Someone flopped down heavily beside him. It was Davis, out of breath and looking strained.

'Got to push through to the next bend,' he blurted out. 'What's going on?'

Harrison gave Davis a hurried briefing, not that he knew much himself. Warning him to be careful of the snipers – 'For Lord's sake, keep your eyes skinned' – he watched Davis lead his men forward. They scurried ahead, sticking to either flank of the road where it cut through the rock. As they darted ever upwards, 'there was a sudden, deafening concussion.' In an instant, Davis and his men, and the expanse of road, had been swallowed in a 'cloud of smoke and dust'. Two figures stumbled backwards, emerging with their 'hands to their eyes'. For a moment they hesitated, before turning uphill again and dashing ahead. 'When the dust had subsided and the smoke cleared away there was no sign of anyone,' Harrison noted, bleakly.

Another figure appeared at his side. At the sound of that powerful blast, Poat had come rushing forward. 'What's happened?' he demanded.

'Those Jerry mortars were smack on Peter and his section,' Harrison explained.

There was only one thing to do, Poat reasoned. If, as seemed likely, Davis and his men were pinned down and burdened with casualties, they had to try to go to their aid. Right now, Davis's patrol were the most advanced troops of any of Mayne's force. The only way to relieve them was to bypass the road, scaling the precipitous slopes to either side, in an effort to take out that enemy mortar platoon. If not, they could rain down bombs onto Davis and his men at their leisure and finish the lot of them.

Harrison got his section on the move, as Poat called for his to join in the hunt. Even as they slipped off the road and into the intensively terraced land to either side – where vines thick with grapes clung to the soil – so another cry went up. Harrison's corporal, James 'Jim' McDiarmid, an outstanding warrior and an SAS original, had been wounded. Hit in the ankle by a sniper's round, he'd continued to fight his way up the hill, before 'pain and loss of blood forced him to stop'.

Shortly, the vine groves gave out, as the slope became too bare and rocky to sustain any crops. Here, only stunted, gnarled trees offered the barest cover. Still Harrison and Poat were drawn onwards by the beat of the enemy mortars, as they thumped out the rounds. Each blast of an exploding mortar bomb sent shivers through them – not for themselves, for as yet they were undetected, but for Davis and his men, whose position right then had to be sheer hell.

Davis's section had been struck bang in the middle of their line of march by that initial mortar barrage. The first bombs had torn into the road forty yards to Davis's rear, showering him with blasted rocks and debris. He glanced back to see that half his patrol had disappeared in a whirlwind of dust and smoke. Almost instantly, the 'sharp wicked roar of a fast-firing Spandau' had hammered out its death rattle, as Davis had yelled for his men to follow him. The only possible cover was a tiny peasant cottage, set some fifty yards away, just beside the road. How Davis and those with him made it there, he would never know, as the 'terrifying, vicious r-r-r-rip of the light machine gun dinned in our ears . . . as we ran for our lives'.

Just before reaching that precious shelter, they found a wire fence barring their way. Diving into the shade of a tall cactus-like plant, Davis cried for Andy Storey, his platoon sergeant, to pass him his wire-cutters. But even Storey – a 'hard-headed Yorkshireman, slow but infinitely sound; nothing could perturb him' – seemed stunned by the speed and ferocity of the enemy onslaught. As bullets ricocheted off the road and ripped through the bushes, so he seemed to be acting in a 'dazed, stupefied way'.

Davis yelled at him again: 'Give me your wire-cutters!'

'Oh, wire-cutters,' Storey repeated numbly, before fumbling around and finally fishing them out of a pocket.

Moments later Davis had the fencing sliced apart, and they had dashed inside the shelter of the building. 'What the hell was the matter with you back on the road?' Davis demanded. 'Were you deaf?'

'Oh no, sir,' Storey replied, in his typical slow and stolid fashion. 'I heard you the first time but . . . I was taking out the wire-cutters when a bullet made a furrow in the road about an inch from my hand!'

Davis sent Storey to check on the others, who were arriving in dribs and drabs. There was Bill McNinch, the man who'd kept their spirits stiffened with song during Mayne's ferocious training marches. Then came 'Hair, Telford, Ashurst, Sandy Davidson, Eddie Wilson, and Smith', the last-named being Davis's Bren gunner, plus there was Tideswell too. Close on their heels came Private Charlie Tobin, a hugely popular figure in the unit. One of Mayne's fighting Irish, Tobin hailed from Tipperary, and was a former builder's labourer and a No. 8 (Guards) Commando veteran. The twenty-three-year-old had volunteered for the SAS in October 1942, and at one point had served as the bait in a trap set for some Egyptian arms traffickers. Last but not least came the two Johns – Stone and Tunstall – the latter also being a dab hand with the Bren.

With that they seemed complete, or as complete as they could hope to be right now. The mortar barrage had split Davis's patrol in two. Half had dashed forward with Davis, heading for this farmer's hovel. The remainder, under Corporal Mitchell – the man who'd 'played' the pianola so convincingly back at Augusta – were somewhere back down the road, and very possibly dead or injured. Doing a head count, Davis had thirteen men, himself included. To one side of the shelter ran the road – the killing ground. To the other a series of open terraces dropped away like giant steps cut into the hillside. Either route was murderously exposed.

All he could think of doing was getting his men into the best defensive positions possible, given there was no route out of there. Peeping through the window of the hovel, he scrutinised the heights above. The enemy were no more than 250 yards away, and from their vantage point they dominated the terrain below. No more Spandau fire seemed to be hitting them, but savage bursts of tracer kept lancing out across the hillside, as the enemy spotted movement somewhere below. Plus the mortar barrage seemed to be more or less continuous, although the bombs were swishing overhead, as they targeted the town. One hit the church tower, causing the bell to ring furiously, sounding eerie and menacing in their present setting.

Together with McNinch, Davis used a pair of field glasses to sweep the hillside, searching for the enemy's hidden positions – but not a thing could he discern. Finally, he spied a lone head bob up from behind a wall, as a figure emerged munching away on an apple.

'Let me have a go at him,' McNinch pleaded, making a move towards the Bren.

'Not with that,' Davis retorted. A burst with the Bren was sure to draw a barrage of enemy fire, and as Davis well appreciated, one careful mortar round could pretty much do for the lot of them. By the time McNinch had grabbed his rifle, the apple-muncher had disappeared.

'Never mind,' Tobin mocked, in his broad Irish tones, 'you wouldn't have hit him anyway.' It was good that the humour was still sparking.

Tobin turned to Davis. 'Let me have a bang at them, sir!' he begged, fingering his EY Rifle, an old Mk 1 Lee Enfield rifle converted into a grenade-launcher. EY was short for 'EmergencY', and the crude device had a maximum range of 200 yards, besides which Tobin would be launching them uphill. Even so, he was typically bullish. 'Look, just let me put a couple of grenades over there with this. I'm sure I can wake them up and give them something to think about.'

Davis reassured the Irishman that his 'opportunity would come soon enough', but best to wait until the enemy were at least within range.

They kept trying their radio. Zero response. Apparently, the hills all about were playing havoc with reception. Finally, after a good hour, Davis decided he simply had to get word to headquarters. He sent a lone runner, Johnny Hair, back the way they had come, telling him to keep off the road as he went. On reaching HQ, he was to report their position – that the enemy were in the hills up above, and to get mortar fire called down on them. As Davis cautioned, if the enemy closed the trap around the tiny farmhouse, 'we will have had it with a vengeance'.

With Hair safely departed, a cry went up that a figure had been spotted coming up the road from below. Sure enough, an Italian famer – 'old, shabbily-dressed' – was sauntering towards their position, his movements drawing not a sniff of enemy fire. He passed, continued to climb, and when he'd made about twenty-five yards he just slipped suddenly from view. It was most odd. The only thing that made any sense was that he must have turned off onto some kind of a side road or path. If he had, then that had to be investigated, for it might offer them an escape route out of there.

Davis decided to check. He'd lead a three-man patrol and they would follow as best they could the old man's tracks. He called for volunteers. Sergeant Storey – his phlegmatic Yorkshireman – and Charlie Tobin, his fighting Irishman, stepped forward. Explaining what he had in mind, Davis turned to McNinch, whom he would leave in command. Plan sorted, he turned back to Tobin and Storey, only to discover that they had disappeared. In the heat of the moment they'd misunderstood him, and Storey had led the two-man patrol out, leaving Davis behind. Even as he realised this, Davis heard a 'long, wicked burst from that mur-derous Spandau', which sounded horribly close.

He felt a kick to his heart, as he was gripped by a paralysing horror. Had that stab of fire been aimed at Storey and Tobin? He could only imagine it had. Throwing caution to the wind, Davis and his men began to yell out the two men's names, but the only answer was another, longer burst from that hated enemy machinegun. After five minutes spent yelling in vain, Davis tried to crawl around one side of the house, in the hope that he might be able to see something. All he got for his pains was a 'devilishly accurate' burst, which sent him diving for the cover of the building again.

Finally, another savage blast of fire raked the road, before Storey came sprinting towards them, 'bullets whizzing off the road a few inches from his heels', as he vaulted the wire and tumbled into cover. But of Charlie Tobin there was no sign, and not the barest sniff of any answer as they called out his name. They could only imagine that he had been cut down, even as he'd bravely tried to find a route of escape. Swept up with bitter anger at Tobin's loss, they felt a surge of rage take hold of them all, as they decided to fight back with all the 'strength we could muster'.

Wielding the Bren, McNinch and Tunstall started hammering out fire, aiming for the thickest patches of brush where the enemy gunners just had to be hiding. With a surge of 'malicious pleasure', they saw the tracer spark flame, as the brushwood caught fire and began to burn. But equally swiftly, the Spandau gunner answered. It was now that they realised what a battle-winning advantage the enemy gunner truly had. The SAS's red tracer – such a bonus when fighting at night, as all had intended on this mission – had the opposite effect in broad daylight, for it simply directed the enemy right onto the Bren's position. In short order, bullets were churning up the ground all around, flinging shattered stone and grit into the men's faces, and blasting all asunder.

A second Spandau joined in the onslaught, firing from slightly further up the slope and to the north. Davis and his men found themselves pinned behind a low wall, which was all that was shielding them from the withering onslaught. The slightest movement would spell death, as Sandy Davison was about to demonstrate most powerfully. Suffering from leg cramp, he tried straightening the offending limb, only for a bullet to rip though the material of his trousers. For what seemed like an age, the enemy gunners kept pouring in belts of ammo, until finally Tunstall lost patience. His eyes glinting, his face 'pale with fury', he started to crawl towards the Bren gun.

'I've had enough . . .' he growled. 'I am not going to let those bastards do this to us.'

Taking up position behind the Bren, and with a stout length of board as a makeshift shield, Tunstall began to take aim. Davis and McNinch tried to talk him out of it, yelling over that he shouldn't be 'such a bloody fool'. But as there was clearly no dissuading Tunstall, McNinch finally crawled over to join him. Moments later the Bren barked, the tongue of fiery tracer burning off in the enemy's direction. While it gave Davis and the others a momentary kick of joy to see it, all feared how it would end.

All of a sudden, as if lifted up by an almighty hand, McNinch and Tunstall were hurled backwards, coming to rest almost on top of where Davis and the others were lying. As he landed, Tunstall let out the 'most dreadful dry gurgling sounds', as blood streamed from his mouth. Dragging him into cover, McNinch did his best to patch up Tunstall's wounds, even as the rounds continued to fly, bullets hammering in from all sides. There was nothing any of them could do to retaliate.

While Tunstall was in a bad way, he'd actually had a very lucky escape. The burst of fire had struck the ground right in front of the chunk of wood, flinging blasted grit into his eyes, while a fragment of bullet had sliced through his cheek. In terrible pain, plagued by flies as the smell of blood drew them, at least he was alive. Amid the chaos, Davis's binoculars had tumbled to the ground. Each time he tried to venture out and retrieve them, he was driven back by a savage burst, which sent him diving into the cover of the wall.

They were pinned down, with the slightest movement attracting 'a hail of bullets'. Stalemate. Eventually, the German gunners must have dropped their vigilance for a second, for Davis was able to dash out and retrieve the battered Bren, plus his binoculars. Back in shelter, they examined the gun. The barrel was choked with dirt, plus the bipod was bent, but they soon had it clean and serviceable again. That way, if the Germans did try to advance down the road, at least they could welcome them with a storm of fire.

Glancing back down the road, Davis spied figures. Somehow, the remnants of the tail end of his section were advancing up the road, Corporal Mitchell – that 'shrewd and excellent soldier'; the pianola virtuoso – in the lead. Mitchell seemed oblivious to the storm of fire that Davis and his men had been enduring, and that he was walking into a trap. The Spandau gunners would be able to see Mitchell and his men already – they had to be waiting for them to reach the perfect killing zone, just as Tobin had done, an hour or so earlier.

'Get down, Mitchell!' Davis yelled. 'Get down, they've got every inch of the road covered. For God's sake get off the road and don't try to reach us!'

In response to Davis's cry, Mitchell and his men scattered. As there wasn't a shred of cover on that accursed road, they were forced to turn tail and run. Instantly, the enemy gunners – seeing they were being 'cheated of their prey' – opened fire. For Davis and his men it felt like the worst ever nightmare, watching the vicious hail of bullets 'getting closer and closer to the swiftly running men'. The leading figures reached the nearest bend and dashed around it, but then one of the last was hit and keeled over, while another also fell. Somehow, they too managed to drag themselves around the corner and were gone. Fire continued to hammer into the position where they had gone to ground.

One of the Spandau gunners returned his attention to the little white house sheltering Davis and his troops. For twenty minutes bullets tore into it, before eventually the fire died down, 'the Germans obviously well satisfied that they had wiped us out completely,' noted Davis. They got the Bren sighted to cover the road, in case the enemy did try to close in. The heat of day built, until it was like a furnace. Tunstall was finding it unbearable, especially all the flies. They feared he'd been blinded, for his eyes appeared 'dull and lifeless'. With infinite care, McNinch tried to sponge them, but all that did was to cause Tunstall agony.

Davis tried to collect his 'numbed and scattered senses'. It was late morning by now. To go forward was impossible, as poor Tobin had proved. To go back would be equally suicidal, as Corporal Mitchell and his men had demonstrated.

He could only imagine lying exactly where they were, to try to last until nightfall, at which point they could hope to slip away.

Chapter Twelve

DAY OF TERROR

In Bagnara Calabra itself, Mayne was aware just what a perilous battle space they'd stumbled into. Under cover of darkness, their job would have been difficult enough. In broad daylight, and with the enemy dominating the high ground, it was proving a nightmare. Wherever his men were visible across the town, they attracted a barrage of 4-inch mortar rounds, plus machinegun fire. Every movement drew a barrage of bombs from the clear blue skies, bringing the 'threat of death'. Mayne's HQ was being particularly badly hit, as each runner – Sergeant Frame included, who'd brought back the grim news about Davis's patrol – brought down a volley of rounds on their heads.

As for Alex Muirhead and his mortar platoon, they too were playing a deadly game with the enemy. All the cards lay with the Germans. They had the high ground and dominated all. Their positions were so well-hidden, they proved invisible to Muirhead and his men. By contrast, the only decent fire point in town was an open square, but any attempt to unleash bombs from there provoked a storm of return fire. Eventually, Muirhead selected a small garden. By darting out, lobbing off a barrage and dashing back into cover, he and his men could just about manage to fight.

As a testament to their skill, sheer fitness and raw courage, they would fire off some 300 mortar rounds that long day.

To make matters worse for Mayne and his men, once again their radios were proving largely useless. His signallers had managed to contact headquarters once only, at the outset of the mission, but after that all further attempts had proved futile. No one could blame a dousing in seawater this time. In short, the radios simply weren't up to the task in hand.

Inevitably, the raiders were taking casualties. As the War Diary recorded of Bill Fraser's patrol, which had been the first to be hit: 'No. 1 Troop move up to 584670 where they meet heavy MG [machinegun] and mortar fire (2 killed, several wounded).' They had been taken by utter surprise, being hit with deadly accurate fire, the first mortar bombs landing 'fair and square' where they were cooking up. Although they'd suffered seven injured, Fraser himself remained unhurt, his typical luck seeming to shield him from harm, even in the midst of frying up his breakfast.

Two of Fraser's men had been killed outright. One of those, Corporal Charles Richards, had worked as a chemist before the war. Thirty-five years of age, he was comparatively ancient among the youthful ranks of the SAS. Shortly after war's outbreak, Richards had married Nadine Gauntlett, but neither his age nor their marriage would stop him volunteering for the SAS. The second man killed, Private William Howell, had been with the unit for barely three months, but even in that short time he'd earned the reputation of being 'liked by the boys . . . always smiling, always ready to help'.

After that first mortar salvo, the dead and wounded were left lying where they fell, as the enemy continued to unleash a barrage of fire. Anyone who tried to go to the aid of the fallen was likewise targeted. But one man, Private Richard Higham, figured he could see a way. A narrow gutter ran along one side of the road. Dropping into it, he'd inched his way uphill and managed to bring back the first of the wounded. By then, Phil Gunn was on the scene, and he'd got busy right away giving first aid. Higham then turned around, crawled back, and one by one he fetched the rest of the injured in. Gunn showed 'great bravery' as he 'dressed and bandaged them under heavy fire'.

Corporal Mitchell's party – the second half of Davis's section – were in an even more perilous predicament, positioned as they were on a bend higher up the road. All but two of Mitchell's men were wounded. Worse still, after they'd tried to reach Davis at the white house, and drawn that terrible barrage of Spandau fire, they found themselves pinned down in a shallow drain by the edge of the road. For them, too, making the barest move-ment drew 'a mass of fire'. But unless the wounded could make it back to Gunn's makeshift aid station, their prospects looked grim indeed.

For so many – especially for Davis and his patrol – the situ-ation was looking dire indeed. The only option open to Mayne was to use his remaining forces to try to outflank the enemy by scaling the slopes above, to silence their fire. Thankfully, cliff-climbing had been a regular aspect of their training, and of course they were all relatively fresh from scaling Mount Etna several times over. If they could remain unseen and undetected, scrambling up the slopes above should be well within their grasp. Poat and Harrison were out there already, leading the charge. Mayne dispatched further patrols, their mission being not only to spike the enemy's guns, but to relieve the siege on Davis and his patrol at the white house, as a priority.

For his part, Davis was consumed by guilt that he'd blithely led his men into a trap. All he'd managed to do was to get one of his best men, Tobin, killed, and Tunstall badly wounded, and with no hope of getting him proper medical attention. Plus his corporal's party – Mitchell's patrol – must have taken horrendous casualties. Blaming himself, his spirits plummeted and he could do nothing to lift them. They were 'wretchedly alone on this bare mountainside', and he would have given anything to hand over command to 'someone more confident and more capable'.

To make matters worse, Davis heard the sudden, ominous death-rattle of enemy fire, this time coming from directly above where they were hunkered down. But just as quickly there was the answering rasp of a Bren. Rifle fire and the distinctive rat-tat-tat of an M1 carbine cut through the air, which had to spell trouble for the enemy. Davis allowed himself a moment of impossible-seeming hope, imagining one of their sections scaling the hillside above, 'in an effort to give some help'.

Sure enough, up above the white house Harrison and Poat's patrols were inching through the sparse tree cover, and the dry terrain, drawn ever upwards by the sound of enemy mortar and machinegun. They'd reached a point where the view extended as far as Pellegrina, the neighbouring settlement, lying some two kilometres further up the coast. Yet still the enemy guns weren't visible. Suddenly, a platoon of German troops hove into view. They were moving south from Pellegrina, heading for Bagnara Calabra, which would bring them winding down the road towards Davis's position. As Harrison realised, their intention had to be to 'mop up Peter's section'.

It was at the extreme end of the Bren's accurate range – 1,850 yards – but even so, they presented a great target. 'The Brens chattered into life,' Harrison noted. The effect on that German patrol was instantaneous. Hit by surprise, within seconds the neat ranks of marchers broke, as they dashed about in confusion. Finally, the survivors hurried back the way they had come, chased by fire all the way. 'They did not try again.' Indeed, the next hint of any action was to come from a totally different direction.

Sharp bursts of fire echoed up from the opposite side of where Harrison and his men were perched, the noise coming from the south of Bagnara Calabra, reverberating across the slopes. With Mayne's raiders having landed behind enemy lines, the threat could come from any direction, of course. In truth, this was Mayne's No. 3 Troop in action, meeting fire with cold steel. Leading the charge were Captain Edward 'Ted' Lepine and Lieutenant John Elliot Tonkin, a former member of the Long Range Desert Group (LRDG) who was blessed with a wildly offbeat sense of humour. Spotted by a force of the enemy on the southern fringes of the town, their section had got pounded by deadly accurate mortar and machinegun fire. Sensing they were about to get pinned down, Lepine and Tonkin had launched an immediate counter-attack, charging down the enemy guns.

By the sheer speed and ferocity of their assault, they had overrun the German positions, the battle descending into a fierce and bloody struggle at close quarters. As the enemy line broke, they fell back in fragmented groups, abandoning their mortars and their heavier machineguns. Ten had been killed, there were more wounded, and dozens had been taken prisoner. The survivors fled into a tunnel, one of a series that burrowed through the cliffs, taking the coastal rail line south.

Tonkin and Lepine had scored a signal victory, but did it

signify the turning of the tide of the battle for Bagnara Calabra? Certainly, from Harrison and Poat's vantage point that appeared unlikely. It was around 2 p.m. by now, and heavier shells had started raining down upon Bagnara Calabra, adding their punch to the enemy's mortar barrage. As they went shrieking overhead, one fell short, slamming into Harrison's exact position. Four men were blasted off the hillside, and buried in the debris of that explosion. Miraculously, Harrison and Poat managed to get them dug out alive, and mostly uninjured.

No one doubted that it been a stray round, but even so Harrison grabbed his binoculars, and scanned the heights above for any potential firing points. Nothing: just rock, bush and 'trees, trees . . . trees'. Then, something caught his eye – a grey boulder that somehow struck him as seeming odd. As he studied it, the boulder moved. It resolved itself into a 'rather fat German in field grey' who was crawling along the slope on hands and knees. One by one, ten others emerged doing likewise, but spread out at decent intervals. The lead figure crawled through the trees, before disappearing into a hidden hollow that seemed to be tunnelled into a rocky bank. The rest followed.

Taking infinite care not to spook the enemy, Harrison pointed out the hollow to his two Bren gunners. Each emptied a full magazine of tracer into the target. 'The shots slammed straight home.' While it wasn't a mortar pit or Spandau post, at least it was a start. Whether it was due to those bursts of Bren fire or something else, no one knew, but the enemy must have got a sense of where Harrison and Poat's patrols were situated. As Poat issued some orders, a tracer round tore through the trees, passing right through Poat's thigh pocket, and setting alight the bundle of maps he carried in there. In classic Poat fashion, he patted out the flames and went back to his briefing, as if nothing much had happened.

By a stroke of ill fortune, the bullet had found its mark. One of Poat's signallers had been standing nearby. Having set Poat's maps aflame, the round had ploughed onwards and hit that man. Twenty-three-year-old Private Thomas Parris had been a butcher before the war, and he'd fought in the ill-fated defence of France, surviving the Dunkirk evacuations. A year later he'd married Edna Bramble, and a year after that he'd volunteered for the SAS. He'd been with the unit for three months. The tracer round that had so narrowly missed Poat killed him outright.

Down at the white house, the Grim Reaper had also been at work. Sensing Davis's distress, and that he blamed himself for their dire situation, some of his men had tried to strike up a little banter, in an effort to lift the 'gloomy silence'. It didn't work. Seeking to know the worst, Andy Storey – Davis's solid, implacable Yorkshireman – climbed onto an upturned wooden box. With it set well back from the window, it offered a vantage point from where he could see a little further up the road, but without being spotted by the enemy. Perched on that box, Storey was able to spy Tobin's body. The Irishman was very clearly dead, 'the dust and foliage mingled in his dulled hair'. He lay where he had fallen, in full view of the enemy; they couldn't even bring his body in.

Tobin was one of those talismanic figures – a touchstone for all that was good and right about this war. In Tobin's paybook would be found his will, in which he'd left all his worldly possessions to his pals in the unit – 'a few shillings here, a few pounds there'.

As that interminable afternoon dragged on, neither Davis nor his men knew if they would reach nightfall alive. In the intense afternoon heat, someone had the bright idea of brewing up. Tea, to lift the spirits. There was just enough water remaining in their bottles to boil up a mess tin. Once ready, the steaming billy was handed to Tunstall, who was suffering terribly from his wounds. A sip of tea worked wonders, 'but we did not dare allow ourselves to hope too much,' Davis noted. The sun began to sink towards the hills in the east. A lone figure was spotted, winding his way up the road from far below. It resolved itself to be Lance Corporal F. Sylvester, one of Alex Muirhead's mortar men. Davis was 'horrified', and again he yelled out his warnings, but Sylvester kept on coming.

Wondering if the man was mad, they were glued to his climb, at every moment expecting to see him cut down in a swathe of fire. Momentarily, Sylvester was seen to pause, so he could exchange words with someone hidden by the roadside. Then he pressed on, and somehow – inexplicably – he reached the white house without provoking a sniff of enemy fire.

'Message from headquarters,' Sylvester announced, calmly, as if he'd just been out on an afternoon's stroll. 'You are to remain in your present position throughout the night. Further orders will be issued in the morning . . . By the way,' he added, 'one of your men, Lowson . . . is lying in the road beneath the wall . . . he's not wounded, but he refuses to move and told me that I was mad to come up to you.'

Privately, Davis and his men agreed with Lowson's verdict – Sylvester was either cracked or blessed with the luck of the devil. Their view was underscored by the way in which Sylvester sauntered back down the road, somehow without attracting the slightest burst of fire from the enemy. Had the German gunners pulled out, Davis wondered? Had those exchanges of fire that they'd heard ringing out above signified that one or another SAS patrol had driven them off? There was no way of knowing. More to the point, they now had their orders direct from Mayne: they were to stay put and hunker down for the night hours. That had to mean they were serving some kind of a purpose here – presumably blocking the road to the enemy.

At last the evening drew in, the hillside growing darker and less distinct as the night thickened. The first stars blinked in the sky. Davis decided they had to get Tunstall out, at least, and to a place where his wounds could be treated. He gave orders for all to prepare to pull back silently, but they were only to move once the full effect of the gathering night was upon them. They could always return, under cover of darkness, and take up their positions again, should their orders still stand.

They mustered at the rear of the white house. With his eleven men widely spaced, Davis led the way as they crept downhill, silently slipping through the night. After swinging around a few bends, they reached the most forward section of their troops. With McNinch to keep him company, Tunstall was hurried down to Phil Gunn's Aid Post, which he'd established in the town. All seemed to know exactly what Davis and his men had endured, and were amazed they had suffered so few casualties. Being met with 'sympathy and understanding' on all sides, Davis felt his spirits lift. Those 'remarks and sentiments cheered me, for I was taking Tobin's death and the other casualties very hard.'

The nearest troops got busy preparing a hot meal and a 'brew of welcome tea'. Bit by bit, the horrors and the knife-edge tension began to ebb away. Davis's mood lightened still further as he learned of the amazing good fortune of the other half of his patrol. Corporal Mitchell had been hit in the side right beneath his arm, and while he'd lost a great deal of blood he'd been stabilised. Private J. Paddy Glacken – another of Mayne's Irishmen – had been shot in the back, but luckily the bullet was a 'through and through', passing in and out without doing any lethal damage. Four more men had suffered leg and arm wounds, but the sense was that they had every chance of recovering swiftly.

Shortly, there was to be even better news. A runner arrived from Mayne's HQ. The advanced elements of Monty's Eighth Army were even then rolling into Bagnara Calabra town. They would have made it earlier, but had been held up by the dyna- mited bridges. As word was passed around, this was cause for serious jubilation. 'The longer our small unit remained behind enemy lines,' Davis remarked, the greater the threat of being 'overwhelmed by some powerful enemy counter-attack.' On the back of that good news, stretcher-bearers appeared out of the gloaming, to carry away the last of the wounded. Those medics may well have been 'non-combatants', remarked Davis, yet they possessed the 'guts, the bravery and the endurance of first-class fighting men'.

Wrapped in a few old blankets retrieved from a nearby house, Davis and his men settled down to sleep. But it was an age before they could do so, their nerves were so on edge. Eventually, utterly exhausted, they fell into a 'fitful sleep'. Yet even when he'd drifted off, Davis awoke again and again, 'my heart racing and a cold sweat on my brow'. Images of Charlie Tobin being gunned down flashed through his tortured dreams.

Davis awoke with a start, at first light, as a mortar bomb exploded not thirty yards beyond their position. But shortly, the SAS's mortars and machineguns roared into life, hitting 'the same targets as the previous day, silencing MGs and scoring successive hits'. Finally, the enemy guns seemed to fall silent. With the Eighth Army in town, that final mortar barrage appeared to be the enemy's last hurrah as they pulled back north towards safety. Mid-morning, the order came that all had been expecting: they were to move back into town, in preparation for their withdrawal from Bagnara Calabra, job done.

There was one last thing that Davis needed to do before pulling out. Taking McNinch and three others, he again climbed that road, one replete with such 'dread and vivid memories'. It began to rain – the first they had seen since leaving North Africa – the glowering clouds and thick mist lending the entire scene a sombre aspect. Reaching the white house, they set about digging a grave in the shallow, rocky soil, among a patch of grape vines. Retrieving Tobin's body, they laid him gently to rest. A rough cross of sorts had been cobbled together from a couple of pieces of wood, on which they etched Tobin's name, rank and number. It was left to mark the grave.

After a minute's silence at the graveside, the sad little party made their way back downhill. McNinch was at Davis's side, and the SAS lieutenant was shocked to see this 'hardened and usually so cheerful soldier' overburdened with emotion. McNinch turned to him, remarking, 'You know, sir, it's funny that it's always the best who catch it. Charlie Tobin was the kindest-hearted man in the section – he would never say a hard word about anyone – and they have to go and kill him. And here I am, a drunken old reprobate, and am still alive.'

Even as Davis and his party had laid Tobin to rest, Harrison and a small group of men were still out in the hills above Bagnara Calabra, hunting. Moving on foot, his patrol had pushed north-north-east, seeking out the location of the German 88mm gun that had been lobbing rounds into Bagnara Calabra. Moving deeper into the hills, they'd slipped through a wooded area, reaching a tiny hamlet, woodsmoke curling into the mist. There, the villagers welcomed them seemingly as liberators, the Germans having just pulled out. Swinging north, they had advanced as far as Pellegrina, the village at which Harrison had spied that German patrol trying to get to Davis's position, the previous day. There, they found what remained of that 88mm gun post, surrounded by spent shell casings. But of the gun crew there was no sign.

Nearby, they rifled through what remained of the local German headquarters, gathering up 'several documents of interest', before moving on. As they began to descend from Pellegrina, heading back towards the town, two Italian soldiers gave themselves up, 'kits packed, ready and waiting to be taken prisoner' at the roadside. Moments later, a burst of shots rang out over their heads. Flinging themselves down, Harrison and his small force proceeded to run 'the culprits to earth', winkling out a pair of men manning a Spandau, set in a foxhole with commanding views over the town below.

The sun was setting by the time Harrison's patrol made it back into town, together with their four prisoners, only to discover that they had been given up for dead. Early that morning, Harrison had managed to get a report back to headquarters, but after that their radios had stopped working, hence their being listed as missing, presumed 'killed or taken prisoner'. Dropping their four captives and the enemy documents at the main army headquarters, they squatted on the kerbside and wolfed down their first hot meal in an age, for they were famished.

Shortly, the entire squadron would be pulled out by LCI.

Before that could happen, Mayne had Corporal Geordie Corps try to execute a 'demolition scheme' on the town's post office and the safe it contained. But bereft of Bill Deakins's explosives expertise, they clearly didn't quite have the knack or know-how. As recorded in the unit's chronicle, their exploits of the 'night of September 5 . . . failed to open the safe'. Of course, Mayne had introduced his anti-looting orders, so presumably he and Corps had been seeking enemy documentation, but who knows what else that safe might have contained.

A storm had blown up off the Italian coast, and so it was amid crashing waves that the men had to wade out to the waiting LCIs. There were fears that the anchors might give way in the heavy seas, and one or other of the vessels might turn broadside on to the coast and be driven ashore. As it was, the Royal Navy crews did a fine job holding their ships firm and all were able to clamber aboard. With that, the pair of vessels turned towards the south-west and set out into the storm-tossed seas.

As the LCIs steamed towards whatever fate might next hold in store, so Mayne and his men reflected upon the last forty-eight hours. No doubt about it, they had accomplished their mission and against all odds. As Davis remarked of the moment, 'Paddy had pulled the rabbit out of the hat once again, in spite of the fact that the Navy had landed us far too late and . . . in the wrong place.' But even in that twist of apparent ill fortune, Lady Luck may well have been watching over them. As they'd subsequently learned, the enemy had been dug in with 'strong defensive positions' overlooking the very stretch of beach upon which the SAS had intended to land. 'There is no judging the . . . seemingly meaningless ways of Destiny!' Davis concluded.

As for their losses, they could have – perhaps should have – been far worse. The SAS War Diary listed 'Total casualties: 22 . . .' This included: Richards and Howell, 'Killed in action 4/9/43. Buried at 584670 . . . below the road in garden at alleyway between two houses'; Parris, 'Killed in action 4/9/43. Buried . . . above bend of road, behind corner house in garden.'; and, of course, 'C. Tobin. Killed in action 4/9/43. Buried at 587670 . . . below solitary house on firm terrace.' A fourth man was also listed as 'died from wounds in action 4/9/43'.

That last man was Lance Corporal John Henry Ball, who was just twenty years old. Ball, a former builder's labourer from Northwick, in Gloucestershire, had falsified his details so as to join up early. Just over a month before the Bagnara Calabra mission, he'd won his 'Operational Wings', signifying that he'd completed at least three missions behind enemy lines. Ball had formed part of Bill Fraser's patrol, and he had been wounded in the initial mortar and machinegun onslaught. He'd died from those wounds the following day. His epitaph would read: 'Happy and smiling, always content, loved and respected wherever he went.'

Unsurprisingly, Phil Gunn, the unit's medic, would be awarded a Military Cross for his heroic endeavours at Bagnara Calabra as he endeavoured to save the lives of the wounded while under fire. It was also entirely proper that Bill McNinch, Davis's deputy, would be awarded a Military Medal, for the role he had played during the long and bloody siege of the white house. So too would Jim McDiarmid, the man who'd been shot in the ankle but carried on fighting, until the loss of blood forced him to retire from the battle.

But perhaps the most fitting accolade of all would go to Private Richard Higham, the man who had crawled through the roadside ditch repeatedly, to rescue his wounded comrades under fire. He too was awarded the MM. And, for his spirited resistance facing such ferocious fire at the white house, John Tunstall, Davis's Bren gunner, would also receive the MM. Sadly, Tunstall would be plagued by his injuries. After twelve months in hospital he was medically discharged from the Army, deemed unfit for military service.

There would be one other unexpected casualty of the battle for Bagnara Calabra. At the wheel of his Bedford truck, Bill Deakins had set forth, seeking to be reunited with the squadron. First by sea, then overland, Deakins had endeavoured to track down the elusive SAS, though no one seemed to even know who they were, let alone where they might be. 'The name was enough to cause some confusion, many had never seen our cap badge and our style of uniform was so very different.' Sharing his 'rations and water with my female companion' – Tiny – he pressed on, sleeping in the truck cab at night, with the dog 'lying across my legs, as she did back in Kabrit [the SAS's Egypt base]'.

Failing to track down his elusive unit, Deakins had set sail in an LCI bound for Bagnara Calabra. As those aboard watched 'the foaming wash and wake of the ship', someone absent-mindedly tossed an empty cigarette packet over the stern. In a flash, Tiny leapt overboard, seeking to retrieve the packet, which she presumed had been launched into the sea 'for her benefit'. The LCI couldn't stop, for fear of enemy submarines. Tiny was left 'in the distance, frantically trying to catch up with the ship'. Deakins was utterly mortified. He and Geordie Corps, Tiny's supposed owner, would never once discuss how exactly the little dog had been lost. It was simply too heartrending.

As for the enemy the SAS had faced at Bagnara Calabra,

Mayne concluded they had suffered over eighty casualties, 'all ranks German and Italian'. Of those troops, the vast majority 'were German and only a few Italians were seen . . . In general, German troops were of good physique, and experienced. Some had fought in Africa and some in Russia. One prisoner belonging to the Jaeger [light infantry] battalion stated that his unit was equipped with British vehicles.' Of course, those British vehicles would have been captured in previous battles, and very likely in the North African desert, which was the SAS's previous stomping ground.

By the end of the first week of September 1943, the Allies had wrested a foothold in southern Italy. Slowly, painfully slowly, the tables were starting to turn. In crowbarring open enemy-occupied Europe, the SAS had served a vital role. In both Sicily and now Italy itself, the seas and cliffs had been bathed in glory and courage beyond measure, but also baptised in their own and the enemy's blood. Crucially, across three back-to-back missions, all objectives had been taken, and arguably, the SAS raiders had played their part to perfection under the leadership of Blair 'Paddy' Mayne.

But unbeknown to all, their greatest battle – and their greatest trial – was yet to come.

Chapter Thirteen

BLOODY, BUT UNBOW'D

Gallico was as fine a place as any in which to attempt to wind down and to rearm for war. Set just over twenty kilometres south along the coast from Bagnara Calabra, it was firmly in Allied hands. The transport section of 1 SAS, complete with admin team, plus cooks and bottle-washers, had caught up with Mayne's raiders by now, and in fact they had been the first to reach Gallico. As a result an officer's billet had been requisitioned and suitably stocked with wine, or so they'd thought. But not content with the supplies provided, Mayne tasked Geordie Corps to check out a store of wine that had just been discovered. You could never have enough vino on hand, and especially when you had need to drink to the fallen. There was also mail to be read, and as many of these men had not been home for three years they hungered for news.

That first night in Gallico, Mayne and his section commanders sat on the balcony of their DIY officer's mess, glasses in hand, as they gazed out over the streets. The stormy weather had abated, and it was a warm and balmy early September evening. A turquoise sea lapped the white sands of the crescent-shaped beach which formed the seafront stretching out far below. While it looked paradisical, there was something decidedly untoward in the air. The church bells began to peal wildly, as figures dashed hither and thither shouting and singing excitedly. Crowds of young men and women hurried through the streets, waving Italian flags to and fro. Many were holding hands.

In the distance, a series of Very lights – flare rounds – arced into the sky, forming 'lazily-moving balls of coloured flame'. The twinkling flames of distant bonfires lit the dusk, as figures gathered to celebrate something momentous, but what exactly? Then the cry went up from the crowd, rendered both in Italian and English, which made all on that balcony suddenly understand, although sadly they didn't quite share in the wild exuberance and joy of the locals. With wise heads and war-bitten – some might argue, cynical – hearts, they knew it wasn't quite as simple as the crowd were given to believe it might be.

'The war is over – peace, peace, at last!'

Around and around went the joyous cry, but the watchers remained unconvinced. It was 8 September 1943, and Italy had just capitulated to the Allies, but that didn't mean for one moment that the Germans were going to follow suit. Indeed, if the forces of Nazi Germany opted not to withdraw to the borders of Italy, the country was very likely to get 'ravaged by the horrors of war; their fair cities blasted to destruction and their vineyards soaked in the blood of soldier and civilian alike'. Still, with that 'bubbling light-heartedness' that so defined the unit, Mayne and his men figured this was cause for celebration. A barrel was broken out. Several more followed. Late into the night, a flurry of Very lights were sent whooshing off the balcony, to the wild delight of the locals.

Along the beach, someone spied 'an attractive young lady . . .

offering her services'. Some of the men slipped away, unable to resist. Bill Deakins – now reunited with the squadron – demurred. 'I was not a complete prude,' he would write of the moment, but the words of caution offered by his father flashed through his mind: 'If one could get there, so could others.'

By the following morning, some of the less savoury ramifications of the Italian surrender were made known to the squadron. Mayne gathered his men. An order had come down from on high, he explained. In theory the Italians were now allies – the Armistice of Cassibile having been signed into law – which meant that from now on they were under orders to salute Italian military officers. Mayne lowered his voice, as he eyed his men: 'Do not let me catch any of you doing so.' He left no one in any doubt what would happen if they were ever seen saluting an Italian officer. Under his command they would do what they deemed was right, not what they had been ordered, or what would ingratiate them with the top brass. And damn the consequences.

All were of a similar mind. As Deakins would note in his diary, 'one moment one is trained to beat the enemy by any means . . . go through tremendous hardships and difficulties to achieve this aim, to lose many friends, killed or injured; then, like after a football match, have a bath or shower, shake hands and all go home. One cannot hate for ever but this seemed all too much for most of us . . .'

That same day, Phil Gunn set out for the nearby city of Reggio Calabria, to check on the wounded. Davis went with him, as it was his section that had suffered perhaps the worst of all during the battle for Bagnara. What he found in the city's hospital proved immensely cheering. Nearly all of his men were recovering well and their spirits remained high. Nearly all would be back to serve with him in the weeks and months to come. There was one exception. Private Kirk, one of those in Corporal Mitchell's patrol, had had a nerve severed in his leg. It was feared it would take many months to heal.

In the same hospital ward there was a German corporal who'd been shot and wounded during the fighting. As Davis, the former student of modern languages, spoke good German, he couldn't resist going to have a few words. The patient was a young lad hailing from the Rhineland area of western Germany, and he certainly didn't strike Davis as being the typical 'arrogant, fanatical Nazi' about whom they had all heard so much. As they got chatting, Davis asked if the landings at Bagnara had taken him and his comrades by surprise.

'Yes, indeed,' the German replied, 'even after you had been firing at us for some time, we still thought you were Italians.'

Davis asked him how he felt, now he was a prisoner and no longer in the frontline. He found the man's reply astonishing.

'Very glad. At least I can feel safe now, which I was never able to do before.'

'And what do you think are Germany's chances of winning the war now? Another year?'

The German shook his head. 'Scarcely.'

Davis left his company feeling distinctly unsettled. 'Why were we fighting decent people like that?' he wondered. That young man was no 'ardent Nazi, with puffed up ideas about the master race. He was just a simple country boy, stolid . . . and good-natured.' What struck Davis more than anything was the incongruity of it all. Just a few days earlier, he had been crouching on a hillside with 'murder in my heart, frantically encouraging my section to kill this very man'.

The next day the SAS boarded their LCIs for a journey that took them, by stages, past Bagnara, and on towards the new frontline. Eventually, they dropped anchor at Scalea, a stunningly beautiful ancient coastal town, lying some 210 kilometres north of their last battleground. They were chasing the frontline, for in the immediate aftermath of the Italian surrender the Axis front seemed to buckle and disintegrate. But then, as if to telegraph his intent, Hitler delivered a masterstroke, in a mission that would have done the SAS proud, had they been tasked to deliver a similar kind of coup.

It was a cloudy afternoon on 12 September 1943, when a flight of German DFS 230 gliders – the inspiration for the British Hotspur – descended onto the peak of Gran Sasso, in Italy's Apennine Mountains. Packed with troops, they landed on the snowy slopes at some 7,000 feet of altitude. There, in the largely deserted ski resort of Campo Imperatore, Mussolini was being held captive by the Italians under close guard. Alighting from the gliders, squads of heavily armed German paratroopers made a dash for the building, bringing with them Italian general Fernando Soleti, held at gunpoint, with instructions to prevent his men from putting up any resistance.

The ruse worked, the 200-strong Italian guard force offering almost no fight, and so leaving Colonel Otto Skorzeny, the commander of the SS contingent, standing below Mussolini's window, crying out in unison with his men: 'Viva Il Duce!'

A diminutive Fieseler Fi 156 Storch spotter plane landed on a sixpence nearby, and Mussolini was whisked aboard. With Skorzeny as his personal escort, Il Duce was spirited north, and onwards by stages to be reunited with Hitler at his Wolf's Lair headquarters.

That same day, Skorzeny gave a triumphant radio broadcast from Germany. 'I liberated Mussolini,' he declared. His exploits and his name had just passed into military legend, Skorzeny becoming Nazi Germany's nearest equivalent to David Stirling, or perhaps, with Stirling in captivity, Paddy Mayne.

Mayne received the news of the daring snatch mission with a mixture of grudging admiration and dismay. 'Why didn't our bright boys at H.Q. think of something like that?' he demanded, his voice laced with irony. 'It would have been just our cup of tea.'

He was right, of course. Seizing Il Duce before Skorzeny and his men could do so would have been just the SAS's kind of thing. In many ways, these two men – Skorzeny and Mayne; German and Irish – were so very alike. Both were powerfully built sportsmen and warriors, and both boasted legendary martial reputations. Both were 'determined and ruthless', but equally they could be 'as gentle as lambs' with those they had vanquished. But with Skorzeny's success, and Mussolini being reunited with Hitler, it spelled bad news for the Italian campaign. For those Italian Fascists still with the fight left in them, they now had a figure to whom to rally. Il Duce was back in business, dancing to Hitler's tune.

Skorzeny – the greatest proponent in Germany of commando-style special operations and unconventional warfare – commanded a unit that was the nearest German equivalent to the SAS, the SS-Jäger-Battalion 502. The dramatic seizure of Mussolini would prove to be his single greatest triumph. Ironically, David Stirling had long advocated for the SAS – his 'Professionals,' as he called his men – to be allowed a shot at seizing General Erwin Rommel in similar style. As Rommel was widely believed to have turned a blind eye to Hitler's Commando Order, the intention was to capture, as opposed to assassinate, him. But no such mission was ever greenlit for the SAS, and now Skorzeny had shown them how it really should have been done.

Springing Mussolini signified one thing to Mayne and his men above all else: Nazi Germany had thrown down the gauntlet. The battle for Italy was likely going to be long and hard-fought. In truth, Hitler had vowed that Italy would not fall, and to fight for every inch of Italian soil. He'd drafted in one of his favourite commanders, Field Marshal Albert Kesselring, as his supreme commander in Italy, complete with some of his most battle-hardened forces. Kesselring, a decorated First World War veteran, had distinguished himself in the Spanish civil war, before spear-heading operations against Poland, Holland and France. He'd gone on to oversee the invasion of the Soviet Union, earning Hitler's very highest regard. Even Allied commanders were said to respect Kesselring's military acumen.

Sensing what challenges lay ahead, Mayne and his men ran over the lessons they'd learned from the battle for Bagnara Calabra. More than half of their casualties had been caused by mortars. So, no matter what the terrain or the challenges they faced, they would have to keep well off the main highways. With their hard, exposed surfaces, they were the ideal killing zones. From now on, they vowed to keep off roads as if they were 'poison'. If pinned down, in the way Davis's section had become, they would need a more potent source of firepower to break any such siege. Accordingly, each section was issued with a 2-inch mortar, not quite as potent as Alex Muirhead's 3.2 inch, but considerably less burdensome to carry.

Yet as the entries in the SAS War Diary made clear, at Scalea they were likewise intent on resting up and recharging their batteries, in preparation for the next battle. Mayne eased off on driving the squadron so relentlessly and urging them to be the best of the best. Knowing that they were battle-weary and in need of serious recuperation, he allowed the training to take a back seat, for now . . . 'In billets. Reorganisation and refitting,' read one War Diary entry. The next day: 'Rest and refitting.' The next: 'Move cancelled. Rest.'

Worn-out bodies needed to be properly revitalised; ripped and torn clothing needed patching. Bill Deakins found a local family – a lady and her daughter – who in return for chocolate and some rations would work wonders, 'sewing and darning, almost dry cleaning and pressing, and laundering my underwear'. They lived in a tiny house with a dirt floor, and they seemed immensely grateful for whatever Deakins could spare them. 'These Italians I would salute,' he concluded of the way they looked after him.

Under the guiding hand of the canny Geordie Corps, the needs of the flesh were also supposed to be seen to. Crossing a field towards a farmhouse, Deakins reflected on how it was 'always interesting to know what he [Geordie] was up to'. It turned out that Corps had found a 'farm lady who would be overly friendly for a supply of food'. But left alone with her in the kitchen, Deakins just couldn't bring himself to indulge his carnal desires, especially as 'her two young children were laughing and playing with Geordie in the next room'. While he could have been wrong, Deakins figured the lady of the house was most concerned with 'the survival of her children'. He gave her his bars of chocolate anyway. 'Women, and men for that matter, sell themselves for so many reasons.'

General Dempsey dropped by to pay Mayne a visit. The two

men had formed a real, genuine friendship, one anchored in the qualities they shared – 'determination, shrewdness, a quiet and calculating common sense, and a real brilliance in anticipating the thoughts and actions of the opposing commander'. Superficially, it seemed odd, due to the gulf between them socially, and in terms of age and rank. Dempsey, educated at Shrewsbury boarding school, was a decorated veteran of the First World War. He'd been gassed by the Germans, forcing him to have one lung removed. The grandson of Major-General Henry de la Fosse on his mother's side, he traced his forebears back to the O'Dempsey clan, in southern Ireland, one of whom, Terence O'Dempsey, had been knighted on the field of battle by Robert Devereux, 2nd Earl of Sussex, in 1599. Perhaps that was his and Mayne's secret bond: both were at heart fighting Irishmen.

As the shy, quiet-spoken Dempsey made clear, he for one didn't see Mayne as a misfit or an outsider. The results of the last three missions spoke for themselves: these were the finest men he had ever had the privilege to command. Dempsey's visit served to put Mayne in fine spirits. That evening, the sergeants were called to the makeshift officer's mess, a requisitioned Scalea town house. Glasses were filled, and the chat and the banter began, interspersed with wild guffaws and laughter. Mayne was totally in his element during evenings such as these. He was never happier. Perennially inventive, he was always dreaming up some new topic of conversation, some new 'diversion to keep everyone active'. Trials of strength were a favourite. Two men would lie facing each other, as each tried to wrestle the other's arm to the floor, 'with beads of sweat standing out on their brows'. Or they'd have a session of 'cock fighting', in which the simple rule was the first to wrestle an opponent to the ground was the winner.

When all tired of that, they'd compete to see who could balance a glass of wine on his forehead, and manage to get down until he was lying flat on the floor, and then back up again, without spilling a drop.

But eventually the moment arrived when Mayne decreed it was time to sing. Pushing back his chair, with a 'wicked grin on his face' and 'gazing fixedly in front', and clutching a glass of whisky in one hand, he opened with 'Eileen Alannah', perhaps his favourite Irish folk song. Of course, Mayne knew he couldn't sing, so he would seem more to chant the words, occasionally hitting a sweet note, holding it for a second, before losing it again. Nine-tenths was delivered in that chanting monotone, but with some indefinable 'timing and cadence about it, as if in the singer's ears he was being accompanied by a mighty orchestra imported direct from the Emerald Isle'.

Few of the men ever got to know the entire tune or the words to 'Eileen', with the exception of Corporal B. Taggart, the Irish mess cook, and he was not letting on. No, 'Eileen' was Mayne's song, and he would only ever start to sing it when he was well-inebriated, and by that point his Irish brogue was so pronounced that few could make out much of what he was saying. The opening lines seemed to be these:

Eileen Alannah, Eileen Asthore,
Light of my soul and its Queen evermore,
It seems years have lingered since last we did part,
Eileen Alannah, the pride of my heart . . .

After that it all became a bit befuddled, not that it mattered much. The singing of 'Eileen' was a signifier, a milestone in any evening. It signalled that the time to sing was upon them. But more than that, it indicated that tonight all was well with the world, as far as Mayne was concerned. As Corporal Taggart, their grizzled cook, had explained to Davis, opening with 'Eileen' was a very good sign. It set the tone for the rest of the evening. 'Eileen' indicated that they were in for a relatively quiet and peaceful night. It was quite different if Mayne opened with 'Mush Mush' – otherwise known as 'Tread on the Tail of Me Coat' – for that was a fighting song:

> Oh, 'twas there I learned readin' and writin'
> At Bill Bracket's where I went to school
> And 'twas there I learned howlin' and fightin'
> From my schoolmaster Mr O'Toole . . .

Corporal Taggart had seen too many of his fellow Irishmen 'succumb to liquor', as he'd explained to Davis, so he was teetotal. But he knew Mayne's moods and his ways intimately, especially when he had been drinking. A rendition of 'Tread on the Tail of Me Coat' invariably ended with Mayne bringing his fist down with a crash on the table, sending the glasses flying. That in turn would put the idea and the thought of fighting into his head, and it generally boded ill.

Once the final lines of 'Eileen' had drifted away, it was time for the partying proper to begin. Mayne called for Geordie Corps, for he had a fine, rich tenor voice. Singing tended to take Corps back to his own Celtic roots, his voice taking up a strong Irish timbre. But while Corps loved to sing, he also liked to hold out for a while against 'the CO's arbitrary demands'. Once he'd demurred a little, and honour was seen to be satisfied, Corps launched into 'the sad, haunting air of Kevin Barry ... one of Paddy's favourite rebel songs'. Regardless of the words, it was enough to move men like these to tears.

Next up was Bob Bennett, offering a few rousing tunes on his mouth organ, before crooning out a 'popular sentimental song', which tended to turn minds to thoughts of loved ones back home. Then Private 'Killer' Casey would get to his feet – not so long out of fronting up to the padre, when seeking loot in Augusta – and in a 'rough, tuneless voice' he would deliver a rendition of one of Mayne's all-time favourites, 'Garden Where the Praties Grow', written by Irish entertainer and circus act Johnny Patterson. ('Praties' are of course potatoes.)

That rousing, boisterous, swing-along Irish love song got hearts thumping, and spirits soaring, and was perfect to join in:

> Have you ever been in love, me boys,
> Did you ever feel the pain?
> I'd rather be in jail,
> I would, than be in love again.
>
> Now the girl I loved was beautiful
> I'll have you all to know.
> And I met her in the garden
> Where the praties grow.

Promising a humorous break from the singing, Bill McNinch – not so long out of weathering the siege of the white house – stepped forward. A past master at the hilarious art of the monologue, he sat back in his chair, glass in hand, and 'without a flicker of an eyelid, and with a face completely devoid of expression' he 'let the mirth-provoking words roll off his tongue'. McNinch's lengthy, rambling, roundabout tale was certainly not fit to be heard in polite company, but it 'kept us all convulsed in laughter', Davis noted in his diary, the speaker letting nothing disturb his 'granite-like expression and slow, regular delivery'. Normally, of course, Mayne wasn't one for swearing or smut, but with McNinch – whom he'd known since the earliest days of 11 Commando – he made an exception, for the battle-hardened corporal was a master storyteller.

As McNinch signed off with his final punchline, another figure took centre stage, Sergeant Ernest Edward Goldsmith, a man who was known to all simply as 'Buttercup Joe'. Goldsmith, with his honest, open features and broad boxer's nose, had something of an archetypal résumé for many an SAS soldier. The son of a farm labourer, and the eldest of six children, the twenty-nine-year-old had lied about his age to sign up, having left school at fourteen. Raised in Winchelsea, just outside Rye, in East Sussex, he'd had the one teacher for all of his Winchelsea education, and while being 'a lively, self-confident lad' he was forever getting into trouble with the local bobby. The military had cured all that, channelling Goldsmith's energy and high spirits into boxing, at which the youngster had excelled.

Then had come the outbreak of war and the battle for France. Goldsmith was serving in the Royal Sussex Regiment at the time, which had suffered heavy casualties in fierce fighting first around Belgium, before being driven back finally to Dunkirk. There, Goldsmith was one of the lucky ones, being pulled out of the water by a French trawler and spirited back to British shores. Incredibly, just over a month later he had volunteered for Special

Service, going into No. 8 (Guards) Commando. The 'Blue Bloods' or the 'House of Lords', as they were known, 8 Commando boasted not only David Stirling, but Randolph Churchill, the prime minister's son, in its ranks.

Mixing with the high-born, the titled and the famous – including the writer Evelyn Waugh – Goldsmith, with his rural upbringing and broad Sussex burr, was something of an oddity. But he never let it bother him much, not even when the men of the Commando nicknamed him 'Buttercup Joe', after the century-old English folk song of that title, which parodied and mocked the rustic ways and accent of the song's subject, a likeable rural fellow named Joe. Embracing his newfound identity, Goldsmith had become universally known as 'Joe', taking that name with him into the SAS, which he volunteered to join in September 1942. He even kept a copy of the lyrics of 'Buttercup Joe', self-typed on a piece of yellowing paper – complete with errors – neatly folded in one pocket, for the song had become not only his namesake, but his signature act, whenever the men were called upon to sing:

Now I be a raw bred country chap,
Me vether cums from Sarum.
Me mother she cums vrom I no's where,
But she sure no's how to rare em.

Now some calls I a turnip top,
And tothers call I Ted,
But I can prove that I'm no vool,
Although I'm country bred.

After the first two uproarious verses came the chorus, which most knew off-by-heart, and was as good an excuse as any for a rousing, raucous singalong:

Vor I can old a plow,
And milk a cow.
I can rip or mow,
I'm as vresh as the daisies growing in the vield,
And they call I Buttercup Joe.

The song went on to tell of 'our Mary', Joe's sweetheart, a dairy maid who was famous for her delicious dumplings: 'By God you awt to try em/ And ask her how she'd like to wed/ A country lad like I am.' Chorus to follow, with gusto. 'Joe was always bursting into song,' one of his comrades would remark, 'people like him made it so much fun.'

During one unforgettable evening, they'd been drinking in a Cairo nightclub jam-packed with Allied troops. The moment had come when Goldsmith figured it was time for his act. He'd climbed onto the stage – set ten feet above the floor, for safety reasons; there was a wild, lawless feel to the place – and persuaded the band to play his signature tune, after which he was soon 'singing away merrily'. He finished to wild applause, forgot he was ten feet off the ground, fell onto a table crowded with Australian soldiers and scattered their beers. The place exploded. 'Bottles and chairs and fists flew,' but Goldsmith and his pals managed to slip away just before the military police arrived. It was 'another night to remember', as all had concluded, heartily.

The final star turn for that magical evening at Scalea was

Sergeant Major Johnny Rose, the former Woolworths store manager. Blessed with the finest singing voice of any man present, all the hubbub and hilarity resulting from McNinch's monologue and Goldsmith's comical ditty died to an enraptured quiet when Rose began. There was a hauntingly soft sentiment to Rose's melodies, and largely due to this striking gift Mayne had appointed him as one of his key deputies. The room fell silent as Rose struck up the evocative, soulful tones of 'Mother Machree', a pre-war Irish-American song made popular in several movies, with its unforgettable chorus:

Oh I love the dear silver that shines in your hair,
And the brow that's all furrowed and wrinkled with care.
I kiss the dear fingers so toil worn for me,
Oh God bless you and keep you, Mother Machree.

A few more numbers from Rose, and then they reached the absolute zenith, which never failed to hit the mark. Rose struck up the iconic, martial, marching-beat timbre of 'Lili Marlene', that German soldier's lovesick lament, but of course transformed into the SAS's own version, what had become their regimental song. Borrowed from Rommel's Afrika Corps, few were the men in the days of the SAS's desert raids who hadn't sat out of an evening, poised to attack, yet hearing those haunting tones drift across the desert sands, as the German garrison gave voice. Though they'd heard it so many times before, to a man they were enraptured as Rose sang this evening, tapping 'time to the music with their toes or fingertips, soaking in . . . those words . . . which belonged to us so completely':

There was a song we always used to hear,
Out in the desert, romantic, soft and clear,
Over the ether, came the strain,
That soft refrain, each night again,
To you, Lili Marlene, to you Lili Marlene.

Check you're in position; see your guns are right,
Wait until the convoy comes creeping through the night,
Now you can pull the trigger, son,
And blow the Hun to Kingdom come,
And Lili Marlene's boyfriend will never see Marlene . . .

Twenty thousand rounds of trace and ball,
Forty thousand rounds of the stuff that makes 'em fall,
Finish your strafing, drive, drive away,
And live to fight another day,
But Lili Marlene's boyfriend will never see Marlene.

Creeping into Fuka, forty planes ahead,
Belching ammunition, and filling them with lead,
A 'flamer' for you, a grave for Fritz,
He's like his planes, all shot to bits,
And Lili Marlene's boyfriend will never see Marlene.

Afrika Korps has sunk into the dust,
Gone are the Stukas, its Panzers lie in rust,
No more we'll hear that haunting strain,
That soft refrain, each night again,
For Lili Marlene's boyfriend will never see Marlene.

As Rose's final words faded away, there was a taut silence in that room, hung as it was with a smog of cigarette smoke, the old hands – those who had made the renown of the regiment so widely known through their 'daring desert battles' – lost in their thoughts and in memories of fallen friends. But gradually the mood lightened and the murmur of voices filled the air again, gently at first, but then with the first hints of returning mirth and laughter, as glasses were refilled, after which the party went on 'until the morning sun streamed through the windows'.

That party at Scalea was one of the good ones, but they weren't always thus. As Sergeant Albert Youngman, another of Mayne's Italy raiders, would remark, in drink Mayne could be 'dangerous . . . When he was sober he had only two things in mind: the job we had to do and the safety and welfare of his men . . . He was terrific, because a) you knew he'd never tell you to do anything he wouldn't do himself, b) he would always lead from the front, and c) he'd never leave anyone behind. He was really special. A born warrior.' But in his cups Mayne could be something quite different. 'I was never nervous around him when he was sober. But certainly nervous when he was drunk, because he was so unpredictable. You didn't know what he was going to do or say . . . he was quite likely to walk around the tents, wake somebody up and say, "Sing!" . . . you wake up in the middle of the night . . . you're going to sing anything, aren't you? "Not that! Sing an Irish song!" Mayne would interject.'

Davis concurred. If 'Tread on the Tail of Me Coat' was heard of an evening, that promised only one thing: 'chaos was let loose. No one would be safe . . . Glasses and bottles would fly and raids would be made on neighbouring billets and rooms . . . if Paddy took it into his head that he wanted someone's presence, distance would be no deterrent to him, and the unfortunate victim sought out and forced to present himself.' Sadly, as the regiment's losses grew – as Mayne failed to safeguard more of his men, his friends, those whom he'd nurtured so personally over the months and years – so his mood tended to darken. In that way, 'Tread on the Tail of Me Coat' began to supplant 'Beautiful Eileen', as he endeavoured to bury the loss and the trauma – his failure to protect – in drink.

Hugely well-read, Mayne was rarely to be found without a good book in his hand. Indeed, he would become renowned for carrying an anthology of poetry – *Other Men's Flowers*, by Lord Wavell – into battle. Under the subtitle 'Good Fighting', the anthology boasted heroic, martial compositions, such as 'The Pilgrim' by John Bunyan, 'The Last Hero' by G. K. Chesterton, 'The Eve of Waterloo' by Lord Byron, and W. E. Henley's 'Invictus', the last of which could almost have been written with Mayne and his raiders in mind.

> Out of the night that covers me,
> Black as the pit from pole to pole,
> I thank whatever gods may be
> For my unconquerable soul.
>
> In the fell clutch of circumstance
> I have not winced nor cried aloud.
> Under the bludgeonings of chance,
> My head is bloody, but unbow'd.

Beyond this place of wrath and tears
Looms but the Horror of the shade,
And yet the menace of the years
Finds and shall find me unafraid.

It matters not how strait the gate,
How charged with punishments the scroll,
I am the master of my fate;
I am the captain of my soul.

The anthology's compiler, General Archibald Wavell, Lord Wavell, was actually Mayne's former commander-in-chief, at the time of 11 Commando's heroic actions during the Litani River battle. But Wavell's anthology – 'published in the darkest days of the war' – also contained a plethora of material that was far from typically military-minded. There were large sections entitled 'Music, Mystery and Magic', 'Love and All That', 'The Call of the Wild', 'Hymns of Hate', 'Ragbag' and, finally, 'The Last Post'. This was a rich, eclectic, diverse, unorthodox, thinking man's anthology, and in that it typified Mayne and many of those he commanded.

It underscored another aspect of Mayne's character, one that caused him to find death – especially of those that he cared for – immensely troubling. In an instant Mayne could flip from poetry to killing, 'from offering succour to mass destruction so rapidly and so effectively'. Such moments of instant action propelled Mayne into a 'trance state' – just as any intensely focused state of attention is akin to a trance. So many factors contributed to that trance: duty, service, doing what was right, the training, the need to safeguard his men, but also the driving imperative of survival. Once that trance was broken, the wider ramifications of the action would crowd in. Mayne was a deep thinker, someone drawn to music, verse and writing from an early age. He did not choose to 'skim across the surface of life'. Rather, he would delve deep into his thoughts and emotions, and the impacts of his actions, both from his own worldview and 'through the eyes of others, too'.

That didn't mean that Mayne regretted those actions or questioned the overall aims of the war they were fighting, but the sheer 'enormity of what . . . he had done and the losses suffered, would . . . have increased with time', and especially as he 'stepped away from the immediacy of the "trance" . . .' Over time, the ghosts would draw closer. The one way to banish those ghosts – at least, temporarily – was through the oblivion of drink. But for now, here at Scalea, they were riding the crest of the wave of their Italy successes; the darkness had yet to truly descend.

In fact, for many, while they recalled how 'Paddy used to drive us, chivvy us . . . towards his aim of making . . . us a first-class fighting unit', their Italian missions proved that they had made it. The pride all felt in being members of such an 'efficient fighting force under so trusted a leader, was one of the finest emotions that can ever stir the heart of a soldier'. More than that, noted Davis, 'we were men – men working with a will toward a common objective, free to make our own decisions and use our initiative . . .' Very many had exchanged their 'sheltered, monotonous lives with an existence full of activity and variety', joining 'an ever increasing circle of comrades and friends'.

Of course, that delightful Scalea interlude couldn't last. Barely had they been there for a week when the unit climbed back aboard the LCIs. Rumours of a coming operation 'flickered into life, smouldered . . . then went out'. Oddly, after leaving the shores of Scalea, the ships swung south, which made not the slightest bit of sense. If they were to chase the frontline, they would need to push north up the coast of Italy, towards Salerno and Naples, beyond which lay Rome. But not a bit of it.

Instead, the LCIs steamed southwards, spiriting all away from the war.

Chapter Fourteen

BRIDGE OVER THE BIFERNO

The fleet of three ships 'butted their way doggedly' onwards, 'riding the heavy swell'. Above, a bank of low, glowering clouds – heavy, black and menacing – blocked out all sign of the heavens. The wind stiffened, as the first blasts of a freezing rain hammered across the deck, menacingly. Behind, tossed about wildly on the seas, rode a clutch of diminutive LCAs, of the same type that had spirited the raiders ashore from the *Ulster Monarch*. Those small craft were being towed into battle, just in case. By rights, their services shouldn't be needed, for the LCI mothership would drop her steel walkway, just as at Bagnara Calabra, to speed the raiders ashore.

There was a certain degree of dark fatalism aboard the lead LCI that evening, as it struggled ever northwards against the rough seas. They were down to 207 men, all ranks, for the rate of attrition had taken its toll. Worse still, bearing in mind the calibre of the enemy they were going up against, and the vital strategic importance of their target, the odds did not seem to favour the raiders. But what did they know? Not for the first time, there were precious few accurate forecasts as to the strength of the enemy, or their fighting spirit. As Davis noted in his diary, 'once again, the job was no more than a gamble.' Many aboard were filled with 'foreboding that all would not go well with us', and that 'hard fighting and many casualties' lay ahead.

One man aboard ship had reasons to be relatively cheerful. Christy O'Dowd – Mayne's southern Irish comrade; he and O'Dowd had a joint raiding history that went way back – had just received official news that he was being awarded the Military Medal. This was for the September 1942 raid on Benghazi, when O'Dowd had served as the Vickers-K gunner on Mayne's jeep. Driving into a massive enemy ambush, Mayne and his crew had stood firm, buying time for the vast convoy of vehicles behind them to execute a series of about-turns and flee. In part, it was O'Dowd's sterling work, burning through pan after pan of ammo in a 'devastating' counter-attack, that had won the day – hence his MM.

Another figure aboard that ship was in a far less positive frame of mind. As he crouched on the deck, trying to find some shelter from the rain, Lance Corporal John 'Ginger' Hodgkinson didn't look at all happy. Someone asked why. The grim answer reflected Hodgkinson's darkening mood: 'I've got a sneaking feeling I won't be coming back from this one.' This wasn't like Ginger Hodgkinson at all. Hailing from Hull, and a nationally renowned junior footballer before the war, Hodgkinson had signed up with the Royal Artillery aged fifteen, going on to fight with the British Expeditionary Force in France. Undaunted by that crushing June 1940 defeat, he'd volunteered for the Commandos and subsequently for the SAS. In short, he was a highly experienced and spirited soldier, but one who seemed unaccountably spooked right now.

It was a month to the day since their 3 September raid on

Bagnara, and much exasperation and angst had attended the weeks of indecision and delay in between. As ever, there had been a series of on-again-off-again missions, the cumulative frustration of which had led Mayne to a standout 'Tread on the Tail of Me Coat' kind of a moment. One night, a 'terrific din' had awoken all, bedded down as they were on the patio of the townhouse at which they'd made their temporary billet. Worried it sounded like an air raid, they'd realised that actually 'it was only Paddy'. From the French doors of his room Mayne had begun to hurl down flower pots that 'burst with a crash . . . on the hard paving stones', noted Davis.

As Davis and his fellow officers dragged their blankets closer, praying they wouldn't get hit, matters had worsened. A series of massive earthenware pots, each full of soil, were heaved off the balcony by Mayne, although each had to weigh at least twice the weight of an average male. As they burst with a 'sickening explosion' on the paving, figures ran for cover. Come morning, a scene of 'incomparable chaos' was revealed. When the authorities came to investigate the cause of so much carnage, so extensive was the destruction that it was easy enough to pass it off as bomb damage for real.

But typically, once the present mission had crystallised, Mayne reverted to being the ultimate leader of men. His orders for 'Operation Devon', as the present mission was codenamed, read: 'land at termoli 822784, with objectives bridges at 852737 and 822698.' To put that in context, Termoli was a port town lying on the eastern – Adriatic – coast of Italy, hence the squadron's journey south from Scalea, to round the toe of Italy, after which they'd steamed north by stages, to where they were now. Termoli was also situated marginally north of Rome – latitudinally – so landing there would allow the Allies to introduce 'a serious threat to the north of Rome'. Success in this mission 'would turn the hinge pin of the enemy line at a crucial point in the Allied advance,' ran a report in the SAS War Diary – but only if the SAS could get ashore and seize their targets.

Thankfully, tonight they were not alone. Riding in the two sister LCIs of that three-ship fleet were several hundred men of No. 3 Commando and No. 40 (Royal Marine) Commando. While the Commandos were to take the town, the SAS would flit beyond that, to seize the bridges, which forded the all-important Biferno river. In the second and third weeks of September, Allied forces had landed at Salerno, another step on the march towards Rome. As the German military fell back, so the Biferno had become a strategic line along which the enemy would make their next stand. Also known as the Viktor Line, the defences stretched right across the breadth of Italy. Hence the aim of the present mission – to outflank the Viktor Line, by landing on the northern side of the river, and capturing the key bridges that would enable the Allies to surge across in strength.

The Termoli landings would be truly a great leap forward, but only if they were successful. Seizing the town with its harbour should allow further forces to be ferried in by sea, so strengthening the bridgehead. But right now, less than a thousand men-at-arms were crowded aboard those three landing ships, and in the coming days it was their line – their ranks – that would have to hold firm.

At 2.30 a.m. on 3 October 1943, LCI 179 (the ship carrying the SAS) turned towards shore. Fully loaded with kit and weaponry, the ranks of men stood in absolute silence, legs braced against the roll of the ship as she ploughed ahead. The only sound was the slap of the sea spray and the hollow thud of the waves against the ship's hull, plus the occasional sharp clink of a rifle or Tommy gun as it swung against the vessel's rail. Just visible off the port (left) side of the ship lay a knoll of land, jutting out to sea, on the higher ground of which the town itself was situated. This time the Navy's navigation looked to be spot on, and all felt a surge of pride in how the ship's crew – the same as had landed them at Bagnara – had risen to the challenge of such operations.

Silently, moving at a dead slow, the ship approached shore. There was a faint judder from below, as the hull made contact with the seabed. They had arrived. But as the captain of LCI 179 could see from his perch atop the bridge, they had not made landfall. There had to be some kind of hidden obstruction or sandbar, and it was on that they had run aground. It left them fifty feet from the landing beach, with no way ahead. It was now that plan B kicked in, the LCAs, which had far shallower draught, being dragged forward. Mayne leapt into the lead craft, ready to oversee the difficult operation of loading men and kit aboard. While maintaining silence and surprise was key, time was also of the essence, for dawn was not far away. It was also crucial to keep ammo and weaponry – and their radios – dry.

Amid the chill drift of the rain, the crashing waves and the darkness, the landings had all the potential of becoming a disaster, especially as the narrow stretch of beach was crowded with the men of 40 Commando too. 'Heavy storm clouds were banking up to the northeast and the night was already very dark,' recorded a report in the SAS War Diary. Shortly, 'a violent rain squall, with wind force 5 set in'. Yet amazingly, the ferrying to shore 'proceeded blindly . . . without losing station'.

One by one the four LCAs nudged up onto the shoreline. 'Sqn [Squadron] landed from LCAs and advance to top of beach ridge, over railway,' noted the SAS War Diary.

The coastal railway snaked through a deep cutting. There the men mustered. At first Commandos were intermixed with SAS, and terse passwords were cried out, as one band of heavily armed men bumped into another. At one point the commander of No. 3 Commando, Major Brian Morton Franks – himself a future colonel commandant of the SAS – called out the challenge: 'Jack Hobbs!' The correct response was supposed to be 'Surrey and England'. But the figure he was challenging happened to be Lieutenant John Tonkin, not so long out of his bayonet charge at Bagnara.

'Sorry, sir,' came Tonkin's reply, drifting through the curtain of rain and darkness, 'Hobbs is not in this section. This is the SRS here.'

Tonkin had recognised Franks's voice immediately, and his singular reply very likely owed much to his offbeat sense of humour.

Teaming up with Alex Muirhead's mortar section, Derrick Harrison led his patrol west, clambering up out of the railway cutting. Their objective lay four miles inland – a ridge of high wooded ground that overlooked the main road. So positioned, they would be able to 'have a smack at the Germans as they retreated', while the Commandos went about clearing the town. Scrambling out of that railway cutting proved a real challenge, as their rubber-soled boot 'slithered and slipped in slimy mud'. The mortars proved the greatest burden, sliding back time after time, but eventually they were over the lip, and began heading inland on a compass bearing.

Harrison found he was leading his men across a freshly ploughed field, and with each step he was 'sinking in well over the ankles'. The thick, heavy mud clung to their boots, which felt like lead weights. As for Muirhead's mortar section, they faced a seemingly impossible challenge. Each of Muirhead's 'carriers' was laden with twelve ten-pound bombs. With well over a hundredweight (51kg) on their backs, it was a crushing load. But if they failed to make the cover of that wooded ridge, and were caught in the open come daybreak, it would be the very worst for them. The carriers fought their way onwards. One man, diminutive in build, was bent double under his load. With 'tears of desperation in his eyes', he struggled on a few steps, fell, was helped up again, before falling once more. Yet he would simply not give up or give in.

Eventually, the straps of one of the mortar-carriers' packs broke. Davis's patrol, moving in behind Harrison's and Muirhead's, came across that man staring at the muddied heap of his broken pack dejectedly, and wondering what he should do. Davis told him there was only one possible option: abandon his load, attach himself to Davis's patrol and head for the objective. As they pressed on, Davis found his mind drifting to thoughts of the others. Two Troops, Nos 1 and 3, had a far greater challenge before them. Their task was to seize the Biferno river bridges, which lay twice the distance from the landing beach. They were infinitely worse off, Davis reasoned, for what chance did they stand of reaching their objectives under cover of darkness?

A mile or so inland, they were supposed to reach a minor road, or so the maps indicated. Where was it? On one side lay a clump of trees, but there was none shown on any of their charts. Harrison concluded their maps had to be wrong. A dog barked frenziedly from an isolated farmhouse. Skirting around it, they finally reached the road. Hurrying across it and into open fields, a harsh burst of rifle fire erupted. For a moment, Harrison feared they'd been spotted, before he heard the answering chatter of Tommy gun fire. It was the Commandos going into action in Termoli town.

Ahead, Harrison spied their objective, a 'tree-crested hill rising into the misty dawn'. Within minutes they'd reached a narrow valley that ran directly into the higher ground. Spotting a remote farmstead nestling in a fold in the terrain, Harrison pointed it out to Muirhead. 'That looks like a likely place for your mortars.'

No sooner were the words out of his mouth than a stab of green tracer lanced towards them. Diving into the cover of a sunken track, they scrutinised that farmstead. A figure dashed inside. More fire erupted from doors and windows, bullets cutting through the pre-dawn air. A thick hedgerow ran up to the farmstead. That would be the cover they'd use to assault it. Slipping into its lower reaches, Muirhead broke out his 3-inch mortar. The first bomb slammed into the farmyard, with three more landing on top of it in rapid succession.

Raising himself on his elbows, Harrison studied the position with his binoculars. Wherever the enemy were, they were well hidden.

'Look,' Muirhead exclaimed. 'About a third of the way down the hill. Whole column of them.'

Harrison moved his binoculars a little lower. 'There's twenty or so of them making their way towards us,' he confirmed.

'OK. I'll give them a smoke bomb for luck.' Muirhead turned to his mortar crew. 'One round smoke – fire!'

The bomb flew through the air, impacting thirty yards ahead of the column, darts of burning phosphor igniting in a 'cloud of white'. The distant figures started to run for cover.

'Good Lord!' Harrison exclaimed. 'They're women and children.'

They came to a halt huddled beneath a thick grove of trees. At the risk of drawing enemy fire, Harrison and Muirhead blew their whistles, yelled, and gestured for those twenty terrified figures to come down and join them. At first they seemed too frightened to move. Then one or two brave souls ventured forth, the others following at a safer distance. At the vanguard came a 'grey-haired farmhand'. He waved a greeting, but from the farmhouse behind came the crack of an angry bullet.

With the civilians safely gathered, the assault on the farm proceeded. As Muirhead kept the enemy soldiers' heads down with mortars, Harrison led his patrol up the cover of the hedge, to attack from the left flank. This they did, moving in extended line, 'rifles and Tommy guns ready'. Warily, they slipped into the farmyard. It was a mess of blasted feathers and dead chickens, testament to the accuracy of Muirhead's mortar barrage. Moving cautiously, they slipped into the farmhouse itself. Not a hint of any Germans anywhere. But signs of their recent presence everywhere. They'd turned the farm into 'a nice little fortress', complete with sniping positions in the attic. Harrison took it over, for now making it their temporary headquarters.

There was a shout from behind the building. Some of his men appeared, dragging with them a German soldier dressed in the distinctive uniform of a parachutist. As Harrison noted, he was sporting a white armband with the word '*KRETA*' embroidered in gold lettering. That signified he was a veteran of the battle for

Crete, in which massed ranks of German troops had launched a daring airborne assault – then the largest such operation of the war - seizing the island in a swift and hard-fought campaign. It was 'the first inkling . . . we were up against the fellows who had dropped in Crete', noted Harrison. Dragged from their sleep by the mortar blasts, eight further captives were brought in. Found 'skulking around' in outhouses, they appeared to be 'a good type of soldier, smart and intelligent', Harrison remarked, but they had been taken by utter surprise.

Harrison's signaller got on the radio. Typically, reception was awful, but he managed to receive a garbled message of sorts from Mayne's HQ. 'They're saying something about Major Melot being wounded.'

'How badly?' Harrison asked.

'Don't know. They're very weak. I can only just hear them.'

That was worrying. Bob Melot – their 'fighting intelligence officer, ex-Belgian flying ace of the 1914–18 war', as Harrison described him – was a talismanic figure within the unit. Strictly speaking, Melot served as Mayne's intelligence officer, so by rights he had every reason not to be in the cut and thrust of combat. But there was no keeping the old warrior down.

Harrison asked his signaller for the coordinates of the HQ. Try as he might, he just couldn't get the gist over the radio. Instead, headquarters put up a Very light. It sailed high over the treetops, 'hung for a moment, and dived out of sight'. Using that as their marker and moving in single file, Harrison led the patrol off to deliver their captives. They found the HQ sited in a farm not dissimilar to the one they had left. A German officer was standing in the lee of a haystack. He seemed utterly bewildered. 'It was not war as he understood it.' Indeed, none of the Germans seemed to have a clue where the raiders could have come from, this far behind their frontline.

The sun was up by now, and in the kitchen the woman of the house was busy frying sausages and eggs. The German stared in disbelief as the SAS lined up, officers mixed willy-nilly with the ranks, mess tins grasped in hand. But that was as nothing compared to the shock of what happened next. One of the men grabbed the German, dragged him towards the line, thrust a mess tin into his hands and gestured for him to get stuck in.

'Come on, Fritz. Better grab something before it's all gone.'

Confused he may have been, but he was equally hungry. Within five minutes the captive was 'one of the family', tucking in gratefully, while smiling uncomprehendingly at all around him.

But as news filtered in over the radio, it became clear that those tasked to seize the bridges had run into serious trouble. The worst of the fighting seemed to have fallen to No. 3 Troop, and Lieutenant John Tonkin's section in particular, most of whom seemed to be missing. Word was that dozens had been taken prisoner, Tonkin included.

After wolfing down his breakfast, Harrison studied his map. While it was far from perfect, it did seem to show the main roads and towns accurately enough. He tried to figure out where the enemy would take Tonkin and his men, once captured. Inland of Termoli lay Guglionesi, the next major town. It was closer to the Biferno river and the enemy's frontline. If Harrison were the enemy commander, that's where he would move his captives. Harrison asked permission to take his patrol and go after them. 'I had an idea that that would be where John Tonkin's section would have been taken . . . If we could catch up with them,' he noted, then there was at least a chance to spring them free.

Harrison got the green light to try. Davis's patrol would move in parallel with his own, so they could watch each other's flank. With that sorted they set out, heading into the next, knife-cut valley, braving a steep descent by hanging onto the odd 'straggling bush and tuft of tall reedy grass'. Pushing through that ravine, they began to climb to the ridge on the far side. At its summit stood an isolated farmhouse. A young Italian girl – 'about eighteen', and hurriedly combing her hair at the approach of the British troops – indicated where the enemy had moved to. Atop the next ridge, half-a-dozen German soldiers could be seen digging in.

Flitting ahead, Harrison and his men slipped by that first enemy position, all the while making for the direction of Guglionesi. A mile or so further on, they came across the distinctive marks of some kind of tracked vehicle. Pausing to study them – it looked as if the German forces had been through this way very recently – three elderly Italians emerged from the trees. Simple, rural folk, they confirmed what Harrison suspected – the Germans had been through here, making for Guglionesi just a mile or two beyond.

'English?' Harrison probed. Did they see any English soldiers?

'Yes, yes, *Inglesi.*' They had British troops – captives – with them.

That was it then. It could only be Tonkin and his men. And if the Germans were moving them in tracked vehicles, Harrison reasoned, there was no way he and his patrol could catch them.

Back at their headquarters, the story of the grim fortunes of Tonkin's patrol was filtering in – partly via radio reports, but partly from those few who had escaped. Moving at the very tip of the SAS spearhead, at first things had gone swimmingly for

Tonkin and his section. Pushing hard inland, they'd spotted their first German troops. It was just starting to get light, and the enemy were trying to take cover in a ditch, adjacent to a bridge. Dashing forward, Tonkin and his unit took all of them captive, and without a shot being fired. Next, a convoy of five trucks were spotted, nosing cautiously down the nearby road. In the gathering light, they made easy targets.

Zeroing in their 2-inch mortar, Tonkin's gunners let rip. The first barrage of rounds set a truck alight, as figures baled out. One officer was killed outright and others were wounded, as the bewildered German soldiers began to raise their hands in surrender. Facing a hidden enemy hitting them by surprise in the semi-darkness, and in what should have been utterly safe territory, they literally did not know what had hit them. So far, so very good. More voices were heard – a German foot patrol. Ambushed by a concerted barrage of Bren fire, the enemy were forced to turn tail and run, dragging their wounded with them. Mustering his men, Tonkin urged them on.

They reached a seemingly deserted farmstead, but as they moved in all hell let loose. The building was a hotbed of enemy activity, the occupiers pouring in 'a hail of heavy fire' from hidden positions. They responded with mortars and blasts from their Brens, but the situation rapidly worsened for the raiders as a light field gun began to lob in shells. Reacting swiftly, Tonkin ordered a withdrawal to the cover of a nearby ditch. It was as they slipped into it under heavy fire that their fortunes truly plummeted. A second group of enemy soldiers began to hit them from the opposite direction.

In an instant, Tonkin realised they were pinned down and sur-rounded, not to mention 'outnumbered as well as outgunned'. It would soon be fully light, and in the remaining minutes of semi-darkness they had to execute some kind of an escape. Even as the battle raged, Tonkin faced the terrible realisation that many of his men had simply 'ran out of ammo'. They were also isolated from the rest of their patrol. 'Penetrated too deep, too fast and by daylight was hopelessly cut off,' he concluded.

Finally, Tonkin gave the only order possible right then: 'Every man for himself!' Maybe, moving in ones and twos, they could slip the net.

Lance Corporal Joseph 'Joe' Fassam was one of the first to make a move. Heaving himself over the lip of the ditch, he came face to face with a group of waiting German troops. Undaunted, Fassam unleashed a long burst of fire at the enemy, before making a dash for freedom. His incredibly courageous actions would cost Fassam dear, as he was cut down in a hail of fire, but it would buy any number of the others the chance to break away. Amid the shock and confusion of Fassam's one-man charge, half a dozen of Tonkin's men managed to slip the enemy trap. Incredibly, they dragged with them the German prisoners they'd seized earlier, refusing to be deprived of their prize.

Joe Fassam lay where he had fallen – their first casualty of the battle for Termoli. A former butcher hailing from Plymouth, Fassam was a No. 8 (Guards) Commando veteran, who'd already survived one epic escape from behind enemy lines in the Libyan desert. With their vehicle out of action, his patrol had set off on foot seeking to reach the nearest friendly position, but Fassam had lost the others during the hours of darkness. He'd been found by a roving patrol of the Long Range Desert Group. They left him with a jerrycan of water and a map, as they set off to rescue his comrades.

Fassam had survived that gruelling solo escape, but not this one at Termoli. He was mortally wounded. One of those whom Fassam's brave actions had enabled to escape was Corporal Russell Jessiman, who along with Syd Payne had crawled into a hidden patch of scrub. Together, they'd stayed where they were, lying 'doggo' for hours, even as the enemy yelled out warnings and sprayed the bushes with bullets. In due course, Jessiman would write to Fassam's father, describing how, during all the time they'd served together, he'd never come across anyone who 'did not like and admire Joe'. But at the moment Fassam had fallen, no one could risk going to his aid, or dragging him in.

Seeing that some at least had broken free, Staff Sergeant James Arthur 'Nobby' Clark led a fighting thrust through the ditch, provoking a ferocious firefight. During that intense battle, Clark himself was struck in the head by a fragment of shrapnel. Even as the blood streamed down, he refused to give himself up, as did others who were likewise nursing injuries. Pounded by heavy machinegun fire, and with some of his men showing clear signs of severe 'shellshock' – today, more accurately known as a form of post-traumatic stress disorder (PTSD) – Clarke vowed to fight on.

It was then that a second section of No. 3 Troop came to their rescue. Executing a swift advance, pushing into the very heart of the hornet's nest with all guns blazing, two of their number were wounded, but they dished out more than they received. That force killed five enemy troops, wounded more and seized nine prisoners. It was a pivotal moment for Sergeant Clark and his men, for the two groups were able to link up. Among the wounded was Bob Melot, who'd been in the vanguard of the fight. As the reunited force mustered, and gathered their wounded, one man, Lance Corporal Edward Ralphs, dashed forward with a Bren. Crossing open ground under heavy fire, Ralphs found a spot from where he could cover his comrades, especially the wounded.

With the breathing space Ralphs's actions had won them, Sergeant Ernest Goldsmith – 'Buttercup Joe' – was able to get the most badly wounded to safety. Grabbing Melot, Goldsmith heaved the Belgian up and 'evacuated him under heavy fire'. He'd been shot through the shoulder, only one of many wounds that Melot had suffered during two world wars. Injured first when serving with Belgian forces in 1917, he'd been all but left for dead after the SAS's disastrous September 1942 Benghazi raid. Blown up by a grenade while attacking the enemy's wireless station, he'd made it out of there alive, going on to become 'worshipped' by the men. An icon of 'patience and tolerance', as Davis noted of Melot, the men would go to great lengths to 'not let him down'. Despite his advanced years, Melot was also 'more capable of enduring hardship and pain than most', as events at Termoli were to prove.

Not content with that one act of heroism, Joe Goldsmith returned through the ditch to organise 'stretcher parties to evacuate' more of the wounded. Thus the injured were extracted, even as what remained of the section pushed on through the guts of that ditch, going after the enemy. At the far end they stumbled upon piles of kit and weaponry, which were clearly of the type that their own troops carried. It was ominous and did not bode well for Tonkin and the rest of his patrol.

With nothing left with which to fight, Tonkin and the two dozen men still with him had had no option but to give themselves up. As noted in the War Diary: 'Germans surrounded section and captured them.' As matters transpired, their adversaries turned out to be the 'very experienced and battle hardened troops' of the German 1st Parachute Division, many of whom sported the *KRETA* armband. Having been taken prisoner, Tonkin and his men were spirited west towards the town of Guglionesi, as Harrison would later confirm.

Meanwhile, what remained of No. 3 Troop pushed on towards the bridge over the Biferno. Moving towards their own objective, Bill Fraser's No. 1 Troop were also in the thick of the action. Advancing almost due south, using the coast road as a route to approach their target – the bridge up ahead – they'd rounded a bend, only to come across an odd-looking vehicle. It was a Sd.Kfz.2, a half-track motorcycle combo, with a front wheel and handlebars, plus tracks in the rear. Behind it sat a 10.5cm light howitzer in tow. Crammed onto the Sd.Kfz.2 were some twenty enemy soldiers, all of whom seemed oblivious to the fact that British troops had landed thereabouts.

Slipping into a roadside ditch half-full of water, Reg Seekings prepared a snap ambush. When he gave the word, his section let rip. 'I've never experienced fire like it,' Seekings would remark of the moment. 'Those lads of mine were bloody magnificent. They opened up and the air was thick with lead. Practically cut chunks out of it.' The half-track's driver was killed outright, the soldiers riding on the vehicle were shot to pieces – 'all of 'em, in seconds' – before the 10.5cm gun was raked with fire and put out of action.

What happened next was both macabre and bizarre in the extreme. An enemy position lay up ahead. Seeing what a horrific fate had befallen their comrades, the nearest German troops climbed out of their positions, hands raised in surrender. But just as quickly, a force of enemy sited to their rear opened fire, aiming to cut down their brethren – to prevent them from surrendering – as well as the SAS. Those troops were hunkered down in a well-defended farmhouse, which dominated the bend in the road. During a battle that raged back and forth, and in which the farmhouse was hit repeatedly with mortar fire, the enemy fell back to a second fortified farmstead, but still the SAS kept coming.

Eventually, realising that only 'surrender or death' awaited, the survivors took the former course of action. To a man, those German troops who gave themselves up were injured. Their commander, a massive parachute major, had suffered several flesh wounds. But he was far from the worst. One bloodied figure – a lieutenant – lay on a stretcher beside him, with his 'stomach all blown out'.

The major indicated the badly wounded man, and said something in German. Seekings couldn't understand, but Johnny Wiseman most likely could, as he spoke some German. Wiseman was called over, and the major repeated himself: 'Please, shoot him. He's beyond it.'

As all could see, the injured man did indeed seem beyond any help. As the major then revealed, it was actually his younger brother, hence his asking for the mercy killing.

'I suppose I had better do it,' Wiseman conceded.

But it was then that another figure stepped forward. 'Leave it to me,' Sergeant Frederick 'Chalky' White announced. As Wiseman stood by, White 'put the man out of his torment. It was very decent of him.'

The German major seemed torn. By White's actions, his brother had been saved any further suffering, but it also meant that he was now dead. He blinked back his emotion. 'The trouble is with you people, you are too hard,' he remarked.

'Well, that's good, coming from people like you!' Seekings retorted, once he'd been made to understand the major's words.

It was then that the major seemed to notice Seekings and White's insignia. 'Ah! SAS,' he remarked. 'I said to my men, "This is strange, I've never known men to fight this hard." If I had known, we would never have fought like this.'

'Why not?' Seekings asked.

'What? Good men kill good men? Our job is to kill the ordinary troops . . . the tank people, the infantry. But you don't kill each other.'

Seekings was left perplexed, but there was little time to ponder the major's words right then.

Along with the prisoners already taken, some vehicles had been seized, and the raiders set to making good use of them. Loading the worst of the wounded and the prisoners aboard, one party left, heading back towards Termoli, while the others sped onwards. They reached the bridge over the Biferno only to have their hopes dashed. They were too late. It had been blown, and by the looks of things just recently. A thorough search of the area revealed no enemy troops thereabouts, and so Fraser's men set up defensive positions to await whatever the day might bring. Once the main British forces got there, they should be able to sling a pontoon (floating) bridge over the Biferno, and cross the river that way. Or so the men hoped.

It was approaching midday by the time Mayne's raiders delivered the first of their prisoners to LCI 179. The ship had pulled into Termoli harbour, the town having been cleared of the enemy. At one stage earlier that morning, Mayne's headquarters unit had

271

been in action 'Hun-hunting', as they'd faced a forty-strong force armed with mortars. That violent confrontation had happened at a bend in the road, as Mayne and his men had been moving back towards Termoli, to consolidate their command. Facing the fierce resistance they were coming to expect from the calibre of enemy troops hereabouts, Mayne had set out on a solo outflanking manoeuvre, without so much as a word to the others.

Managing to appear by surprise on the enemy's flank over-looking their position, he unleashed a grenade. Lobbed in among the enemy mortar crew, it knocked out their main source of firepower. After that Mayne raised a Bren to his shoulder, and wielding the eleven-kilogram weapon in his favourite fashion, he unleashed repeated bursts, cutting down the rest. A dozen enemy were killed, and with 40 Commando's help the remainder were driven off or captured. That was what those under his leadership most appreciated about Mayne: despite being in a position of command, at crucial moments he chose to fight at the forefront of the battle.

'He was idealised by his men,' wrote Fraser McLuskey, the regiment's future padre. 'More than that, he was both loved and trusted by them to a unique degree. Everyone knew Paddy would be in it too – there with the men he loved, where the going was toughest, and the danger greatest. Paddy did more than send someone – he went himself too.'

With the town cleared, the docks were secure – at least from any threat from land. But not so from the air. Even as the first of some 300 German POWs were loaded aboard the waiting LCIs, the air was filled with the roar of aeroengines, as a flight of German warplanes swooped in to attack. The air assault would last for a further thirty-six hours, as the enemy moved hell and

Instead of facing troops eager to surrender, Mayne – pictured, above left – was forced to lead his men on a daylight landing, in the teeth of the enemy's guns. Facing bloody street-to-street fighting, plus enemy armour, it was now that Lieutenant Derrick Harrison (above right, in action) fully justified the faith Mayne had put in this relatively fresh recruit.

The SAS's prized medic, Captain Malcolm Pleydell (fourth from left, above) along with (L-R) Troopers Jeff and Cattell, plus Sergeant Bob Lilley and Lieutenant Johnny Wiseman. By the time of the Augusta landings, Pleydell had been hospitalised with exhaustion. He had been replaced by Captain Phil Gunn (above right, hands in pocket, with Mayne's key deputy, the unshakeable Major Harry Poat). At Augusta, Gunn would tend to the wounded under intense enemy fire, proving himself to be amongst the bravest of the brave.

Having taken and held Augusta against all odds, Mayne's warriors seized a rare moment to relax. Grabbing armfuls of Italian wine and with a pianola dragged onto the street, the party spirit took hold. Meanwhile, Mayne took Bill Deakins, his demolitions expert, to the town's main bank to blow up its safe. The results are pictured above, in a sketch by Deakins.

With precious little time to serenade the fallen, Mayne, (right of picture, with key deputy John Tonkin), was thrust into action once more, as the SAS spearheaded the Allied landings on the Italian mainland. Their target was Bagnara, the gateway to the Eighth Army's advance on Rome.

Captured on film by the RAF's photo reconnaissance unit, Bagnara (above) would prove a bloody trial by fire, especially as the Germans held all the high ground.

The battle for Bagnara proved especially tough for Lieutenant Peter Davis, (above left, with dog, flanked by Ron Grierson on his right, and Derrick Harrison on his left). As Davis' patrol tried to scale the heights above the town, Irish Trooper Charlie Tobin, 'the kindest-hearted man in the section,' was killed. He was buried where he'd fallen, as were others.

But nothing could prepare Mayne and his men for the cauldron of Termoli. Landing by surprise in a daring outflanking manoeuvre, the battle descended into horrific close-quarter combat, reducing much of the town to ruins. Mayne and his small force faced the might of the 16 Panzer Division (Wehrmacht), a crack armoured unit ordered to retake the town at all costs and drive the defenders back into the sea. The SAS barricaded the streets against the enemy's armour but the German officers drove their troops forward in human waves.

With Termoli's defenders running desperately short of food and ammo, Bill Deakins (above left, third from left) commandeered a cart to ferry supplies to a ship, which would run the gauntlet into Termoli. A second siege-breaker, Captain Roy Farran, (pictured above right, with white belt, alongside Mayne) made it through overland, bringing vital food, men-at-arms and firepower, leading a patrol of the newly formed 2 SAS Regiment.

Termoli was under intense shelling, and a truck convoy crammed with SAS suffered a direct hit. A row of graves would need to be dug in the town's main park, to bury the fallen. It was a devastating blow, putting Mayne and his men in desperate straits. The 2 SAS siege-breakers arrived by heavily armed jeeps and by sea in a fleet of Italian fishing boats (caïques), in the nick of time.

Fighting north through Italy, 2 SAS, commanded by Major Oswald Cary-Elwes (left above, with Corporal Eric Mills), had executed a string of daredevil missions. At one stage they seized a train, steamed into enemy territory, raided a concentration camp and rescued the prisoners, before racing back to friendly lines. During Termoli's last-ditch defence, a train packed with explosives was to be detonated, to stop the enemy's Tiger tanks in their tracks. Seizing Termoli proved a double victory: not only did it outflank the enemy's key defensive line, it enabled the SAS to launch their fleet of caïques, sailing north to the aid of thousands of Allied POWs (as shown).

"SECRET" MEDALS

"We've Been Around" Say the Men With the Parachutists' Wings

Two of the Special Air Service men who received decorations at a recent investiture. (Left to right) Sergeant F. White, D.C.M., of Manchester, with his aunt, Miss P. White, and Corporal T. W. Moore, M.M., of Battersea.

Evening Standard Reporter

Sergeant Fred (Chalky) White and Corporal Terry Moore are members of the Special Air Services.

They are two of the men who, during the North African campaign, landed far behind the enemy lines, destroying enemy airplanes on their landing fields and equipment at their bases.

But when they came up to London to receive their medals from the King—a D.C.M. and M.M. for White and M.M. for Moore—all they would say about their secret exploits was: "Well, we've been around."

Sergeant White comes from Manchester. Soon after being awarded his "secret" M.M. he got married.

"The King seemed surprised when I told him I had been three and a half years in the Commandos," he said.

Now Sergt. White wears the parachutists' wings below his medal ribbons.

Corp. Moore, of High-street, Battersea, was equally reticent about his M.M. and his wings. But he told me he is a keen amateur photographer, and he will have an interesting album to show me after the war.

My two friends after receiving their Decorations.
I should have been with them, but was in Hospital

Lt.-Col. Paddy Mayne of S.A.S.

New facts about the most daring men of the war

TODAY it is announced that Lieut.-Colonel Robert Blair (Paddy) Mayne, chief of the Special Air Service Regiment, has been on a short visit to London. This picture of the legendary leader of the most daring fighting force of the war was taken during his visit.

For three years men have talked about the exploits of S.A.S.—of their courage and self-sacrifice, of their cheek and cunning. Their adventures read like a mixture of Bulldog Drummond and Robin Hood. Lieut.-Colonel Mayne is 6ft. 6in. tall. He was an Irish lawyer and amateur boxer and Rugby footballer.

Led them through German lines

A month after D-Day he was parachuted into France with only a mental map of the country.

With the help of the Maquis he set up headquarters for his army of 200 whom he met in Normandy. This army of Special Air Service operators piled into 50 jeeps and Mayne led them through the German lines to Nievre, south-east of Paris.

From there he harassed enemy troop and supply columns going to pressure points in Normandy, and intercepted and disorganised Germans when they retreated after the American break-through. He and his men wrecked more than 1,000 Nazi supply trucks during this operation.

Time bombs put in Nazi planes

Mayne has conducted this type of guerilla warfare since the North African campaign, where he and his men attacked airfields, destroying enemy planes by planting time bombs in the petrol tanks.

Mayne himself destroyed 47 in one lightning attack in jeeps. The Special Air Service men drove in and out of lines of parked planes, strafing them with incendiary bullets.

The Special Air Service started the invasion of Sicily. Next came Italy, where Special Air Service continued their attacks. It was in Italy they drove a captured Italian train into enemy territory to 5 concentration camp, captured the guards, released the prisoners and brought the whole party back by the train—including the Italian colonel-commandant.

In pride of place in his wartime scrapbook, Mayne's stalwart, Doug Goldsmith, pasted two news clippings. One showed his comrades getting their medals, on which he noted 'I should have been with them, but was in Hospital.' The other profiled their revered commander, Mayne, and the exploits of those he lead – 'the most daring men of the war.' But before Churchill could lay the final wreaths of victory and remembrance – with the erect figure of Cary-Elwes standing by – Mayne would need to lead his raiders on the D-Day missions and the march into the Fatherland that followed.

high water to retake Termoli and its vital port. For now, LCI 179 – together with her two sister ships – steamed out to sea, where they would be more able to take evasive action. But so 'persistent were the attacks,' ran a report in the SAS War Diary, 'the gunners ate and slept at their posts . . . the enemy knew well the value of the craft and were willing to pay heavily to get them out of the way.'

Indeed, if those LCIs could be sunk, crippled or driven off, that would leave the men of the SAS and the Commandos stranded, should they ever seek to withdraw. And that was exactly as the German high command intended it should be. At the behest of an enraged Führer, and a Field Marshal Kesselring who felt blindsided, and was angry and smarting, even now a grand plan was being put in place to retake all of the terrain that had been lost, annihilating their adversaries in the process. The raiders were to be corralled in Termoli and crushed by an overwhelming force of arms.

In short, the battle for Termoli had barely begun.

Chapter Fifteen

THE ENEMY AT THE GATES

Davis awoke at dawn on day two of the Termoli operation to an absolutely glorious sight. By the early morning light, he could see a stream of foot soldiers and light vehicles moving up the coast road towards the port town. Overnight, the first of the relief troops had started to stream in. 'The army had arrived, and our worries were over,' Davis noted. Catching the spirit of the moment, he and his men gathered in front of the barn where they had spent the night, kindled a large fire and began to cook breakfast. Little did they realise that they were under close observation from a well-placed and powerful enemy.

The first hint was the shriek of an incoming shell, followed by a 'shattering explosion' that shook the ground, throwing up a massive column of dust. The previous day they'd cleared the terrain of hostile forces for miles around, so surely the enemy gunners had to be firing from a great distance, and doing so blind. But seconds later came a 'tearing, roaring whine' as a second shell 'compressed the air over our heads and sent us flat on our faces'. Hurriedly packing up and moving out, Davis and his men were chased by artillery and mortar rounds all the way back to Termoli. With the main army pouring in to relieve them, it didn't seem to make the slightest bit of sense.

Davis's patrol was the last to reach Termoli, apart from John Tonkin's of course, twenty-three of whom were listed as 'missing', Tonkin included. In addition, the squadron had lost one man, Joe Fassam, 'Killed in action 3/10/43', and three were badly wounded, one of whom was Bob Melot. Typically, the stubborn Belgian was refusing to retire from the field of battle, not that anyone believed there was much fighting to be done anymore A team of surgeons had accompanied the Commandos, and they'd set up an Aid Post in town. Mayne tried to persuade his friend to get his wounds seen to. The bullet had torn through Melot's shoulder, exiting through his back. But the Belgian sensed that there was more to be done, and he wanted a part of it. So too did Sergeant Nobby Clark, with his head wound.

Mayne had stationed his men in the town's monastery, the Seminario Vescovile, a cold, bare, cheerless place with scrubbed flagstone floors and rooms like cells. In an abandoned townhouse nearby he'd established an officer's billet-cum-headquarters. From somewhere he'd retrieved an ancient gramophone, and through the house drifted the plaintive tones of 'Lili Marlene' – a 'scratchy recording in Italian'. Shortly afterwards, Davis arrived there. Being one of the last in, he found himself collared by Mayne. There were rumours of a threatened counter-attack, Mayne told him. What, if anything, had Davis seen? Davis related the story of being chased back to Termoli by shells and mortars, but otherwise all had seemed peaceful enough, especially with the main army moving in. Mayne revealed that there were reports of Tiger tanks – the German army's main heavy tank, just short of 60 tonnes when fully battle-loaded – being seen. That could explain what had been lobbing shells at Davis's patrol, they reasoned.

Overnight, Davis had questioned the one prisoner they had seized here at Termoli, a young German soldier around nineteen years of age. The interrogation had proved revealing, as he outlined to Mayne. Together with a fellow paratrooper, the German had swum a river, carrying a machinegun and magazines of ammo, in an attempt to escape, but his friend had been killed. All told, there had been some 800 airborne troops stationed in the area – a potent force – and that young fellow was not at all happy at having been caught. Facing one of the real 'Nazi brood' – he was 'arrogant and haughty' even in defeat – Davis had delivered a pep talk about German aggression, for they had invaded first Western Europe and then Russia. But he was wasting his breath.

'You must in any case admit the German campaign in Poland was a model of military skill,' the young soldier had retorted, proudly. 'Why in merely twenty-one days we had conquered the whole Polish army.'

Appalled, Davis had called over to his men, explaining what the 'cheeky young devil' had just said. There was a roar of laughter. 'Tell him about Sicily,' someone said. 'It hardly took us more than twenty-one days to conquer that!'

Davis did just that, before demanding if the young soldier really believed that Nazi Germany could still win the war.

'It's possible,' he insisted.

That was the calibre of men they were up against – a blind fanaticism ran through their ranks. The incident in which Fraser's patrol had witnessed German troops firing on their fellow soldiers, to dissuade them from surrendering, had been repeated several times during the previous day's fighting. All things considered, Mayne reckoned the cost to the squadron of taking their objectives had been remarkably light. All had feared worse, Davis included. While the enemy were high-calibre troops, and had fought ferociously, they'd given ground when faced by the kind of men Mayne commanded.

Earlier that morning, Lance Corporal Douglas Ridler, who served in Mayne's intelligence unit, had been escorting a group of German prisoners through Termoli. He'd been ambushed by a group of enemy troops and caught in a fierce battle at close quarters. As he returned fire with his Tommy gun, the weapon had jammed. Moving lightning fast, Ridler had grabbed a grenade and tossed it into the midst of the enemy. For a brief moment, it had sent them to ground. Unaware of how incredibly lucky he had been – two rounds had gone right through his beret, but without doing him any harm – Ridler fell back on the powers of deception. Yelling out to his imaginary comrades – 'Section A, flank right! Section B, flank left!' – he'd managed to convince his adversaries that they faced a far superior force. Eventually, five Germans had stood up, dropped their arms and surrendered.

But the most interesting thing was the weapons they were carrying. They were equipped with the FG 42, a super-advanced battle rifle with the power of a light machinegun. One of the most cutting-edge weapons of the war, the FG 42 would become the model for modern-day assault rifles. Back then, only the elite of Nazi Germany's paratroopers were equipped with the FG 42. It was that very weapon that had put the holes in Ridler's beret. The capture of those men and their weaponry had helped Mayne establish exactly who their adversaries might be. These troops hailed from the German 1st Parachute Division, formed by *Generalmajor* - Major-General - Kurt Student in 1938. Among other battles, they had spearheaded the lightning May 1940 airborne thrust into the Low Countries, the seizure of Crete a year later, and then finally the siege of Leningrad.

Facing such forces as these, Mayne had received requests from the brigadier commanding the inbound Allied troops to help bolster their frontline defences. Mayne had refused, and for several reasons. First, they had their dead to bury and to mourn. Second, Mayne was adamant that after several days on the go – moving in aboard the LCI, and then immersed in the full-on flood of combat – his small, battle-weary force was in need of rest and recuperation. Thirdly, this was not the deal he'd cut with General Dempsey. They were to take Termoli and the river, until relieved by the main army. By guile and martial spirit, they had done as asked. By rights, they were due to be withdrawn. They were due to be loaded aboard their LCI, to face whatever the next mission might bring.

Mayne had a hunch as to what that might be. Some sixty kilometres north of Termoli lay the Sangro river, the next obvious step on the enemy's defensive line. A plan had been mooted for Mayne to lead a party of raiders to forge a way across the Sangro. He and Reg Seekings were to swim the waters under cover of darkness, dragging a line with them, so a rope could be hauled across, after which the rest of the men would follow.

Whether dispatched on that mission or not, right now they needed to bury Joe Fassam, and ready themselves to withdraw. Some of the men went to fetch Fassam's body in. At a crossroads just to the south of Termoli, Padre Lunt held a sombre service. Corporal Jessiman, one of those whose escape had been aided by

Fassam's courageous actions, described how they placed a simple wreath beside the cross marking his grave.

As Mayne also appreciated, once the pontoon bridges across the Biferno had been stabilised, heavy armour would follow, with American M4 Sherman tanks in the van. Plus the calibre of the troops they were expecting, who hailed from the 78th (Battleaxe) Division, was as good as it got, and especially those who were scheduled to land at Termoli port. Shortly, 11th, 36th and 38th (Irish) Brigades – plus the 56th Reconnaissance Regiment – were to be shipped in, units that had distinguished themselves most recently during the battle for Centuripe, a Sicilian mountain-top fortress. Studying the terrain, General Montgomery had declared such a move 'impossible!' Spearheading the assault, the 38th (Irish) Infantry Brigade had proved him wrong.

That evening, 4 October 1943, Mayne and his men settled down to rest, confident in the knowledge that the main army was holding the perimeter, and that heavier forces were inbound. Bottles of vino were uncorked, as voices were raised in song, serenading the lost, but also celebrating a battle well-fought and won. Unfortunately, that night the weather took a turn for the worse. The storms that had threatened to wreak such havoc during their landings returned with a vengeance. As the wind howled and the rain hammered against the monastery's windows, so the Biferno was transformed into a swirling torrent. The pontoon bridges that had replaced those blown by the enemy were in 'danger of being swept away in the flood'.

By contrast, the forces of the enemy were moving on good roads and faced no such impediments. In short, the route of advance for the 16th Panzer Division (Wehrmacht) was open and clear. Fresh out of the battle for Salerno, this crack German armoured division was under direct orders from Field Marshal Kesselring: they were to recapture Termoli at any cost, driving the Allied forces back into the sea. Veterans of the Eastern Front, during one epic battle the 16th had destroyed 295 Soviet battle tanks, and had played a crucial role in the capture of 650,000 Soviet troops during the battle of Kiev. Reformed and dispatched to Italy, the 16th had fought tenaciously at Salerno, inflicting heavy losses on the Allies, before being driven back by Allied naval gunfire.

Over the night of the 4/5 October, the *Kampfgruppen* – the battle groups – of the 16th threw a ring of steel around Termoli. Even as those forces were drawing the noose ever tighter, so Bill Deakins had received his marching orders. Left in the rear – still 'declared unfit' due to his injuries – Deakins had been given the role of overseeing the unit's supply chain. At Manfredonia, a coastal town set 150 kilometres to the south of Termoli, he found himself guarding two warehouses full of rations and other assorted kit, even as the main force had gone in to attack. With Termoli taken, he'd been ordered to load up all supplies into a waiting LCI, and to steam north to rejoin his unit.

Commandeering a horse and cart – there was no other transport available – Deakins got the stores loaded aboard the waiting ship. In the half-light of dawn, they cast off and steamed at full speed for Termoli. Expecting to dock as soon as they got there, instead, 'from the shore came the sounds of all types of firing: rifle, Bren, artillery, mortars', as Termoli's defenders 'were fighting valiantly to hold the frontline'. Ordered to sail north, the LCI headed off to create a diversion, acting as if another Allied landing was under way. Once within range of shore, the LCI's cannons opened fire, strafing the coastal railway line, the 'hits on rolling stock' clearly visible, as buildings were set ablaze.

The enemy response was swift and menacing. A flight of 'Stukas' – the hated Junkers Ju 87 dive bombers – pounced on the ship, 'diving down with the all too familiar . . . almost terrifying whine'. The first bombs fell wide, but then much closer, as Deakins 'got down into as much cover as possible', the ship lurching violently from the near-misses, which threw up a 'huge column of water', men and ship being covered in a 'heavy splattering of mud'. Having run the aerial gauntlet, the LCI turned back towards Termoli, braving shellfire from land. The ship would make it into port unscathed, to unload its much-needed supplies. For the last forty-eight hours, the men of the SAS had been basically 'living off the land'.

The previous evening, Davis had retired to an exhausted sleep, secure in the knowledge that Mayne believed his men had done quite enough, and that he would not be sending them into action again until he himself was sure that it 'was fully necessary'. At first light Davis was jerked awake from a deep, deep slumber, to the least expected of sounds: 'the slow steady rattle of a Bren', which was answered by 'the roaring burst' of a machinegun, one that he recognised instantly as German. Worse still, the fire sounded close, less than half a mile away. Moments later there came the sound of a shell 'tearing the air', followed by a deafening crash. The rumours of a counter-attack appeared all too true.

Dragging himself from his bed, Davis rushed to join the others. The atmosphere proved 'strained and oppressive'. It matched the mood of the weather outside, as heavy rain and gusts swept through the town. The cloud cover was down so low, few warplanes would be able to fly, but that did little to bolster the raiders' fortunes. All reports were that the Biferno was swollen and impassable, so cutting off the spearhead of the advance from their supply columns and heavy armour. Reportedly, the front-line artillery and mortar units were running out of ammo, so low were their supplies.

Confirmation of much of this was about to come from a most unlikely-seeming source. While Deakins had been left to bring in the majority of their stores by sea, the unit's motor transport officer (MTO), Captain E. 'Franco' Francis, had risked the route by land. His truck had been one of the only vehicles to attempt to cross the Biferno. Overnight, the river had been transformed into a muddy, churning surge. Creeping across the swaying, groaning pontoon bridge at a dead slow, Francis had managed to brave the torrent. Even though all had warned him it was suicide, he had proceeded to run the gauntlet of the main road leading into Termoli, the entire length of which was menaced by the enemy's guns. Not even the Sherman tanks would dare such a thing – not that they could cross the river right then. Somehow, Francis had made it through. He'd brought a much-needed resupply of cigarettes, plus mortar bombs.

Apparently, the enemy had retaken all the high ground surrounding Termoli, those ridges and valleys that Harrison, Muirhead, Davis and others had done so much to clear the day before. More worryingly still, in places the thin line of troops slung around Termoli was in danger of buckling. Those forces first into the bridgehead had found themselves outnumbered and outgunned, and were in many cases lacking in combat experience. Few seemed to doubt that shortly, rather than pulling out of Termoli, the men of the SAS would be sent forward, in order to bolster the defensive lines. All that Mayne was waiting for was a proper sense of where the threat was greatest, and where his forces could best be used.

As others milled about, nervously killing time, Bill Fraser gave the impression of absolute cool and calm. Over and over again he played that 'Lili Marlene' record, all morning long. Outside, the shells were crashing into the town, the barrage seeming to creep ever closer, as all braced for a direct hit. But Fraser did not seem to care one jot. As long as the gramophone would spin and 'Lili Marlene' continued to play, he seemed quite content. Many envied his extraordinary sang-froid, for he seemed utterly unperturbed by the 'furious battle' raging all around. As with Mayne, he never seemed calmer or more centred than at the moment when danger was near at hand.

The first to get Mayne's orders to deploy was Harry Poat – 'as brave as a lion'. Poat took with him three patrols, those led by Harrison, Sandy Wilson – the officer whose clumsy feet had earned him the sobriquet 'Oh, Sandy!' – plus Captain John 'Tony' Marsh, 'young, bouncing, blond and extremely good looking', as Davis would describe him. Seemingly always up to one trick or another, the irrepressible high spirits of Marsh, who loved to play the eccentric, served as a foil to hide his hugely professional and fearless approach to soldiering. In fact, no one was more conscientious than Marsh, for he knew everything that was worth knowing regarding 'training and handling men'. A veteran of Mayne's A Squadron and the Great Sand Sea raids, Marsh had proved himself time and again where it mattered, in the heat of battle.

Poat, Harrison, Wilson and Marsh loaded their troops into a convoy of waiting trucks, which rumbled out of town just as the sun was going down. They reached a ridge lying on the northern outskirts of Termoli, overlooking the coastal railroad. A line of trees running along the high ground 'stood out clearly against a rapidly darkening sky'. A troop of 40 Commando were digging in nearby. They waved a greeting, but no one spoke much. Amid the gathering darkness, Poat directed each patrol to its position. Spread out along the ridge, the men prepared to dig in around a couple of farmhouses, with Sandy Wilson and his men taking the far eastern flank, nearest to the railway line and the sea.

Harrison and Marsh went with Wilson to check out his location – the last in the line. That way, all would know where the others were situated, shielding each other's flanks right down to the shoreline. At Wilson's position, a blocky farm building set to his rear 'merged awkwardly with the night sky', while the beach – a 'gleam of sand' – was clearly visible off to the right.

'Cheerio. See you later,' Harrison and Marsh whispered, as they turned to go back the way they had come. Little did they know that this was the last time they would see Sandy Wilson alive.

Returning to his own stretch of high ground, Harrison grabbed his patrol sergeant, F. Ridler – same surname, but not the same man whose earlier ruse had tricked the enemy into surrender – to execute a quick recce. In the dying light, they crawled towards the very lip of the ridgeline. Inching their way forward, they gazed into the terrain beyond. An open field dropped away in the direction of the enemy. Hugging the earth, Harrison surveyed the terrain. He figured the only way to avoid being sky-lined on the ridge was to drop down onto the front slope and dig in. But when they tried that, the earth was rock-hard.

They dropped back to their side of the ridge. Cut into it, and running parallel with the ridgeline, was a path. It looked perfect.

From the cover of its upper bank, they could command a clear field of fire, and anyone topping the ridge would be outlined against the sky. Working swiftly in the gathering darkness, they strengthened the position as best they could and set a watch rota. As Harrison had been warned, shortly after nightfall the LCI fleet was to steam up the coast to create another diversion. Laying a smokescreen close to shore, they were to pour in fire to an enemy outpost at Marina di Montenero, as if landing troops there under the cover of that smoke.

Bang on cue, Harrison heard 'the distant crackling of the Oerlikons', as the ships' cannons opened fire. Four LCIs were in action, the combined firepower of their sixteen 20mm guns creating a 'very creditable barrage', as reported in the SAS War Diary. For ten solid minutes they tore up the shoreline. Tracer sparked fires, which glimmered through the thick haze of the smoke. At the same time the ships exchanged frenzied radio calls, 'in the hope the enemy would assume that a landing was imminent'.

Acting on the assumption that the German forces would decide not to assault the ridgeline that night, for they were facing what appeared to be a fresh seaborne threat, Harrison rolled into his one blanket and settled down to sleep on that path. But in the bitter cold and wet he found himself shivering uncontrollably, and ended up passing one of the 'longest and most miserable nights' ever.

Back at the SAS's austere Termoli monastery billet, Sergeant Joe Goldsmith snatched a few moments to write a letter to his real-life sweetheart. This was no dairy-worker called Mary with her scrumptious dumplings, of 'Buttercup Joe' fame. Linda Rolfe was a restaurant manager from Hastings, a town lying a thirty-minute drive from Goldsmith's hometown of Winchelsea. They'd met in a whirlwind romance following his miraculous escape from the Dunkirk beaches, and they were engaged to be married. Normally, his letters were imbued with a typically upbeat spirit.

In the spring of 1943 he'd written about how proud he was to have been awarded his SAS wings, the highest accolade that one could achieve in the wartime SAS, as far as the men were concerned. In rapturous terms, he'd gone on to tell Linda all about 'the boys with whom I work. They are the finest band of lads you could ever go into action with . . . we know one another off by heart and there's not one who would not lay his life down for his mate, and they are all mates to each other.' But over the long months at war there had also been the drip, drip, drip effect of trauma. Here at Termoli it seemed to be getting to Joe Goldsmith, as it was to any number of others, much as they might try to hide it.

Deployed with David Stirling's B Squadron in the winter of 1942/3, Goldsmith and his fellows had harried the enemy's supply lines across North Africa, but they had done so facing a vengeful enemy and hostile locals and across terrible terrain. The losses among B Squadron had been punishingly high, and Goldsmith had seen scores of his comrades killed or captured. A real low point had come when their patrol had shot up what they believed to be an Italian officer's convoy. The luxury vehicles had turned out to be a mobile brothel, and to be packed full of Italian women. That 'horrific incident' had left Goldsmith troubled. More recently, events had transpired to fan the flames of their disquiet – his and his fiancée's – when Linda had read in the newspapers of what she believed was his death. It had taken an official letter from the British military's Infantry Records Office to put her mind at rest, assuring her it was a mistake and that 'you will soon hear from your fiancé direct'.

Tonight in Termoli, as the legions of the enemy massed on the outskirts of town, Goldsmith's sentiments seemed markedly downbeat. The letter he wrote Linda seemed to reflect a fear that his long run of good fortune – from spring 1940 at Dunkirk until now – was about to run out. 'I only hope that my luck is as good as you wish it and that I am one of the chosen few to get away from here; you know, if I do not do another op' I reckon I have had my share of thrills . . .' Those were uncharacteristically dark sentiments, but they would come to embody the terrible ill fortune that was about to grip all of those bracing themselves to face the enemy onslaught.

Come first light, Harrison and his men stamped life into frozen limbs at their ridgetop position. From a nearby farmhouse, a whisp of smoke curled into the sky. Harrison sent two men to the house, with rations, to see if the family might cook them some breakfast. While they were gone, he took one of his Bren gun teams to a patch of woodland, just forward of the ridge. From there, they could send warning of any impending attack, and put out the first stabs of countering fire. That sorted, Harrison and Ridler went to eat. Eight or nine ragged children watched them closely, as the eldest girl helped her mother cook, and grandpa enjoyed an English cigarette at the fireside. Once he'd eaten, Harrison tried to convince the family to leave. Trouble was coming, he warned. Smiling fatalistically, they demurred. This was their home. They would stay.

Harrison gave up trying to persuade them otherwise and returned to the Bren position. Using his binoculars, he studied the terrain stretching north, and especially the far ridge. Running his glasses along the heights, he spied small groups of German troops, but they were well out of range. Dropping his binoculars a fraction, he let his gaze follow the coast road, and the railway line on the right of it, to where they crossed over a small bridge. Beside it lay a whitewashed building, with a wooden signal box on the far side.

Suddenly, he noticed movement at the rear of the building. Four figures emerged. Harrison might have missed them, except for the fact that one, an officer, was carrying a map board, and the 'sun flashed from its polished surface like a heliograph' (a signalling device that uses movable mirrors to reflect sunlight). As Harrison watched, the senior figure gestured towards their very ridgeline, and he was obviously giving orders to his junior officers.

'Range sixteen hundred, right of arc, white house . . . four men,' Harrison cried out his fire orders.

When the Bren gunner confirmed he was on target, he gave the order. 'Fire!'

The Bren's muzzle spat smoke. The distant group of figures scattered. At the corner of the house one fell. The other three dived for some bushes, and Harrison's gunner gave them a long burst. 'There was no more movement.'

The Bren fell silent. Distant figures darted hither and thither on the far ridge, but Harrison could do no more than make a guess as to what they might be up to.

Sergeant Ridler came scurrying over to find him. 'Still no sign of our relief, sir. Wonder what's happened to them?' They were supposed to have handed over their positions to the regular army come dawn.

'Expect they were late getting through . . .' Harrison replied.

From behind came the distinctive roar of Oerlikons. The LCIs' guns were in action at the port. A German fighter streaked overhead, low and fast. There were the sounds of diving planes: the harbour was under attack. Harrison made a dash for his signaller's position, located along the path where they had set their main defensive line. Once there, he got on the radio. A first shell 'moaned overhead', followed by another and another in 'eerie succession'. Initially, they dropped beyond the ridge, but the enemy gunners began to walk the fire backwards, until the blasts were showering Harrison's position with shrapnel.

Orders via the radio came in: 'Get dug-in, fast.'

There was no sign of any force coming to relieve them any time soon. Between them they had the one shovel, borrowed from the farmhouse. As they were behind-the-lines raiders, shovels did not form a part of their normal load. The ground was hard and unyielding, as they did their best to bolster their defences and the shell-blasts crept closer still.

A message came through from their forward Bren post. The enemy had launched an attack across the valley, and had reached as far as the coast road. There, they'd been caught in a barrage from the defender's '25-pounders' – the Ordnance QF 25-pounder, the British military's fine 87mm field gun, one of the few pieces of heavier firepower that had managed to make it across the Biferno. For now, that had driven the enemy troops back.

Harrison went forward to the Bren position once more, to take a look. As he crept over the ridge, a 'slow tearing sound' ripped through the air, spouts of earth erupting in the valley right before him. That had to be their gunners on the 25-pounders, Harrison thought, putting in another barrage. In fact, he was wrong, as a radio message from Poat was about to reveal.

'Harry? Look, the situation is deteriorating over on your left flank,' Poat told him. 'Get your section over there as fast as you can and see what you can do . . . Better hurry, though.'

Harrison snatched off the headphones. He gathered his men. Tony Marsh held their left flank, so they were heading over to reinforce his position, he explained. No time to lose.

Keeping to the cover of the trees, Harrison dashed across to Marsh's position. He found Poat there, too. Both men looked worried. As Poat explained, heavy armour had broken through on the far left flank of their line. The defenders had faced Tiger tanks with little more than 'Carriers' – the diminutive Universal Carrier, a 3-tonne lightly armoured tracked vehicle, which was armed with a Bren, plus either PIATs or the even more archaic Boys anti-tank rifle, the notorious 'elephant gun'. Against Tiger tanks, it was only marginally better than sitting in a tin can armed with a peashooter.

'Get moving,' Poat told Harrison. 'There'll be infantry following those tanks.'

Thankfully, along this section of the ridge the trees were thicker. Moving in line, Harrison led the advance, as the din of battle echoed through the woodland just ahead of them. They came upon a farmhouse. Lined against the rear wall were the wounded, propped against the masonry or lying down. With earth-shaking impact, heavy shells from the enemy tanks slammed into the far side of the building, as shrapnel ripped apart the air with the 'sickening sound of tearing paper'. Beyond the farm the trees began to thin out. Scattered among them were a few broken Carriers, one torn open like a blasted bean can, others with their tracks blown off.

It was clear that whoever had been manning this position had fought ferociously. The Commando leader explained there were still a few 25-pounder guns out there. If Harrison and his men could reach them, they could maybe still 'make a fight of it'. Flat on their bellies, they wormed their way forward as heavy shells tore overhead. At the very edge of the tree cover, they came upon those field guns. But even at a quick glance it was obvious they would never fire again. The Tigers' 88mm shells had ripped into them. Those operating the 25-pounders – the men of the Royal Artillery – had defended them to the last, many dying at their posts.

Reversing course, Harrison and his men crawled back to rejoin the Commandos. Only the thick tree cover was holding back the German armour now. Even a modest-sized trunk could cause a Tiger to pause, and a mature woodland such as this was basically impassable to armour. But infantry would be there in support of the Tigers, and no one doubted they were massing to attack, just as soon as the big guns had done their worst. Once back with the few Commandos who were still fit to fight, they set up a defensive line, readying themselves 'to meet the German attack'.

A message came through for Harrison to link up with Tony Marsh. Dashing through the trees, he found Marsh's command post, situated beneath a blanket that he had thrown up to form a sort of awning. The two commanders snatched a quick confab as a barrage of mortars began to rain down, tearing into the earth all around. One burst in the treetops, fragments of shrapnel cutting through the blanket above them.

'We can't stay here much longer,' Harrison exclaimed, shouting to make himself heard above the din of battle.

'I know,' Marsh yelled back. 'But we can't withdraw . . .'

'Only one thing for it,' Harrison cried. 'We must go forward. At least it has the advantage it's the last thing Jerry will expect.'

That decided, they readied to move, Harrison dashing back to his men. Hurriedly, he explained the plan, and without so much as a pause they began to crawl through the trees leading into the valley below. Somehow, the mortar barrage seemed to follow their every move. Suddenly, a bomb tore into the earth some five yards in front of Harrison. By chance, he happened to be in a fold in the ground. The shattering blast tore over him, but he was completely unscathed.

Ahead lay a narrow 'sunken track'. It was as good a position as any of them could wish for right then. Organising his men, Harrison led the first of them into it. Unless a mortar dropped directly into its depths, they should be shielded from the blasts. From the cover of the far bank they could pour down fire on the enemy. That sorted, Harrison went to bring in the rest of his patrol. Some seemed to be missing. Where the devil were they? He heard a twig snap. He whirled around, only to find one of his men looking utterly ashen-faced. A mortar round had ploughed into the midst of them, he explained.

Harrison found the victims lying beneath the trees. There were five wounded – four from his patrol, and one from Marsh's. Harrison bent to inspect their wounds. Two were in a very bad way. He broke out his medical kit from his pack, and did the only thing possible right then, injecting both with shots of morphine. Then, grabbing hold of some barn doors and pieces of fencing that had been blown down by the shelling, they wrapped the injured in blankets and lifted them onto their improvised stretchers. Harrison detailed a few of his men to try to get the wounded back to the Aid Post at Termoli. They should head east along the ridge, then take the beach south into town.

With his 'weakened section . . . now further depleted', Harrison and his few surviving men took up their positions along that sunken trackway. The mortaring seemed to grow heavier still as bombs tore up the ground on all sides. They crouched in cover, 'waiting for the inevitable' – the enemy's charge. Together, Marsh and Harrison's patrols were down to some twenty fighting men, as their thin line prepared to face the onslaught.

A shout came ringing through the trees, punctuated by the rasp of Brens firing. 'German infantry coming across the valley. We've broken them up for a bit, but they are getting ready again.'

For long minutes, the two sides traded vicious fire. But as the hordes of enemy pressed ahead, the defenders were forced to fall back. Seeking to link up with any surviving Commandos, Marsh and Harrison figured they'd try to drop down to Sandy Wilson's position, covering the rail and road routes into Termoli town. There, they'd look to make a last stand, with their 'backs to the sea'. They gathered up their scattered weaponry. There was too much to take. They selected the Brens and Tommy guns – the heaviest firepower. Though few in number, by the time they got moving they were a fairly heavily armed band of men, Harrison noted. But it was small comfort, bearing in mind all that they were facing right then.

Back at Mayne's headquarters, they received grim news. Word came in that those holding the line along Termoli's northern ridge had been overrun. If it were true, Poat, Marsh, Harrison and Wilson may have been lost, along with all in their patrols. It was a confused and chaotic battle situation right then, but that was the word from the regular forces who had been holding that section of the line. They'd seen Mayne's men push forward, advancing onto the enemy guns and their armour. It was a suicidally brave move. They'd seen none of them return.

In truth, what remained of that small band of men was still in action, but only just. Halfway to Sandy Wilson's position they'd come across the worst of their wounded. Those carrying them on the improvised stretchers had found the going simply too tough, and so they'd got word to Termoli to send teams of medics. Even now, distant figures could be seen crossing the open ground, their red cross armbands standing out against the green of the grass.

Syd Payne was doing his best to comfort one of the worst of the wounded, who was crying out in agony. It was John 'Ginger' Hodgkinson, the man who'd had the premonition of his own death even as their LCI had crept in towards the landing beaches. Caught in the mortar blast, Hodgkinson was in such pain that he kept calling out for someone to end it all, to put him out of his misery. Instead, Payne got busy bandaging his wounds, to try to stem the flow of blood. But it was clear that unless they got Hodgkinson to the Aid Post, and quickly, he simply couldn't last.

Someone found an old wooden farm cart. Hodgkinson, the former junior football star, was a big man, but maybe using the cart they could get him to the help he so desperately needed. Loading him aboard, the small band of warriors set off once more, the rest of the wounded hefted on their makeshift stretchers, as they pressed onwards. But with each step the enemy shelling seemed to grow ever more intense. 'The German gunners were throwing every type of shell they had at us,' remarked Payne, 'but thankfully the ground was pretty soft,' which served to take the force out of the worst of the explosions.

Harrison noticed the face of one of the wounded was 'deathly grey green'. Nearby a stream rushed down towards the sea, running between steep banks. They slipped into its cover. It felt wonderful to be out of sight once more. Reaching a shallow waterfall, they slithered down it, Harrison realising that the railway line lay just ahead, with the beach beyond that – their route back to Termoli. Still there was zero sign of Sandy Wilson or any of his patrol, who had been holding this section of the line. Harrison could only imagine they had been captured, or forced to retreat.

No option but to press on.

They reached the fringes of the shoreline. A first figure ventured onto it, only for 'a long, dangerous crease' to erupt in the sand just inches from him, as an enemy machinegun opened fire. The beach had been taken, so that way too was barred to them. They did a quick head count. More men seemed to be missing. Marsh asked Harrison to check if there was any route they might use a little inland – could they make it back to Termoli that way? Harrison did as asked, climbing out of the streambed, but the terrain was horribly flat and open. He didn't doubt that as soon as they stepped into the open, burdened as they were with their wounded, they would be cut down in their droves.

He reported back to Marsh: 'pinned down . . . unable to get out . . .' There was heated debate as to what they should do. Some of the stretcher-bearers had joined them by now. They argued they should chance it on the open beach, relying on their red cross insignia to allow them safe passage with the wounded. Harrison and Marsh were dead set against it. The way the battle was looking, the Germans were at the very gates of Termoli. If they allowed the stretcher-bearers to get through, they could report to the town's defenders about the nearest German positions. They just couldn't allow anyone to make it back alive, of that Harrison and Marsh were certain.

Either way, 'darkness was our only hope', they noted, grimly.

Chapter Sixteen

TO THE DEATH

Anchored off Termoli, the LCI fleet came under ferocious bombardment, as the enemy endeavoured to send those landing craft to the bottom. Focke-Wulf FW 190s and Messerschmitt Me 109s dived and weaved overhead, tearing up the seas. A cheer went up from the ships' decks – an aircraft had been hit. It came tumbling out of the skies in a ball of flame. But just as quickly another threat was upon them, with the enemy forces closing in on Termoli itself. The 16th Panzer Division's advance must have brought the LCI fleet within range, for shells started to tear into the seas. As the situation around Termoli worsened, one by one the defenders' field guns fell silent. There were signs of breakthroughs by 'enemy tanks', and the LCI commanders feared the worst.

From the vantage point of their ships, they watched as columns of German infantry advanced to within 'three cables [some 500–600 yards] of the town'. The chief worry now was Termoli's defenders getting cut off, and how to evacuate them before that might happen. A Lieutenant Hylton volunteered to go ashore, to try to ascertain how bad things were. Using an Italian fishing smack – a small boat with sails – boasting a somewhat unusual crew, Hylton made it safely into the harbour as the evening shadows drew in. He returned with a report reflecting how truly dire things had become. Some thirty-odd fishing smacks were anchored nearby, and a hasty plan was put together. Under the blanket of a smokescreen put down by the LCIs, they'd use those boats to ferry the raiders to the motherships, as their 20mm cannons gave covering fire.

As luck would have it, an unusual fleet of fishing smacks – otherwise known as caïques – had only recently docked at Termoli. Unexpectedly for the town's defenders, they had turned out not to be crewed by Italian fishermen, as the boats' appearances might suggest, but by fellow members of the SAS. Even as that mystery fleet of caïques had run the gauntlet, so another force of SAS had made it into the town, this one arriving overland. Under the command of Captain Roy Alexander Farran, they had braved the most incredible risks in an effort to reach the besieged town and their beleaguered brothers in arms.

Captain Farran's reputation went before him. He'd already won an MC during the battle for Crete. Suffering terrible wounds, he'd been captured by the enemy, but had gone on to mastermind one of the most daring escapes of the war. Rejoining Allied forces, Farran had been injured again, this time in North Africa, after which he was dispatched to Britain to face a medical discharge. He'd somehow managed to avoid that, and instead had volunteered for the SAS.

In the spring of 1943, Farran had joined 2 SAS, the second regiment then being raised by Bill Stirling – David Stirling's elder brother – and undergoing training in Algeria. A handful of early missions by 2 SAS – small-scale parachute insertions into Italy – had proved largely disastrous, but then had come a change in tactics. On 9 September 1943, 2 SAS had deployed en masse with their heavily armed jeeps, landing at Taranto, on the heel of Italy, along with the main Allied forces. Once ashore, their task was to chase after the enemy, probe their frontline positions and help the main army beat a path through.

First into action had been the unit's overall commander, the wonderfully named Major Oswald Aloysius Joseph Cary-Elwes. As noted in the SAS War Diary, Cary Elwes's 'Jeep patrol . . . ran into enemy section . . . killed three and took three prisoners without suffering casualties.' In the War Diary there is a map of 2 SAS operations, titled portentously '2 SAS Regiment in Italy from Taranto to Termoli'. Farran had just completed that epic route, some 300 kilometres long, in twenty-five days of hectic driving intermixed with combat. Along the way, some quite spectacular battles had been fought, and some rather unorthodox missions undertaken.

One patrol in 2 SAS, the so-called 'French Squadron', was made up entirely of former French Foreign Legion troops, being commanded by the inimitable 'Captain Jack William Raymond Lee'. Lee was in truth one Raymond Couraud, former Foreign Legionnaire turned Marseille gangster, turned Special Operations Executive agent, and most recently SAS commander. It was during his stint in the SOE that Couraud had been obliged to change his name to Lee, especially after he had deployed on the March 1942 raid on Saint-Nazaire – Operation Chariot – during which he'd been shot in both legs and almost given up for dead.

Part of 2 SAS's covert remit in Italy was to engineer the rescue of escaped Allied POWs, thousands having fled from the prison camps, once the Italian armistice had been declared. Mostly, they were hiding out in the mountains, and with the onset of winter conditions were turning dire. Cary-Elwes and Couraud – Lee – had struck the first blow in those POW-rescue operations, and with unbelievable dash and panache. On 12 September, 2 SAS had seized Chiatona railway station, lying some twenty kilometres to the west of Taranto. There, a 'special train was assembled, manned by the French Squadron', plus a troop of British SAS, together with an Italian officer, Colonel Usai. By then, of course, the Italian armistice was several days old, so Colonel Usai and the SAS were now on the same side.

As Cary-Elwes would remark, 'driving a locomotive was one of the skills we had learned in the course of SAS training,' though perhaps none had never done so with a mission such as this in mind. The train that Cary-Elwes had ordered into action prepared to depart Chiatona bristling with weaponry. It also carried a Polish airborne officer, for a very particular reason. On 13 September it set forth, steaming west into 'enemy country', making for a distant concentration camp that was crammed full of prisoners, a number of whom were Polish. Just as in Nazi Germany, a network of such camps had been strung across Fascist Italy, where the 'enemies of the state' were incarcerated amid inhuman conditions. Situated some eighty kilometres inside German-occupied territory and boasting a guard force commanded by an 'Italian Fascist Colonel', the camp at distant Pisticci was the train's planned destination – that was if it made it through.

As the war-train had gathered pace and steamed westwards, at one of the key crossroads Major Cary-Elwes stood guard with a patrol of SAS jeeps, determined to hold the junction and adjacent railway crossing against all adversaries. In that he had succeeded, the special train steaming through unmolested. On 14 September it reached the Pisticci camp unscathed. Upon arrival the SAS had struck by surprise, bursting out of the train and overpowering the camp guards, before springing free 180 'prisoners of mixed nationalities'. Having loaded the former captives aboard the carriages, the war-train had steamed back towards Chiatona going like the clappers, with Cary-Elwes and his jeep patrol still standing guard, to ensure their safe return. They even brought with them the Fascist commandant of Pisticci camp as a bonus prize. Simply incredible.

One of Cary Elwes's foremost raiders had been recruited in the most unorthodox fashion, and he epitomised the calibre of those under his command. Charles 'Charlie' Hackney had been a tank commander in North Africa. Twice his Crusader tank had been blown up beneath him, Hackney seeing all of his crew killed, while he alone 'was lucky enough to escape'. After the second horrific loss, he'd arrived back at his own lines, only to be ordered straight back out again, and commanding another Crusader and its crew. 'Unshaven, dirty, exhausted from lack of sleep and with his clothes in tatters,' Hackney simply 'refused point blank to do so'. As a consequence he was placed under close arrest and was thrown into the brig, two soldiers with fixed bayonets standing guard.

As he waited, knowing he was up for a court-martial and might well be shot as a deserter, an unexpected figure materialised before Hackney. Tall, ramrod straight and somewhat debonair-looking, with a magnificent moustache, the officer struck Hackney as having a distinctly 'aristocratic air'. It was the inimitable Oswald Cary-Elwes. Having introduced himself, Cary-Elwes asked the condemned man what he was doing in detention. Hackney related his tale, whereupon Cary-Elwes told him that if he wanted out of there and to join the SAS, he was to be outside, kit packed and 'ready to move off in the officer's jeep', double quick. While Hackney barely knew a thing about the SAS, on balance he figured anyone in their 'right mind would have been foolish to reject the offer'.

So it was that Hackney was spirited out of detention by Cary-Elwes and taken almost a thousand miles across the desert to the SAS's camp, then at Kabrit. There he began his training. Shortly afterwards, Hackney's parent regiment, the 4th Hussars, had discovered his whereabouts, and issued orders for him to be returned to their custody 'for court-martial'. David Stirling had concluded that Hackney was worth 'more alive than dead, so told him to keep a low profile and the order was ignored'. In due course, Hackney had been hustled off to join 2 SAS in Algeria, which proved to be the perfect means of keeping the wanted man out of the grasp of those who sought to prosecute him.

Commando-trained before joining the Hussars, Hackney was a soldier of long experience and had proved a fine recruit. In early 1943, he'd embarked as one of a fourteen-man party for a raid on Pantellaria, an island off the coast of Sicily. In a mission codenamed Snapdragon, they'd been dropped by submarine and canoed to shore, seeking to blow up the island's lighthouse, which posed a menace to Allied shipping. As the enemy 'opened up with all they'd got', Hackney had set the charges around the base of the target, after which they'd dashed away into the darkness, carrying their wounded. Hearing the 'lighthouse go up with a loud bang . . . and come crashing down', they'd taken to the seas, the submarine spiriting them back to friendly shores.

Forever grateful to Cary-Elwes, Hackney was an intensely loyal and courageous warrior, and as 2 SAS had pushed into

Italy he'd been at the forefront of a 'series of short sharp battles with the Germans'. Thankfully, their jeeps, boasting 'twin Vickers machine-guns, Browning .50 machine-guns, Bren guns . . . Tommy guns, grenades and explosives, afforded colossal firepower', as all had quickly come to appreciate. Shortly after executing the daring prisoner-rescue mission by train at Pisticci camp, Cary-Elwes was sadly obliged to return to Algeria, to oversee the ongoing training of the remainder of 2 SAS. But as a massive consolation, that had left Captain Roy Farran very much in charge.

From then on a series of daring thrusts and hard-fought battles had propelled their jeeps by stages north, towards Termoli, which had just assumed a very special significance for Farran and his men. Knowing that the bulk of the escaped Allied POWs lay well beyond the German frontline, their rescue would involve bypassing it, and with a means to bring them out en masse. Rather than banking on another war-train steaming through, Farran and his men had set upon the ruse of using a fleet of caïques to pluck the escapees to safety. Sailing under the noses of the enemy, and appearing for all the world as bona fide Italian fishing vessels, they should be able to slip by. For that to be possible, a harbour was needed as near to the German frontline as possible, from which to sally forth on their rescue missions. Once Mayne and his 1 SAS raiders had been dispatched to seize Termoli, that was the only sensible place to head for.

A fleet of four diminutive caïques, plus one tall-masted schooner – a larger wooden sailing ship – had set sail, even as Farran had pressed north overland with his column of jeeps. Farran had reached the town of San Severo, some sixty kilometres south of Termoli, but there had found the massed ranks of Allied military transports clogging up the road. German warplanes attacked, setting several of the trucks ablaze. Desperate to bypass the morass of mired traffic, Farran 'overrode an obstinate military policeman, who refused to let me pass'. In the same breakneck manner he'd continued north towards Termoli, only to find the swollen torrent of the Biferno river barring his way.

A force of Royal Engineers were trying to make good the crossing by pontoon bridge. Telling 'lies about the urgency of my mission' – Farran didn't yet realise how dire matters had become in Termoli – he managed to convince them to ferry him and his men across on rafts. Braving the Biferno and the roads beyond, in that way they had finally made it into town. As Farran would write of his journey's end, it was 'good to see our own winged dagger flaunted on the sand-coloured berets of the S.A.S. in town'. Heading for the harbour, Farran chose a building that overlooked the water as his HQ. As the afternoon drew on, he saw 'four little caïques heeled over against the wind, led in by a tall schooner'. Once the boats – 2 SAS's covert POW-rescue fleet – had tied up, Farran found himself envying the crews, 'with their opportunity to play pirates'.

But shortly, the enemy's attentions were drawn to that pirate fleet. As the SAS War Diary recorded, '4 dive bombing attacks by Focke-Wulfes on harbour ... Caïque of B Squadron struck (1 killed and 5 wounded). Shelling of town ...' The first vessel that had been hit began to sink. Farran, who had rushed down to the waterside, dived in to rescue one of the wounded. But he'd forgotten to remove his 'German jackboots', which filled with water and like lead anklets dragged him down. As a consequence, Farran also had to be rescued. Once he'd recovered from his dousing, and ensured that the wounded were being cared for, Farran returned to his harbourside HQ.

There he came across Major Alexander 'Sandy' Scratchley. Scratchley, an old SAS hand, was part of 2 SAS's headquarters section, so had made it into Termoli with the fleet of little ships. Scratchley proceeded to reprimand Farran for 'sitting idle like a rat in a hole, while Termoli was in acute danger of falling to the enemy'. Chastened, Farran grabbed his twenty men, and taking six Bren guns for maximum firepower, they made their way over to the main HQ. Even that short walk proved 'extremely perilous', with enemy aircraft swooping low and 'shells bursting everywhere'. At one point, Farran had a duel with a Focke-Wulf, as the SAS captain wielded his Tommy gun from the streets below. Arriving at the HQ, Farran discovered just how sorely his force was needed.

Dispatched immediately, he was sent north to plug a gap in the frontline, where the railway line and the goods yard ran down to the sea. Taking up positions on the last ridge of land before the town, Farran reckoned they had a thousand-yard front to hold, with twenty men. To their left, the battle-worn warriors of Mayne's 1 SAS were clinging on, guarding a long section of ridge and bolstered by some Commandos. Farran consoled himself with the thought that their firepower was 'abnormally strong', with those half-a-dozen Brens, plus a 2-inch mortar to hand. But within a short time, they were forced to fall back under the enemy onslaught, as a determined thrust by German troops seized the town's cemetery.

They now had their backs to the goods yard itself. Farran placed his men, ten to either side of the rail tracks, with three Brens apiece. Taking heavy fire from both the direction of the cemetery and the enemy positions to their front, still Farran's force held firm. Sniper rounds snarled 'dangerously close to our heads', while a constant barrage of mortar rounds rained down, crashing into the rail sheds to their backs. Time after time, the enemy tried to rush down the rail tracks, but the range was so short and 'we could not fail to hit a man advancing', Farran would note. 'I am sure we inflicted heavy casualties.'

On one flank of the railway line, Farran had positioned his rock-steady lieutenant, James 'Jim' Mackie, with a ten-man force. Mackie, a medical student prior to the war, was as solid as they came. On the opposite flank was the even more redoubtable Lieutenant Peter Jackson, a man who'd already distinguished himself any number of times during the war. Wounded in North Africa during the final battle of El Alamein, Jackson had spent weeks in hospital. Once he was released he'd rejoined his unit, the Queen's Bays, and earned a Military Cross during the final stages of the desert war. Badly wounded in that battle, a second stint in hospital had followed, after which he'd volunteered for the SAS in August 1943, so a little over a month earlier.

Farran sited his own HQ 'in centre of railway line', as the War Diary noted, from where he could yell orders to his forces on either side. As he and his men had realised, the battle for Termoli had descended into a 'bloody affair', with Mayne's forces and the Commandos suffering 'heavy casualties'. And as Charlie Hackney – one of those helping to hold their perilous position – appreciated, it was Mayne, the 'battle-hardened Irish giant', who was spearheading the resistance and 'especially distinguishing himself in battle'. Though he didn't yet know it – their mail had been delayed by two months – Hackney's mother had died in England just a few weeks earlier. As a result, Hackney was due compassionate leave. Instead, he was here, helping face the onslaught.

With the evening light fading, the enemy were no more than 500 yards away. They kept pouring in long bursts of tracer, in an effort to provoke Farran's forces into revealing their positions. His men held their fire. They weren't about to give anything away, for this was the only means by which to try to conceal themselves from the enemy mortars. They faced another problem too, which was growing ever more serious: 'shortage of ammunition'. The mortars kept coming in, right until last light. Still Farran, Mackie, Jackson, Hackney and the others didn't budge. A 'cold, uncomfortable night' lay ahead. Who knew what the dawn might bring?

As a note in the SAS War Diary recorded for the evening of 5 October: '1900hrs . . . 2 SAS in position around goods yard 819786 . . . The Sqn [squadron] is ordered to repel any offensive action that may occur the next day.' Come sunrise on the 6th, their thin line of steel was to hold firm, no matter what the enemy might decide to throw at them.

Directly ahead of Farran's position, over at the sunken riverbed, Marsh and Harrison's party had somehow managed to hold out. As the battle had raged to either side of their place of hiding, they'd ended up crawling into a culvert – a concrete-sided drain – that ran below the railway line. Sadly, one of their worst-wounded, Ginger Hodgkinson, the champion junior footballer, had died of his injuries, but the other injured men were still clinging on. As the darkness thickened, two men had ventured out from the culvert, to see if the beach was still menaced by the enemy. One was Harrison, accompanied by one of their Commando brethren. Together, they 'crept out among the dunes'.

A hundred yards away, they spied the outline of a German sentry. Slipping their Tommy guns forward in readiness, the two men waited. From behind them, moving with infinite caution, a shadowy column of figures emerged from the culvert, some carrying stretchers. Under the cover of the Tommy guns, they crept south along the beach, until they had merged with the darkness. Pulling back, Harrison and his comrade resumed their covering positions, and in that fashion, bit by bit, the withdrawal was made.

As the fugitives flitted along the beach towards Termoli, for a moment Harrison and the Commando worried they had dropped their guard. A stab of flame cut the night. Rounds tore into the sand. The party 'scattered for cover'. Under sporadic fire, they realised what had happened – they had 'bumped' their own defences. But with shouts exchanged and recognition gained, this small force which had been given up for dead finally made it into their own lines.

A group of men were pulled out of the SAS's frontline positions to help carry the wounded. One was Jim McDiarmid, the man who'd been shot in the ankle during the battle for Bagnara but had carried on fighting regardless. Ripping down doors to fashion DIY stretchers, they picked their way through the narrow streets. One man, Bob McDougall, stopped to light a cigarette, when a shadowy figure leaned out of a window with a Beretta submachine gun. McDougall proved quicker. Grabbing his Bren and firing from the hip, he unleashed a burst, forcing the enemy gunman to dart back inside.

McDiarmid had had quite enough of this. A veteran of the Black Watch (Royal Highlanders), McDiarmid hailed from a regiment that had earned the nickname 'the Ladies from Hell' during the First World War, due to the fact they wore kilts and were such ferocious fighters. In that spirit, he darted inside the building. A few moments later, he was back. There had been no sound of any gunfire, but McDiarmid seemed satisfied.

'He'll fire that Beretta no more,' he growled. 'I wrapped it around his fucking head.'

That done, the wounded were rushed ahead to the Aid Post, which lay in a building to the rear of the railway station. The place was 'heavy with the smell of blood and ether', while the 'grimy windows' were lit with a ghostly light – 'the flames of a burning railway shed'. Soon Marsh and Harrison arrived. They went around to check on their wounded. One man was already on an improvised operating table. Another of those who'd been hit in the mortar strike, Ben McLaughlan, looked to be in a very bad way. McLaughlan, who hailed from Hamilton, a town to the south of Glasgow, was a Gordon Highlander, and he had been with the SAS for over a year.

A surgeon looked Marsh and Harrison up and down. They were 'dirty, unshaven, tired out and wet through', with haggard features and a wildness in their staring eyes.

'You'd better go down to the kitchen and tell them to give you some hot soup,' the surgeon told them, tersely.

Ignoring his advice, they went to find the rest of their fellows. They came across their line, a body here and a body there, each curled tight within a blanket or whatever might offer a modicum of warmth. With not a blanket remaining between them – they'd used them to fashion the makeshift stretchers – Marsh and Harrison curled up on the ground in their sodden clothes. Sleep proved impossible. Their wet clothes froze to their bodies. They went in search of shelter. In the middle of the goods yard they found a small wooden hut. Wrenching a pair of doors from their hinges, Marsh and Harrison laid them between a sink and a table. Climbing onto their makeshift cots, they sunk into a tortured, nightmarish 'dream-filled sleep'.

The Aid Post had seemed jam-packed with the wounded, far more than either man had been expecting. In truth, as the battle for Termoli had raged, the SAS had been struck a terrible blow. Some six hours earlier, the true extent of the threat facing the town had become clear to all. Reg Seekings had watched as a dispatch rider delivered an urgent message to the brigade headquarters. The brigadier had read it once, before declaring: 'We'd better get the SRS onto this.' That message had reported the imminent collapse of the frontline, where Marsh, Harrison, Sandy Wilson and the Commandos had been fighting so valiantly, but against impossible odds.

Seekings hurried over to the monastery to warn the troops. At his headquarters, Mayne gave the order for every available man – cooks and bottle-washers included – to head for that section of the front. A column of captured German trucks pulled up at the entrance to the monastery, on the Via Regina Margherita di Savoia. The first was driven by Bill McNinch, Davis's steely corporal. Due to an injury, he'd been placed on driving duties. It made every sense for Davis and his patrol to clamber aboard his truck. But just as they were doing so, they were ordered off again. Bill Fraser and Johnny Wiseman wanted their troops – arguably the most battle-hardened – in the vanguard. Davis and his men jumped down, while Reg Seekings got a dozen men formed up in their place.

Davis took his party to another empty truck, but as they piled inside the air was cut by the 'frenzied shriek of a heavy shell'.

As if mired in a dark nightmare, chained to the spot and unable to move, Davis and his men heard that inbound projectile. 'The human mind can stand so much,' Davis would note in his diary, especially when 'a horror too great for it suddenly materialises'. That first 105mm shell slammed into a wall directly above the convoy, scattering rubble and dust in all directions. 'As if in a trance, we watched the wall of that house come down, slowly, infinitely slowly it seemed . . .'

There followed the terrible shriek of further incoming rounds, the 'shock of which was such to deprive us of feeling'. Five more shells slammed into their position, as the air became clogged with a thick and choking dust. Not a shout or a scream seemed to have been raised, the artillery strike had been so swift and so murderously accurate. Here and there 'figures . . . vague and indistinct in the dust cloud, appeared, pale and shielding their eyes as they staggered out of the whirlwind.' By now Davis had come to his senses, realising that by some impossible stroke of good fortune his truck seemed unharmed.

Leaping out, he was met by a scene of utter carnage. Huge chunks of masonry and blasted metal littered the road, amid which figures stumbled about in shock and confusion. Then, Davis noticed the truck that McNinch had been driving. The rear half of it had been almost completely vaporised, only a 'twisted and shattered hulk remaining'. To one side lay Bill Fraser, 'limp and motionless, his face an ashen grey'. Beneath his fallen form was Douggie Monteith, the Bren gunner whom Mayne had warned to 'Get down!' during the battle of the Pig's Snout, even as Mayne had cut about wielding his officer's cane.

Monteith had been plucked up by the blast and hurled into the nearby wall, the force of the impact knocking him unconscious.

He'd come to soaked in blood. At first he'd feared it was his own, before realising that it was Bill Fraser's, and that the SAS captain had been blasted down on top of him. Bending over their fallen forms was Phil Gunn, the squadron's indomitable medic, who was even now trying to tend to the most seriously wounded. Gunn seemed to be working away 'coolly . . . methodically, calmly', while more bloodied figures were manhandled across to him.

Reg Seekings had been standing by the rear of McNinch's truck when the shell had torn into it. Thrown backwards by the blast, he'd ended up on the roadside, semi-conscious and badly shaken, but largely unhurt. Clambering to his feet, he'd stumbled over to the twisted remains of the truck. He'd spied McNinch sitting bolt upright behind the steering wheel, as if ready to get moving. Wrenching open the door of the cab to try to drag him out, he'd realised that McNinch was dead. A large piece of metal had been blasted forward from the rear of the truck, going 'straight through McNinch, killing him outright and pinning him in position'.

Seekings next came across a body on the ground. It was Trooper Sydney 'Titch' Davison, the youthful-seeming recruit who'd told General Dempsey to 'stuff it' when he had refused to believe he was really twenty-one. Davison looked almost unhurt, but as Seekings went to lift him, his 'shattered body just fell apart'. Johnny Wiseman appeared, stepping unsteadily through the carnage. He'd been seated beside McNinch in the truck cab, yet he was all but unscathed. He stared about dazedly, trying to work out just exactly whom he had lost from his patrol. Few seemed to have been spared. 'I'd been with those chaps for three months,' he would remark of the moment. 'And with one shell I'd lost them. But what could you do? It was the luck of the draw. It was war.'

Davis mustered his men, 'all stout-hearted lads'. To his utter amazement all were unhurt. Taking four volunteers, he hurried towards what had been McNinch's vehicle. There was Wiseman, surrounded by a vision from hell. Davis spied what he first mistook to be a lump of meat from a butcher's shop. For an instant, his shocked mind wondered if there had been a butcher's nearby. Then he noticed the charred scrap of uniform that adhered to the carcass. With his 'stomach writhing', he saw more blasted bodies scattered around the truck – those who just a minute before had been 'twenty-five brave men in the prime of life, cheerful, strong and good-hearted'.

Here lay a figure 'with half his head blown off', there a severed arm, while the twisted, smoking remains of the truck's rear were a veritable charnel house – 'the dead, piled high, a horrible bloody carnage'. Overhead, a scalp 'hung on the telegraph wires'. It had the curly dark hair that had so marked out Christy O'Dowd, their wild Galway warrior and Mayne's gunner on so many of their previous missions. Blindly, Davis stumbled about, 'his innards revolting' at what he was seeing, knowing even then that 'never would I get over it – never, no matter what happened to me afterwards.'

Without being asked, a young Italian woman wandered over to help. As calmly as though she were 'sitting in her own drawing room', she squatted among the rubble and began to clean the wounds of the less seriously injured. Nearby, Phil Gunn soldiered on, trying to save those whose bodies had been ripped apart. With not a glance at the dead, he applied all his focus on the living, directing their evacuation by stretcher just as soon as he could risk them being moved. As Davis noted, 'we could not fail to admire his splendid coolness, as he worked patiently . . . to mend broken bodies and torn flesh.'

Joe Goldsmith – the man who'd already retrieved several injured men when John Tonkin's patrol had been surrounded – set about rescuing more wounded now, as the column of trucks came under further sporadic fire. The injured were loaded aboard stretchers and hurried inside the monastery. There, they set up a makeshift aid station. Grabbing some of the nuns, Goldsmith got them busy patching up his bloodied comrades, even though the holy sisters were stunned by the savagery of the bombardment and the resulting death and bloodshed. Ripping up sheets, they did their best to stem the bleeding, at least until the wounded could be got to the town's Aid Station.

A ghostly, high-pitched wailing cut through the air outside. A young Italian girl had just discovered the remains of her family, those who had lived in the house that had been hit. She 'fell screaming to the ground' as she saw her father, 'his belly ripped open'. Her mother, dead, lay close by. Two of those lucky enough to have escaped the bombardment led her away. There was worse, much worse to be avoided. A young Italian boy, no more than twelve – presumably her brother - was nearby, his 'guts hanging out'. Reg Seekings did the only thing he could conceive of, right then. 'I had to shoot him . . . you couldn't let anyone suffer like that,' especially a child.

A figure approached Wiseman, dazedly, his hand held to his face. 'Please sir, may I go to the hospital, as I have lost an eye?'

In the midst of all of this hell, Douglas Ridler (Mayne's intelligence officer) came hurrying over. Mayne had gone forward to the frontline, to direct the defences, and he was desperate for news of his reinforcements.

'Major Mayne says you must hurry, and come forward at once,' Ridler explained, speaking to Captain David Barnby, the most senior officer then remaining. 'It is very urgent.'

'Tell Major Mayne we can't possibly come until we have sorted out this mess,' Barnby retorted.

Ridler remained adamant, stressing that the battle was at a turning point.

'Very well, we'll come as soon as possible,' Barnby conceded.

He turned, scrutinising the troops, trying to see which, if any, might possibly be able to go. Seeing this, and reading the desperation on Barnby's face, Davis stepped forwards. His section could go, he volunteered. They moved off on foot, Davis leading a 'shaken, straggled procession' along one of the main streets, their ears straining for the slightest hint of any incoming shells. In that fashion they reached Mayne's forward position, which was set in the garden of a villa lying to one side of the railway.

Immediately, Davis was struck by Mayne's preternatural-seeming calm. He stood in that garden, 'immobile as a mountain, no trace of emotion discernible on his features'. With incredible cool and precision he issued Davis with his orders. 'Take your section over there, by that wall, and get them into good positions,' Mayne directed, indicating with a sweep of his arm where they should deploy. They were to hold that section of the line, come what may.

Davis spread his men along a ditch, upon the front slope of which was a stout stone wall. Right away, he got them busy with their fighting knifes, scraping away mortar, forming peepholes and firing slits. The entire expanse of terrain was under enemy observation, and the slightest movement seemed to draw a burst of fire, or provoked the whine of an inbound 88mm round. As they hunkered behind that wall and the shells slammed down in 'ever increasing numbers', Davis feared that the reactions of all in his patrol had been 'numbed by the horror of what we had experienced', the images of which still plagued his mind.

Word spread along the line. Sherman tanks were backed up on the southern bank of the Biferno, unable to cross the swollen river or to make it through. The one pontoon bridge had been hit by enemy shell fire and blasted away. Repeated and brave attempts to rebuild it had failed, so dominant were the enemy positions on the high ground and so accurate their fire. An attempt had been made to drive a column of tanks directly across the river at its shallowest point. They'd got bogged down mid-stream and were going nowhere. In short, no Allied armour was about to make it into Termoli to relieve them anytime soon.

There were reports of soldiers fleeing, trying to get out of Termoli, fearing that it was doomed to fall. A group had converged on the shoreline, where they tried to board the LCIs. One of the captains had asked just what they thought they were up to. They'd told him the town had fallen, and unless they were evacuated, they and the ships would be caught in the onslaught. All of this was confirmed when the LCI fleet commander managed to get a radio call through to Mayne. By way of response the SAS commander made it quite clear that the line was being held, and that it would hold. His fears put to rest, the LCI commander allowed not a single one of those who had fled to board his vessels.

The mood along Davis's line darkened. No one was talking much, and there was certainly no laughter or joking anymore.

Haunted by images of 'the frightful slaughter' earlier that day, they had been stunned into grim silence. Equally, as all realised, by rights it should have been *their* section in the truck that had taken the direct hit. That made the entire horrific episode 'all the more terrible'. Targeted by intense shelling, a nearby vehicle was hit. Packed with ammunition, it began to explode in spectacular fashion. An adjacent haystack caught fire, and it was transformed into a raging inferno. As the afternoon light ebbed away, so that blazing conflagration acted as a marker for the enemy gunners, attracting yet more of their fire.

All of a sudden, one of Davis's men simply lost it. As his nerve cracked, he 'threw away his fighting knife' and 'lay groaning and sobbing in the ditch', as enemy shells and bullets screamed overhead. The 'poor devil' couldn't be blamed, Davis reflected. Under the kind of strain they had been suffering, it was 'something which could happen to anybody'. But it was still a horribly unsettling sound, and it put the nerves of the rest of his patrol even more on edge. Some yelled at the man to shut up. Then, to either side of him they gradually moved away, until he was left crying in the ditch on his own.

Johnny Wiseman was the first to reach Mayne and break the terrible news, although he hadn't known quite what to say.

'I hear . . . you've had one or two casualties,' Mayne queried.

'I haven't got a section anymore,' Wiseman stated, simply.

Eighteen men were dead, or not expected to survive their wounds. Bill Fraser was injured, hit in the shoulder and out of action. So too were many more. Mayne received Wiseman's words in a cold, icy silence, a terrible death-like stare coming into his eyes. Apprised of the horrific losses, his anger knew no bounds. He muttered some words, which sounded very much like a vow for vengeance: 'I'll make up for this.' But there was no time for revenge right then ... let alone to come to terms with the loss, or even to grieve. In fact, there was no time to process any of this at all. Mayne had to force his mind back onto the job in hand – preventing Termoli from falling to the enemy.

Instructing Wiseman to attach himself and any other survivors to his own headquarters unit, Mayne gathered their small force and headed towards the town's cemetery, where the enemy were threatening to break through. They reached that part of the frontline, to find it taking a pounding from the German guns. As the evening shadows lengthened, so the 16th Panzer Division pressed home their attack, the lumbering great forms of three Tiger tanks rumbling forward along the railway tracks. With just one Ordnance 57mm anti-tank gun and a line of bristling Brens, Mayne and his raiders managed to beat them back, and still their line held.

The SAS War Diary would record the horrific incident of the Termoli truck bombing thus: 'Suffer 18 casualties, almost wiping out remainder of No. 1 Tp [Troop] ...' As Seekings would remark, the experience had been 'shattering'. It was especially so for him, since this was his first time in command of men 'I'd trained ... and moulded them together. And so you had a real rapport with them, and they were good ... And it's been a long campaign ... and they'd become more than just your men; they were your friends, your pals.' In those sentiments, Seekings spoke for so many. But most of all he spoke for their leader, Mayne, a man whose care for those under his command was commensurate with Seekings's words and the view they embodied. Or, as the future SAS padre, Fraser McLuskey, would declare of Mayne, 'he had a natural sensitivity ... with the men he commanded ... if they suffered ... he would suffer with them.'

Mayne was a prolific photographer, and he would record innumerable images of the SAS at war. As his men would remark, he seemed to go into action bearing a weapon in one hand and a camera in the other. He had done so in Termoli, at one stage deliberately taking photos of a mortar section on the frontline – not his own men – to try to spur them into greater efforts. In the SAS War Diary there is one of his photos, a chilling image which shows the remains of the Termoli street where the salvo of shells struck, plus the bomb-blackened carcass of the truck. It was taken some time after the attack, scribbled beside it is a note in Mayne's hand. It reads: 'Termoli, Italy. There were 18 lads killed when a shell hit this truck. We buried them in the churchyard.'

There the fallen might well rest in peace, but there would be little such peace for Mayne's tortured mind.

Chapter Seventeen
BATTLE OF BREN GUN RIDGE

The final battle for Termoli would open with the dawn. It was 6 October and as soon as it was bright enough to see, Mayne was on the move. The sky overhead was dark and angry and pregnant with rain. It seemed to match the SAS commander's mood. Mayne was in the frame of mind for a good long fight. He slipped from hastily dug slit-trench to foxhole, pausing in each to offer a few words to his war-weary men. A battle can hinge on a fateful moment; on a momentary lift in, or collapse of, an army's morale. Mayne's message right now was clear; consistent; unyielding. They would give no quarter. Not a backward step would they make this day.

'We came here to take this place,' he told his men. 'We've taken it and we're staying. What we have we hold on to.'

The night just gone had been long and fraught, but no concerted attack had materialised. As a fillip to the thinly spread defenders – facing an enemy with far superior firepower and numbers – the Royal Engineers had laboured through the hours of darkness, throwing a replacement bridge across the Biferno. As soon as that was done, the first Allied armour had got on the move, edging north into the town. With the earliest hints of light creeping into the streets of Termoli, the lead Shermans manoeuvred into position, four of them filing into gaps in the line of thinly spread troops, SAS intermingled with Commandos.

In addition to the newly arrived armour, Mayne's men had managed to scavenge four anti-tank guns that were still in working order, plus some supplies of ammo. Alex Muirhead had got his mortar platoon bedded in, at a position where it could hammer in fire at the behest of those holding the perimeter. As the light strengthened, Mayne strode from position to position in full view of the enemy, camera in hand, snapping photos. Whenever he came across a scattered group of Commandos, he did the same with them: a quick snap and a few words of encouragement. They'd nicknamed their position 'Bren Gun Ridge'. Today, Bren Gun Ridge would hold. Today, they would give no ground.

At five o'clock the enemy barrage began. Even as the first shells rained down, so the heavens opened, a deluge sweeping across Termoli. There was nothing subtle or strategic about the enemy's attack – this was an all-out blanket bombardment designed to crush the defenders' morale and tear apart their thin line. The first blasts of exploding shells woke Marsh and Harrison from their slumber in the wooden hut at the goods yard. They tumbled off their ripped-down doors – their improvised beds – and hurried forward to bolster the frontline. They joined a force of about a hundred SAS, with Commandos interspersed along their length.

Their line topped a shallow ridge – the last before the town. From there the ground ran away for 200 yards, before dipping out of sight. On their right stretched the railway line, to their left the cemetery, with its fancy ornate tombs. Under the cover of the enemy's ferocious barrage, a phalanx of German troops appeared, as they tried to rush the railway line. They were cut down in a hail of fire, for the defenders boasted around one Bren gun for every third man, plus scores of Tommy guns. Likewise, each time the massed ranks of the enemy reared up above the ridge lying to the SAS's front, 'we blasted away at them, forcing them back,' Harrison noted.

Relieved of his medical duties at the monastery, Joe Goldsmith rushed to the frontline. Upon reaching Bren Gun Ridge, Mayne grabbed him, explaining that he had a special task in mind for Buttercup Joe. The SAS commander wanted him to head for the goods yard, to see how he might bolster Roy Farran's thinly spread forces. Mayne asked Goldsmith to find some kind of vantage point, so as to give Farran and his force the best possible covering fire.

In normal circumstances, such a solo mission might have been daunting, but not now. As with so many then manning Bren Gun Ridge, Goldsmith was driven by a cold, icy fury at the horrific loss of so many of his brother warriors. Having volunteered to deal with the wounded up close and personal – not that he had any formal medical training – he found that their terrible suffering was seared into his mind. That, more than anything, would inspire Goldsmith – and so many more – to superhuman acts of bravery on this day.

There was one other factor that drove Goldsmith on: Paddy Mayne. As with so many then present, he would follow the SAS commander anywhere, for the simple reason that he inspired utter confidence in his men – that they would somehow win through, and that they would emerge unscathed. Goldsmith would have followed Mayne into hell itself, had he asked him to.

As he'd written to his fiancée, Linda, each of these men would lay down their lives for the other, no questions asked. Goldsmith was actually compiling a scrapbook of the war years. On one prominent page, he would paste a newspaper cutting about Mayne, entitled 'Paddy Mayne of the SAS. New facts about the most daring men of the war.' In Goldsmith's eyes, he was 'immensely brave, almost to the point of recklessness, he always led from the front and was idolised by the men he commanded.'

In that spirit, Goldsmith headed for the goods yard, dashing through the enemy fire. As he surveyed the war-ravaged terrain, one place struck him as offering the perfect vantage point – the giant petrol storage tank that dominated the ground. Ignoring the obvious threat – if it were hit, it would very likely explode into a giant inferno – he scaled the tank, getting into a position from where he commanded a magnificent field of view. Of course, he was also highly visible to the enemy. But despite the incoming blasts of rounds, Goldsmith would not be moved, as he put down searing bursts of fire onto those forces rushing the railway line. Goldsmith's incredibly brave actions epitomised the spirit of the thinly spread defenders along Bren Gun Ridge, as Mayne's subsequent praise for him would reflect: 'Took up position on top of 500 gallons of petrol although under heavy fire, as this was the only place from which he could carry out his task.'

The town cemetery remained one of the areas of greatest threat. A lone Sherman shunted into position, where it overlooked that terrain. It began to lob in shells, tombs disappearing in clouds of dust. 'The new dead mingled their bodies with the dead of past years,' Harrison noted. A round from the Sherman scored a direct hit on a large dome of green marble situated at the heart of the cemetery. It disintegrated spectacularly. It was from there that German snipers had been causing the defenders the worst problems. It was fine shooting. A ragged cheer went up from the line. But still the sniper rounds kept coming from that ruined building, the enemy demonstrating a stubbornness that bordered on the fanatical.

Another mass assault materialised, grey-uniformed figures charging forwards, and again it was broken up by fire from Bren Gun Ridge. Attack followed attack, as the German commanders drove their men forward in human waves. Still the defenders held stubbornly firm, 'the enemy being thrown back time after time'. A massive barrage of mortars began. The murderous wall of fire crept across the exposed stretch of land towards the leading edge of Bren Gun Ridge, drawing closer and closer with every second. 'A curtain of mortar bombs . . . It was inexorable. Fifteen yards. Ten yards . . . The barrage lifted.' Out of the dust and smoke emerged the enemy, charging ahead at close range. They ran into a wall of withering fire.

Down at the goods yard, Farran's small force were likewise holding the line, but barely. They'd taken casualties, several being wounded. Still they held firm against the mass of enemy fighters that were gathered at the far end of the railway tracks. The enemy kept coming, driven onwards by their commanders. 'The fighting was intense, ferocious and prolonged.' It was now that Farran received a warning as to just what the rail yard behind him harboured. Parked there was a locomotive and a wagon, the latter of which was stuffed full of high explosives and rigged to be detonated. Should the enemy break through, it was a last line of defence. But equally, if that lethal cargo got hit by a mortar or a shell, Farran and his men would be caught in the blast. It lent an added frisson of fear to the battle.

Lance Corporal Terry Moore, one of Mayne's signallers, was sent forward to an isolated white-walled farmhouse, to act as a radio relay point. From there he weathered a storm of fire, his position seeming to act as the proverbial bullet magnet. It wasn't long before Mayne ordered him to abandon his post, for fear it would be overrun. When Moore managed to make it back, weaving through the enemy fire, Mayne had another task for him. Those lining Bren Gun Ridge were running desperately short of ammo. Mayne needed Moore to serve as his runner, getting a message back to brigade headquarters. They needed to send more ammo supplies, and urgently. Moore was then to scavenge for ammo wherever he might find it, and get it back to the frontline by whatever means possible.

Discovering an abandoned German military BMW motor-cycle and sidecar, Moore set off, zipping through the streets. Eventually he reached a crossroads, which was manned by a lone MP, complete with a very smart-looking jeep. Moore pulled to a halt, for the jeep was just what he needed right then. He could load it with ammo and zip back to the frontline, bearing supplies for his 'beleaguered comrades'. Moore asked to borrow it, or even to swop if for the BMW. The MP seemed entirely unconvinced. Somehow, Moore managed to get his hands on that jeep, and leaving a very 'disgruntled'-seeming military policeman for dust, he sped away in search of supplies.

Having located a munitions dump, Moore loaded up the pur-loined vehicle, before turning around and heading back towards Bren Gun Ridge, resorting to driving along the railway line at breakneck pace, for he figured that offered the most direct route. His arrival at the frontline was both celebrated and a little fraught. Sure enough, the ammo was a godsend, but apparently the Red Caps had learned of the jeep being 'borrowed' and they were on the warpath. Moore was to be arrested for the theft of Army property, the MP commander had declared. No one paid their messages so much as a blind bit of heed. There was a battle to be fought and won.

Three hours into that raging firefight, the nearest German troops made it into the houses fringing the cemetery. Bit by bit, they were gaining ground. Frederick 'Chalky' White – the man who'd put the German airborne major's brother out of his misery some seventy-two hours earlier – pulled his men back, for their position was about to be overrun. But just as soon as he'd done so, he realised his mistake. He'd opened a fateful gap in their line of steel. If the enemy managed to breach Bren Gun Ridge, all would be lost. Dashing back towards the ground that he'd just vacated, White yelled for his men to provide cover. He made it, braving a storm of enemy fire, and from there he continued to hold that lonely outpost, even as a storm of bullets tore into the area and mortars exploded on all sides.

Sensing that the battle was reaching a tipping point, Lieutenant Sandy Wilson's section became the focus of the enemy's ire. Wilson and his men had never once left the frontline, since they had first deployed alongside Harrison and Marsh, some forty-eight hours earlier. As the battle for Termoli raged, Alexander Melville Wilson – tall, shy-seeming, apparently ham-fisted, polite to a fault – had proved himself possessed of a core of inner fortitude that seemed just about unbreakable. He and his patrol had commandeered an abandoned anti-tank gun and set it in the cover of a large haystack, after which their sector of Bren Gun Ridge had been held against all comers. Now, as the sun climbed higher into the sky above Termoli, they were subjected to a savage pounding by mortar fire.

Wilson, whose parent regiment was the Gordon Highlanders, had been singled out in his final report from officer cadet training as being the right material to make a fine platoon commander, once he had gained 'experience . . . and when he overcomes his shyness'. Those words would prove eerily prophetic today. Not long after Wilson had graduated as an officer, his elder brother, John, had been listed as killed in action, when the Fairey Swordfish torpedo bomber that he had been flying had failed to return from a raid on Italian shipping. Shortly thereafter, Sandy Wilson had volunteered for the SAS.

In his application for his Operational Wings – to be worn on his left breast – Wilson had listed the following desert operations. '1. Lt. Sadler and self recce Fort Maddelena . . . 2. Capt. Marsh and self Beurat-Gildalia road blew up 4 x 10-ton trucks and trailers by day with ammo aboard. Strafed coast road by night two trucks set on fire . . . 3. Blew up three trucks and armoured car . . .' He'd been awarded his wings on 23 July 1943, shortly before the SRS had undertaken the Bagnara landings.

Just twenty-two years old, Wilson – a former boarder at Cheltenham College, which is renowned for its sporting and military traditions – kept his gun firing from Bren Gun Ridge, even as the mortars rained down. But one salvo bracketed their position, bombs exploding to either side and raking the terrain with shrapnel. Wilson and all but one of his men were wounded. Amid the hellish carnage, chunks of blasted, red-hot steel had torn into the haystack, setting it ablaze. Even as the fire raged, Wilson and his patrol kept fighting, regardless of their injuries. But eventually, part of that flaming pyre of hay 'collapsed over the gun', trapping Wilson and several of his fellows.

One of Wilson's men, Corporal Robert Joseph Scherzinger, was a decade older than his commander, and was married to Doris, with a daughter, Josephine. A professional wrestler before the war, Bob Scherzinger was a man with a physique that was almost the match of Mayne's. Though wounded himself, Scherzinger – a 'huge chap, a tough bugger', according to Seekings – began to drag the injured out of the worst of the danger. Repeatedly, he dashed back into the fiery conflagration to rescue his comrades. But even as he returned for Wilson, Scherzinger was lost from view, as more of the blazing haystack tumbled down. Both Scherzinger and his patrol commander were trapped as the fire flared and raged.

A second figure took Scherzinger's place in that desperate rescue mission. Again and again, Lance Corporal Duncan McLennon dragged men from the flames, manhandling them back towards the nearest point at which they could get medical aid. Though under fire the entire time, McLennon was the only member of Wilson's section who managed to escape injury, and he was to prove unbreakable. Having rescued all that he could, McLennon was forced to accept that Scherzinger and Wilson were beyond help – those two men would be 'burnt to a cinder'. Undaunted – Sandy Wilson's example of leadership had earned him intense loyalty – McLennon had snatched up a Bren, taken up a position before the burning haystack, and proceeded to beat back the enemy.

McLennon managed to hold off the German infantry for long enough to allow a group of 40 Commando men to come to his aid. In that way, their part of Bren Gun Ridge was held. As the SAS War Diary noted of this tragic loss: '1000 hrs Germans come back into houses and mortar our positions. Capt. Wilson killed and C Sect. [Section] No.1 Tp [Troop] wounded.' Shortly, the enemy mortar unit that had scored such a telling blow would itself be silenced. His position stabilised, McLennon managed to get word back to Mayne of the exact location of the enemy gunners. Thirty minutes after Wilson and Scherzinger had been killed, a counter-barrage from Alex Muirhead's mortar patrol 'silences enemy mortar'.

Harrison heard the news of Sandy Wilson's death, with a deep shock and sadness, plus a grim fatalism. The last he had seen of his friend and fellow commander was when he and Marsh had wished Wilson goodnight, as they'd set their positions along that first stretch of high ground, a way to the north of Bren Gun Ridge. 'Cheerio. See you later,' they had whispered. Now, Sandy Wilson was gone.

By way of response to this tragic loss, Harrison scuttled forward to reach some 'rough, broken ground' at the high side of the railway cutting. From that vantage point he had a view all down the tracks, to the very point where the culvert he had hidden in the previous day cut beneath. Among the dunes on the far side, Harrison spied 'German heads moving about incautiously. I started sniping with a Bren gun.'

Back at his position, Davis spotted a figure wandering along the tracks. It was Tony Marsh. Davis was struck by the shocking transformation of the SAS captain, a man whom he'd always seen as being 'young . . . blond . . . extremely good looking', and blessed with irrepressible high spirits. Now, 'through the mud and grime' his features seemed 'drawn and haggard', his eyes betraying the 'ordeal which he had had to bear'. Worse still, it was only with the greatest difficulty that Marsh could 'keep still for more than a few seconds'. His 'quick, anxious movements and

328

violent reactions to the slightest sound' betrayed how 'his nerves had been strained . . . almost to breaking point'.

Marsh seemed disinclined to talk – 'I'm afraid I'm completely bomb-happy,' he murmured. But he did manage to inform Davis of their most recent, tragic loss. 'Sandy was killed and practically his whole section was killed or wounded, when their position was plastered by Jerry mortars,' Marsh explained, speaking in an odd, disembodied monotone.

This was the first that Davis had heard about the loss of Sandy Wilson, a hugely popular patrol commander. He realised then what hell all had been subjected to along Bren Gun Ridge, and how the courage and steadfastness of those at the tip of the spear was deserving of the very 'highest admiration', as he noted in his diary. Had they fallen back or broken, the battle for Termoli would have been lost, of that he felt certain.

Tony March wandered off to find Alex Muirhead, in order to call in some fire onto the enemy. It was around 2.45 p.m. on the afternoon of the 6th when Muirhead sent up one of his final mortar barrages. Moving through his position came a force of men at arms, who were poised to take the fight to the enemy in strength, and with the martial spirit that they so epitomised. At last, the men of the 78th Division's Irish Brigade – the 1st Royal Irish Fusiliers and the 6th Royal Inniskilling Fusiliers – had made it to Termoli. Not only that, but they had fifteen Sherman tanks in support, plus a unit of field artillery. As their regiments led the way, they did so embodying their long-held fighting-Irish traditions. The Irish Fusiliers' motto was: *Faugh a Ballagh!* – Clear the way! That of the Royal Inniskillings: *Nec Aspera Terrant* – By difficulties undaunted.

The men of 1 and 2 SAS, plus the Commandos and assorted other units, had held on for long enough for the battle to reach its turning point. When Mayne heard news of the troops that were about to move through them at Bren Gun Ridge, the relief he felt was palpable. For the first time in what seemed like an age, a smile spread across his drawn and haggard features. He turned to his battle-weary, bloodied men, whose faces were a portrait of exhaustion. He felt an enormous pride in what they had achieved.

'You'll be all right now, lads,' he declared, with conviction, 'the Irish are coming, and they'll sort it all out for us.'

Down at the goods yard there was a bustle of activity, as the Irish Brigade's jeeps pulled up and soldiers dismounted. A crowd gathered, as Mayne, Farran and the other commanders gave the newcomers a hurried briefing. At five minutes to 3 p.m. a major from the Irish Brigade flopped down beside Harrison, where he was perched atop the railway cutting, still manning his Bren.

'Can you show me their positions?' the major queried. 'My company is attacking through here, between the cemetery and the railway.'

By way of response, Harrison pointed out where the enemy lay.

Three minutes before three o'clock, the line of men holding Bren Gun Ridge began to 'pour a withering fire into the known German positions', with two or three men acting as reloaders, refilling the Bren magazines. 'The barrels became red hot. There was no time to change them.' At three o'clock sharp the Irish Brigade went in to attack. Five minutes later, the major that Harrison had been speaking to was carried back on a stretcher. He'd been shot by a sniper from the cemetery, but still managed a weak wave to Harrison as he passed.

A machinegun section joined Harrison, hungry for targets. He pointed out the enemy among the dunes. They fired off a fierce barrage, before moving into the cemetery to take on the snipers. Minutes later, on the beach stretching ahead of Harrison, hundreds of grey-uniformed figures became visible, as the enemy broke and ran. Alex Muirhead had brought his mortars forward, and he proceeded to chase the enemy with a final salvo of fire. In a way it was entirely fitting that the man and the patrol that had fired the first round at Capo Murro di Porco would fire the last of their rounds here at Termoli.

As the Irish Brigade hounded the enemy, what remained of Mayne and Farran's forces pulled out of Bren Gun Ridge and made their way back into Termoli town. During that weary march – 'with our blackened and unshaven faces, our shambling gait' – Davis was mistaken for an officer leading his men in retreat. A wizened Italian woman, her face a mass of wrinkles, berated Davis, exhorting him to 'turn around again and go back and fight the Germans'. Finally, she was made to understand that the 'hated *Tedeschi* were *finito*', at which she gave a 'cackle of delighted laughter . . . the smiles creasing round her wrinkled old face'.

They reached the monastery to find it largely untouched by the shelling. A hot meal had been readied for them. But before they could eat, padre Captain Lunt came around to have words. As their thin line had fought to hold Bren Gun Ridge, so he had had the unenviable task of collecting up 'the shattered and blasted fragments of what had once been human bodies' – those killed in the truck bombing. With incomparable fortitude, Captain Lunt had completed that 'gruesome and heart-breaking task', laying out the remains beside a neat row of graves, which had been excavated in the town's park, adjacent to the monastery. The burials were to take place right away, he explained.

It was dusk. Ranks of battle-worn figures filed into place, with 'heads bared and softened tread'. The scene brought the horrific memories flooding back. The air was still thick with the stench of burning, 'mixed with the heavy, clinging smell of death'. In a sombre voice the padre read the service, after which the men were dismissed. Wordlessly, in groups of ones and twos, they filed back to their billets, 'spirits heavy, and troubled'.

For Davis and his patrol had come the dreaded confirmation that Bill McNinch, their corporal, was dead. 'I thought of him . . .' Davis noted in his diary, 'of his power over the men, his cheerfulness, and his amazing coolness in an emergency . . . I thought of his words at Bagnara, when he had said to me in a voice full of feeling, "It's always the best that catch it. Charlie [Tobin] was the kindest hearted man in the section . . . and here am I, a drunken old reprobate." And now, he too was gone . . .'

Back at the monastery the gloom and despondency did not last long. Those who served in this unit had developed a particular coping mechanism; a necessary survival skill. It was designed 'not to let the death of our comrades affect our normal life,' as Davis noted, and to blank from their minds the 'memory of their loss'. This didn't mean that the fallen weren't dearly missed or remembered. But as a coping mechanism, it prevented 'gloomy, morbid thoughts' from taking hold, which could destroy the unit's fighting spirit. Once the fallen had been laid to rest, the living were to 'cast the memory' away. In similar fashion, 'while we were all cut-up about the losses . . . and Paddy most of all,' they tried to forget, just as soon as the burial service was over.

Once the meal was eaten, crates of wine were broken out. Exhausted, dazed, 'bomb-happy', the hubbub of voices ran around the echoing room, as groups of men exchanged tales of the fight just won. But then a door would slam and all fell silent. For a moment, they would gaze at each other 'with startled eyes, as if expecting all hell to let loose at any moment', before realising it had only been the slamming of a door. Once that became clear, the chat resumed, with 'sheepish looks' all around. As Terry Moore – Mayne's signaller, fresh out of dashing through the streets of Termoli in that purloined MP's jeep – would recall: 'When you took the first drink it was in relief that you had survived, the second was that you would be able to take part in the next action, and the third was for your fallen comrades who had not been so lucky.' Or as another would describe it, while there were tales to be told, they would do so 'leaving out the bad parts, such as the times we lost so many comrades'.

Tony Marsh related a fabulous story about what they had intended for the town's last-ditch defence. Once the wagon packed with explosives had been discovered in the goods yard, it had been hitched to a locomotive, with murder and mayhem in mind. Had the enemy broken through, they would have 'sent the whole lot snorting up the railway line', with a timer fuse ready to blow the entire train to hell. It would doubtless have caused the enemy 'some surprise, and possibly heavy casualties'. It hadn't quite been decided who would drive the locomotive, and in the final analysis it hadn't proved necessary, but many were those who would have dearly loved to see the train do its stuff.

They would drink hard and long into the morning, in an effort to keep the ghosts of the fallen at bay. As Seekings would relate, 'We stayed awake all that night getting drunk.' Some argued that the Germans must have had a spotter sited in the church tower that dominated Termoli, to call in that fateful barrage of shells on their convoy of trucks. Others disagreed. Johnny Wiseman went to take a look. 'Someone had been up there, but I don't think that was the reason. It was just a lucky shell.' A number of suspected 'spotters' would be rounded up, but the culprit, had there even been one, was never caught.

As the partying went on, Phil Gunn was able to deliver a small bit of welcome news. Bill Fraser's injuries were far less serious than all had at first feared. The amount of blood Fraser had lost had left everyone convinced that he was in a really bad way, but in fact he'd simply taken a fragment of shrapnel to the shoulder. He was apparently in fine form and was expected to rejoin the squadron in a few weeks' time.

Even so, the cost of the battle for Termoli had been devastatingly high. The SRS had suffered nearly 30 per cent casualties. Three sections of troops had been almost wiped out. First, there was John Tonkin's patrol – practically all killed or captured. Then, Johnny Wiseman's section had been caught in that ill-fated blast, an event that constituted the greatest single loss of life the SAS had suffered to date. And finally, Sandy Wilson and his patrol had been all but wiped out in that mortar barrage and the resulting haystack inferno. In addition to that, there had been numerous other casualties.

Indeed, the long list of fatalities and seriously injured would cover an entire page in the SAS War Diary: '21 killed, 24 wounded, 1 injured, 23 missing. Total casualties: 69 all ranks.' Then the names were listed, a long litany that underscored the ferocity of the battle just gone. The dead included a number of iconic figures, including Sandy Wilson, Bob Scherzinger, Bill McNinch,

Cristy O'Dowd and Sydney 'Titch' Davison, plus many more of Mayne's long-standing cohorts.

There was Sergeant John 'Jock' Finlay, a twenty-five-year-old veteran of Mayne's Great Sand Sea raiders and of countless other missions, including Operation Bigamy, the Benghazi battle. As Reg Seekings would recall, Finlay, a Glaswegian who was engaged to be married, was 'absolute first class' and a 'very clever man'. After the truck had been hit, Seekings had discovered Finlay's severed head lying in a flower bed, his face 'unmarked, a grin on it – it had been so sudden'. Of the rest of his body they'd found not a trace.

There was Lance Sergeant John 'Jocky' Henderson, another Glasgow lad, who'd worked in a carpet factory before the war. Signing up with the Scots Guards, Henderson had volunteered for the SAS in May 1942, and would go on to soldier on a string of operations, including the Benghazi wireless station raid during which Bob Melot was injured. Praised for his 'coolness and courage' under fire, at one stage Henderson had led a jeep patrol on a series of daring sabotage operations, before bluffing his way past a phalanx of German armoured cars to make it back to friendly lines. Seekings had discovered Henderson 'hanging upside down with all his chest blown open'. Nearby lay Corporal Charles Grant, aged just twenty-two, who hailed from Liverpool and was discovered in a similarly terrible state. While both men survived for an hour or so, there was no saving them. 'They were good lads,' as Seekings concluded, simply. Tellingly, Henderson's epitaph would read: 'To live in the hearts you left behind is not to die.' Grant's epitaph read simply: 'Stand Fast – *Craigellachie*', Craigellachie being the war cry of the Grant clan.

There was Lance Corporal Clarence Crisp, another

twenty-two-year-old, who had falsified his age to sign up early and had gone on to fight in the 1940 defence of France. Hailing from Pontefract, in Yorkshire, his mother and father would give him the following epitaph: 'We loved him too dearly to ever forget.' There was Lance Corporal John MacDonald, also twenty-two, from Runcorn in Cheshire. Working in a tannery before the war, MacDonald was yet another veteran of Mayne's Great Sand Sea raiders. His epitaph would read: 'Utterly unselfish. And so to the end.' There was Private Simon Silifants, aged twenty-three, a veteran of both the 1940 battle for France and the battle for Crete, after the hell of which he'd volunteered for the SAS. A Lancastrian from Clitheroe, Silifants was one of Bill Fraser's long-standing stalwarts; at one stage they had together captured a German Panzer IV tank in North Africa.

There was Private George 'Georgie' Cassidy, a former plasterer from County Leitrim, in Ireland. Signing up to the Essex Regiment in 1940, Cassidy had volunteered for the Commandos, and then the SAS, joining their ranks in October 1942. Cassidy's epitaph would read: 'Short was your life, Dear, may Jesus in his mercy grant you eternal rest.' There was Private Alan Duncan, of the Black Watch, who hailed from Dundee. Aged twenty-four, Duncan would have the simple epitaph 'Ever remembered.' There was Private Edgar Grimster, of the Gordon Highlanders, a man who'd already been wounded once before in Italy, during the Bagnara landings. There was Private William McAlpin, of Edinburgh, another Gordon Highlander, who'd been a barman before the war. There was Private William Stewart-Johnson, a twenty-two-year-old from Wardley in County Durham, who'd worked as a miner before the outbreak of hostilities. A long-standing veteran of the SAS, Stewart-Johnson had been recommended for his operational wings not long before the Termoli battle, for missions executed in Benghazi, Sirte, Tripoli and Sicily. His epitaph would read: 'Dearly loved we will meet again.'

There was Private William Hearn, a Londoner, who'd volunteered for Special Service in 1940, being posted to the Commandos and undertaking several raids. Stepping forward for the SAS in 1942, Hearn had been posted as 'missing in Libya' in January 1943. His jeep patrol had been ambushed, most of the men being captured or killed. But Hearn, plus the patrol sergeant, Ted Badger, and one other, had managed to fight their way out of the ambush, theirs being the only jeep to slip the trap. Three weeks later, the intrepid trio had made it across the desert and back to friendly lines. There was Alex Geordie Skinner – better known to all as 'Blondie' or 'Jesus' – the man who'd refused to have himself listed as 'wounded', after the Capo Murro di Porco battle, so as to ensure he could carry on serving alongside his fellow warriors. Poor Reg Seekings had been forced to fetch a jug of water from a nearby house to try to douse Skinner's burning body. 'Proud and loving memories of our dear son at rest. Age shall not weary him,' read Skinner's epitaph.

Finally, there was Private Emrys Pocock, who by rights should not have been caught in that terrible blast at all. Pocock, who was from a Monmouthshire mining family, had signed up with the Duke of Cornwall's Light Infantry, and in June 1942 his battalion had been dispatched to help relieve the siege of Tobruk. Totally outgunned, they had been overrun by the 15th Panzer Division. The battalion was virtually wiped out, Pocock being one of the few to survive. Eight months later he had volunteered for the SAS. Serving as Mayne's runner in Termoli, Pocock had dashed down to the truck convoy to pass a message on to Wiseman, just as they were readying themselves to depart. As fate would have it, Wiseman had survived the blast, while Pocock was killed. His epitaph read: 'Hearts that loved you never forget. In memory you are with us yet. Mum, Dad and brothers.'

From captured enemy documents it was clear what an extraordinary victory the SAS had won in Termoli, a place that German forces had been ordered to recapture no matter what the cost. That accounted for why the squadron had taken such a heavy battering, before the enemy were finally forced to turn and run. The thin line had 'held the town against the best German troops, a Panzer Division backed by airborne troops'. As Mayne made clear in the SAS War Diary, the outcome of the battle had hung in the balance, for the enemy's 'attack was abandoned when the threat to the town was greatest'. Had the 16th Panzer Division pressed home their advantage, Bren Gun Ridge might well have fallen.

It had been such a close-run thing.

Chapter Eighteen

THE GHOSTS OF THE FALLEN

In the days after the Termoli battle there would be rumours that Mayne, gripped by an ice-cold fury at the loss of so many of his stalwarts and friends, had embarked upon a solo mission of vengeance. Several accounts suggested that Mayne set forth on his 'own private manhunt, stopping only when he believed he had exacted suitable revenge on the Germans'. What truth there is in this is hard to fathom, but Mayne's sense of loss was undoubtedly deep and heartfelt.

In the aftermath of Termoli he would write to Malcolm Pleydell, sharing some of the sad news. 'Poor old Sandy Wilson was killed in our last operation and Bill Fraser was wounded. I had a letter from Bill today saying he was much better, and I am glad about that. Bob Melot also had a bullet into his chest and out somewhere around his back. With a bit of trouble we managed to get him to hospital, but he came back after a couple of days with a card to say he was fit for full duty! Bob Lilley, Rose and Sgt. Bennett are the steadiest of the old hands. All our officers had been really good. Phil Gunn has done some grand work; he is just what I expected him to be . . .'

Mayne would write with similar sentiments to his sister

Barbara, typically saying nothing of his own role in the epic battle just gone. His letter is replete with a sense of loss, and especially with regret at his inability to safeguard all his men. 'I'm glad you wrote,' he told Barbara.

I wouldn't have liked to have gone through all that mail from HQ and found none for myself. I was looking at an old letter from Frances [the third-oldest sister; the one just above him] tonight. I keep letters for some time and often reread them ... Our unit got cut up a bit in our last operation. It was at Termoli and we had to withstand some heavy counter attacks. We had 29 killed with a series of shells, for it was the only way they could touch us. A very nice wee lad called Canning was wounded there – he comes from Belfast, and had done four raids with me. If you could call around and say he is not too bad – only a flesh-wound and that he did awfully well. I would be so grateful.

As well as solicitude for his troops, Mayne's homesickness – his longing for Ulster and for Ireland – shines through.

You might get Mother to send me her recipe for soda farls [Irish soda bread made with buttermilk]. We have a good cook here from Lisburn [a city in Northern Ireland] who thinks he could make them but he's worried about having no buttermilk. He thinks he can manage with cream of tartar [similar to baking soda] ... Have you heard they have given me a bar to my DSO? – still managing to bluff them. Hope you are as fit as I am. Give my love to Mother. Yours B.

Mayne's self-deprecating humour – *still managing to bluff them* – shines through, as does his sense of being unworthy of all the accolades coming his way, including that bar to his DSO, his second award of that high valour medal so far in the war.

There was one force among the SAS then gathered at Termoli who would set forth hunting, and in the hours directly following victory at Termoli. In a series of daring sorties by caïque, Roy Farran, Raymond Lee (Couraud), and many of the 2 SAS parties they commanded would set sail, venturing north into enemy waters. In that way they would go ashore in search of the thousands of escaped Allied POWs hiding out in the Italian countryside. For weeks after victory at Termoli, the town's port would serve as the headquarters, from which those POW-rescue missions would set sail, and via which hundreds of escaped POWs would be brought back to Allied lines.

One of those 2 SAS men, Charlie Hackney, would not be joining those rescue missions. With a mail delivery had come the sad news of Hackney's mother's death. Even as 'Farran was preparing for the next adventure' – the POW-rescue sorties – so Hackney had received a letter from his brother, Tom, telling him that their mother Elsie had passed away. When he showed the letter to Captain Farran, the SAS commander granted Hackney immediate compassionate leave. A rumour was doing the rounds that Mayne's raiders – their ranks sorely depleted – were slated to return to Britain, to rebuild and refocus on the next stage of the war. Accordingly, Farran released Hackney back to his old unit, 1 SAS, so that he could sail home with them. In that way Hackney was reunited with 'old friends from Kabrit days – Bob Bennett, Johnny Cooper and Reg Seekings'.

Shortly afterwards, General Dempsey, CB, DSO, MC, paid a visit to Termoli, during which the rumoured return of Mayne and his raiders to Britain would be confirmed. Dempsey gathered the surviving men – those who had escaped being killed, captured, or seriously wounded in action – at the monastery, the Seminario Vescovile, to deliver a heartfelt speech. It constituted as glowing an endorsement of the SRS (1 SAS) as ever one could wish for, and in particular of Major Blair 'Paddy' Mayne's powers of leadership and of command. Right at that moment, it was just what all needed to hear, and it 'won him [Dempsey] a place in our hearts'. As they gathered in one of the Seminario Vescovile's large halls, the losses they had suffered were driven home, for as they gazed about the room they noticed how 'sparse were their numbers and how thinly they were spread'.

Dempsey began speaking, his voice ringing with emotion:

It is just three months since we landed in Sicily, and during that time you have carried out four successful operations. [. . .] The first, that at Capo Murro di Porco, was a brilliant operation, brilliantly planned and brilliantly carried out . . . An excellent piece of work . . . You then went on to take Augusta. You had no time for careful planning, but still you were highly successful. Then came Bagnara and finally Termoli. The landing at Termoli completely upset the Germans' schedule and the balance of their forces, by introducing a threat to the north of Rome. They were obliged to bring to the East Coast the 16th Panzer Division . . . They had orders, which have since come into our hands, to recapture Termoli at all costs and to drive the British into the sea. These orders, thanks to you, they were unable to carry out.

Dempsey, a First World War veteran, then delivered the most ringing endorsement imaginable. 'In all my military career, and in my time I have commanded many units, I have never yet met a unit in which I had such confidence as I have in yours. And I mean that!'

Dempsey went on to identify the six reasons why he believed that Mayne's raiders were the superlative warriors that they had proved themselves to be:

> First of all, you take your training seriously. This is one thing that has always impressed me about you. Secondly, you are well-disciplined. Unlike some who undertake this specialist and highly dangerous job . . . Thirdly, you are physically fit and I think I know you well enough to know you will always keep that up. Fourthly, you are completely confident in your abilities – but not to a point of over-confidence. Fifthly, despite that confidence, you plan carefully. Last of all, you have the right spirit, which I hope you will pass on to those who may join you in the future.

Dempsey went on to stress the key tenets by which he'd tried to steer their deployments. He had endeavoured never to use them unless 'the job is worthwhile'. The risks had to be justified by the ends. He had been ready to use all his forces, including tanks and artillery, to relieve them, and especially since 'you always seem to stir up trouble wherever you go'. He had striven to get them out as quickly as possible, once their missions were accomplished, in order to 'refit and reorganise'. Finally, Dempsey regretted very deeply that his command of their unit was now at an end. Mayne's raiders would be returning to Britain, to prepare for the next battles and all that they would bring.

Knowing they were homeward bound, the spirts of the men soared. On the tail of Dempsey's visit there was one from Montgomery. Following a 'Squadron Feast' in honour of his presence – 'Tomato Soup, Roast Turkey, Welsh Rarebit, and fruit' – Monty said a few words. The gist of his message seemed to be that the British general no longer considered the unit to be wild adventurers, that there was much to be done, and that he looked forward to working with them in the future. That was how Bill Deakins – now firmly back within their ranks – interpreted it. Riding on that LCI stacked with rations, the ship's captain had only been able to risk returning to Termoli once the German attackers had been driven off. Since then, Deakins had been assailed by 'dramatic tales of the desperate encounters and engagements, and . . . individual actions'.

As the men of the SAS drank to the fallen and celebrated the news of their impending return to home shores, Deakins witnessed one Scottish soldier who 'liked his "wee dram"' getting somewhat carried away. After delivering a drunken version of the Highland Fling, he'd graduated to his 'celebrated puddle dance'. Performed in the pouring rain, it involved a wild blend of Fling intermingled with the Sword Dance, but with added 'forwards rolls, backward rolls, side rolls . . . until he was soaked, saturated, mud covered and exhausted. He had been cheered on by the laughing onlookers and indeed, this was one of the hilarious moments of the war.'

Shortly, the squadron boarded their fleet of LCIs and began steaming south. They docked at Molfetta, a town situated some two days' sail to the south of Termoli. There, as per usual, an interminable wait began. Billeted in the former Fascist headquarters – a grand, ornate building – boredom and frustration set in.

The town boasted a fine football stadium. A match was organised between an SAS team and the local Italian side. It turned out to be 'perhaps the most extraordinary game of football ever played', remarked Davis. The entire force of SAS gathered, as did crowds of townsfolk, but when the Italian footballers proved themselves to be far more nimble and skilled than the British team, tempers flared. By the end of the match, the 'sportsmanship for which the Englishman is famed' was not much in evidence, and by means of various rugby tackles and chasing their opponents off the field, the SAS had managed to scrape a draw.

For some at that match, it provoked especially difficult and haunting memories. As Joe Goldsmith would write to his fiancée, Linda, he'd gone to the game for 'the fun of the thing . . . you see the lads laughing away and it does them good after the action they went through on the last Op. We lost some good footballers then, the first game making us think of them . . .' By rights, the footie should have been a highlight for him – he had gone for *the fun of the thing*. In the past it always had been fun. His best friend in the SAS, Sergeant Doug Eccles, was one of the finest sportsmen in the unit, being especially talented at football. But now, after Termoli, that ill-tempered kickaround had reminded Goldsmith of just who was missing, and of the ghosts of the fallen.

'I always thought I was a hardboiled clown' – a tough and cynical joker – Goldsmith continued in his letter, but Termoli had made him realise otherwise. 'Am I glad I've got something to come back for,' he wrote, 'my one ambition is to . . . make you happy and for us to forget all this separation.' In fact, Goldsmith was troubled in more ways than even he realised. Their medic, Phil Gunn, had advised him to 'pack in a lot of the things' he enjoyed the most. In short, he'd been rationed to one bottle of beer a week. Any number of the men were drinking too hard in an effort to forget; to numb the sense of loss. 'I am not too bad,' he wrote to Linda, 'but I have got to take care of myself, so I reckon I shall have to go by the doctor's advice.' In truth, Termoli had done for Goldsmith's sunny, genial 'Buttercup Joe' persona. As time wore on, the ghosts would draw ever closer, as they would for so many of those who were unscathed in body, but troubled deep in their minds.

With hopes of more peaceable, joyous relations at Molfetta, a dance was organised. A local lady of some standing was asked to help arrange it, and especially the all-important female contingent. But when the night drew around, the dancehall proved deserted of the members of the fairer sex. Making the best of a bad show, the men thronged the bar, the dance floor remaining deserted, which as it happened was a very good thing. Late into the night, the building reverberated with a 'powerful explosion' and the 'ceiling fell in on us', noted Davis. Luckily, with the dance floor deserted, there were very few casualties. It turned out that the lady 'Countess' who had helped organise the dance was actually a Fascist sympathiser, and sabotage was suspected.

At one stage, Mayne – likewise troubled and haunted – had embarked upon his wildest and darkest drinking binge. It began with a rendition of 'Tread on the Tail of Me Coat', a bad sign, after which a table-load of glasses were swept to the floor. A decanter was hurled at one of his officers, hitting Tony Marsh in the chest, due to Mayne's drunken aim being off, after which there was a 'mad scramble for the door'. Mayne managed to grab their medic, Phil Gunn – a man of whom he was immeasurably fond – and throw him against one wall, damaging Gunn's shoulder. There had then followed the strangest of scenes, as Mayne, sounding as calm and polite as before he had been wild and fearsome, had asked for a road map of Italy.

Announcing that he was off to take a look at Naples, Mayne had made his way to a requisitioned civilian car and driven away. It was the early hours when he set off on that long drive, Naples being some 240 kilometres away. No one had been able to stop him, that was for sure. He'd managed to make about five miles or so, before missing a bend and overturning the vehicle. Alerted by a local, Johnny Wiseman had gone out to search for their missing commander. He'd discovered him lying beneath the vehicle, totally unharmed. Banning himself from drinking thereafter, Mayne had seemed utterly contrite at the incident, and especially of manhandling Phil Gunn.

One thing was for certain – it was high time to get out of Molfetta and head for home. There was one glorious upside to their stay in that town, as unexpected as it was welcome. One day, out of the blue, Lieutenant John Tonkin strolled into their former Fascist headquarters billet. Of course, all were desperate to hear how on earth he was able to rejoin them, for the last anyone had seen of Tonkin was his capture at Termoli, when his patrol had become isolated and surrounded. Tonkin was happy to oblige, regaling all with his tale.

After being taken prisoner by the men of the German 1st Parachute Regiment, Tonkin had at first been treated with great respect, but even he was surprised to be invited to dinner by General Richard Heidrich, a First World War veteran, a paratrooper and the regiment's overall commander. Apparently, Heidrich insisted on dining with all captured Allied parachutists. Tonkin accepted the invitation, and their conversation had encompassed all things war, including the Termoli attack, which the general described admiringly as 'a beautiful stroke' and 'perfectly timed'.

Over cigars, Heidrich had confided that Hitler's decision to declare war on Britain was a grave mistake, but there was to be a sting in the tale. When Tonkin was driven back to his cell, the German escorting officer issued a grave warning. 'It is my duty to inform you that we have orders that we must obey, to hand you over to the special police. I must warn you that from now on the German army cannot guarantee your life.' Under Hitler's Commando Order, Heidrich was obliged to pass men like Tonkin into the custody of the Gestapo, which amounted to a death sentence.

'When a man knows he is about to be shot, it sharpens his mind wonderfully,' Tonkin declared. Loaded aboard a truck, he was driven north into the Italian mountains. There were some twenty fellow captives riding in the vehicle, with two SS guards perched on the tailboard, while a motorcycle-and-sidecar combination took up the rear. The truck jolted along a high ridge, before climbing through a remote and frozen pass. It grew bitterly cold. Snow began to fall. The truck halted, so the guards could take a breather. An hour or so later, they did the same again. Each time Tonkin noted where the guards gathered for their smoke break, at the rear of the truck. As they got going a third time, he busied himself working free the canvas covering at the front, above the vehicle's cab, until it was loose enough to allow him to slip through.

The next time the truck pulled over and the guards gathered at the back, Tonkin crawled under the canvas, moving 'very quietly', and moments later he was 'down on to the bonnet and away down the mountainside'. Slipping into the darkness, he headed south, in the direction of friendly lines. After days moving on foot, creeping ahead at night, he'd come across a mystery patrol. It was only when one of the figures had blundered into something in the dark, and let out a sharp curse in English, that Tonkin had realised they were British troops. That was how he'd found his way back to his parent unit, catching up with them at Molfetta. (Several others of Tonkin's patrol would escape from captivity, although most would be recaptured before they could make it to Allied lines.)

Tonkin's incredible getaway proved a real boost to their collective spirits. So too did the haul of decorations that would result from the epic and costly battle of Termoli. Along with Mayne, Captain Tony Marsh would be awarded the DSO. Staff Sergeant James 'Nobby' Clark – the man who'd led the fighting withdrawal from the point where Tonkin's patrol was surrounded – was awarded a Military Medal, as were seven others. These included: Lance Sergeant White, whose dash back to fill the gap in the line at Bren Gun Ridge had proved so decisive; Joe Goldsmith, the man who had stood firm atop that massive petrol storage tank during the final day of the battle; Corporal Terry Moore, whose madcap ride in the purloined jeep had kept the men charged with ammo; Lance Corporal Douglas Ridler, Mayne's intelligence officer, whose courage had proved legion; Lance Corporal Duncan McLennon, who had dragged so many out of the burning haystack where Sandy Wilson and Bob Scherzinger had perished; and Lance Corporal Edward Ralphs, whose courage with the Bren had saved so many of the wounded when Tonkin's patrol had been overrun.

Yet for Mayne, the dark legacy of the Termoli losses cast a

long shadow, especially as it fell to him to write to the families of the fallen. For a nomadic unit such as theirs, which had for years been perennially on the move, home addresses could be hard to come by. Christy O'Dowd had actually run away from his Galway home, aged eighteen, to join the British military. Mayne's first hint as to where he might send his condolences would come in a letter from O'Dowd's mother, Sarah. In it, she wrote of how shocked she was to learn of her son's death, word coming as it had hard on the heels of the news that he had just won the Military Medal for his actions earlier in the war when serving alongside Mayne. 'I was just after receiving news of him being awarded the Military Medal in the London Gazette, and it gave me such hopes of seeing him again,' she wrote. 'Now I know I will never again see Christopher in this world.'

The grief-stricken mother had so many questions. While she felt certain her son had 'faced death bravely', she wanted to know if he had been able to 'keep in touch with a Chaplain?' She wrote of how 'I often think is there any mark over Christy's lonely grave, or will there ever be a chance of getting a snap of it. I understand that he was buried in Italy.' She asked after her son's personal belongings, if 'there may be some medals or letters that I could have'. Mayne had made a particular habit of photographing the graves of the fallen. Those images fill the SAS War Diary – those at Termoli showing a row of mounds of freshly dug earth, each with a crude wooden cross at one end, and set against a neat green background, the border hedge of the town's botanical gardens. That at least Mayne could help O'Dowd's mother with.

Making a point of writing personally to the next of kin, he began to draft his reply, noting in pencil in the margins of O'Dowd's mother's letter how he might best respond. 'I have been feeling for a long time that I would very much like to write to you, but until lately I have been unable to get your address. I would like to offer to you and your husband and family my sincere sympathy on the death of your son, Christopher. I knew him well and on many raids . . .' When O'Dowd's possessions were gathered up, they were found to amount to precious little: two wristwatches, some letters and a string of rosary beads. 'A soldier of fortune he certainly wasn't,' as one of O'Dowd's family would later write.

For Mayne, perhaps the toughest letter of all was that to Sandy Wilson's folks. As with the others he had written to – twenty-one letters, to the families of twenty-one men killed in action at Termoli – Mayne included photos. Helen Wilson, Sandy's mother, would write back, expressing how much it had meant to her that the SAS commander had thought so highly of her son, and how touched she had been to receive the pictures. She told Mayne of how Sandy was the second son she had lost to the war – the first being John, the Fairey Swordfish pilot killed on operations in the Mediterranean. Sandy had been very proud of his unit, she told Mayne, and Mayne's thoughtful letter had meant a great deal to them at their time of loss.

Yet, as he brooded upon the missing – the holes in their ranks which might never be filled – Mayne could perhaps allow himself a lighter moment; a sense that it had not all been in vain. As he would confide to Pleydell, 'Our future I believe is pretty rosy. I think the chaps will get what they deserve . . . and I don't think they are worrying.' While their four missions in Italy – Capo Murro di Porco, Augusta, Bagnara and Termoli – were very much not archetypal SAS tasks, and very much not what their founders had envisaged, their successes, costly though they had been, had secured the unit's survival, of that Mayne felt certain. With General Dempsey and Montgomery having given the unit their blessing, he could only imagine that their return to Britain heralded great things.

Mayne would be the first to go. As his men set forth for Taranto and then onwards to North Africa, to link up with Bill Stirling's 2 SAS at their Algeria training camp, so Mayne was whisked home directly by air. After a short stopover with 2 SAS, the men of his battle-hardened unit would sail for Britain on Boxing Day 1943, largely because Mayne had pulled strings to get them back as soon as possible. Once again, there was so much to be done. Once again, a new mission and a new set of challenges would have to be faced. The Allies were gearing up for Operation Overlord – the Normandy landings – and the SAS would have a very special role to play. Once again, more men would need to be recruited, to fill the gaps in their ranks. And of course, there was training to get started.

Nursing their memories and collective trauma, the unit would be formally reformed as 1 SAS. With their numbers massively expanded, they would once again be going in at the tip of the spear. But this time, they would be returning to their roots. They would be doing what they arguably did best, and certainly what they had been formed to do. They would be parachuting deep behind enemy lines, to harry and harass the enemy's supply lines, so frustrating their attempts to reinforce and resupply those serving at the Normandy coastline, as the Germans tried to hurl the Allies back into the sea. In some cases, the men of the SAS would be dropping into France just prior to the Normandy landings, in the absolute vanguard.

Thankfully, so many of the old guard would be there, those

who had survived the hell-storm of the Italian operations. Harry Poat would be present, serving as Mayne's right-hand man. Bill Fraser would be there, recovered from his Termoli injuries and hungry for battle. So too would Bob Melot, carrying yet another war wound, but equally undaunted. So too would Bob Bennett, Reg Seekings and Johnny Wiseman, those who'd run the Termoli gauntlet and made it through seemingly unscathed (at least in body, if not in mind). So too would Peter Davis, Derrick Harrison, Tony Marsh, Joe Goldsmith, Bill Deakins and many more, as they prepared for the push into France and into Nazi Germany itself, and the hard fighting that was bound to bring.

Once again, much would be riding upon the success of their missions.

Once again, they would be facing the challenge of a lifetime.

Once again, Mayne and his raiders had better be ready.

The sequel to *SAS Forged in Hell* will tell the story of Blair 'Paddy' Mayne and his band of raiders, as they spearhead the thrust into German-occupied France, and from there into the Fatherland itself during the dying days of the Reich.

It will be published in autumn 2024.

Acknowledgements

First and foremost, thank you to my esteemed readers. You go out and buy my books, in the hope that each will deliver an enjoyable and illuminating read, bringing a moment from history to life in vivid detail. I hope I have managed to deliver that kind of reading experience in this book. Without you, there could be no author such as myself. You enable individuals like me to make a living from writing. You deserve the very first mention.

The second massive thank you is extended to Fiona Ferguson (née Mayne) and her husband, Norman, for inviting me into your family home, so that I might delve into Lieutenant Colonel Robert Blair Mayne's war chest and the plethora of other wartime memorabilia you offered so generously, and to discuss with you his wartime and post-war story. I have gained invaluable insight in the process. Your unconditional welcome and your openness were hugely appreciated, as is the correspondence we have shared over the years that it has taken for this book to come to fruition. I am most grateful.

I owe another debt of gratitude to Peter Forbes and his wife, Sally, and their children, who hosted me in their home in Northern Ireland and who, in Peter's case, first alerted me to the wealth of private family archives held by Lieutenant Colonel

Robert Blair Mayne's family. Peter, you are in your own right an expert and an authority on the life and soldiering of this great war hero, and I have been privileged to have been given access to your own extensive personal archive and to your unnerving wisdom and advice. You have been enormously generous with your hospitality, not to mention your time and expertise.

I extend my enormous thanks to John O'Neill, great-nephew of Lieutenant Colonel Robert Blair Mayne and author of *Legendary Warrior of the SAS*, for entrusting me with me your extraordinary private family archive concerning your great-uncle's war years, and also for offering such personal insight into your great-uncle's wider character and what troubled him post-war. John, you remind me so much of your great-uncle – physically, of course, but also in your soft-spoken tones, your offbeat humour and your laughing eyes. I am hugely grateful for all of your help and support.

Enormous thanks to Doug Goldsmith, and his wife, Annie, for inviting me into your wonderful Devon home and for allowing me to peruse your late father Ernest 'Joe' Goldsmith's war records, memorabilia, letters and the like. Again, this proved hugely insightful, and especially for the relating of the story as it has been told in this book.

Very great thanks to Paul Davis, for our phone calls and our correspondence about your father, Peter Davis MC's wartime service, and for graciously allowing me to use some of the photographs from your father's collection in this book, and for reading an early draft of this manuscript and for your comments thereon.

Enormous thanks to Nabil Lawrence Jamal, the grandson of Derrick Harrison, and to the wider Harrison family, for corresponding with me as you have, for reading and commenting on the manuscript of this book, and for the kind permission to use those quotes from Derrick Harrison's excellent book, *These Men Are Dangerous*, and also for the photos I have used. This proved invaluable.

Huge thanks once more to Alison Smartt, for sharing with me the long correspondence regarding your father Captain Malcolm Pleydell MC's wartime service, for allowing me to quote from the Pleydell family papers, and to have access to the rich materials held therein. I'm so glad I finally got to meet you at last, and your husband, Tim.

Huge thanks to Gary Hull, the son of SAS operator Billy Hull, for inviting me into your home and for sharing with me your stories and recollections about both your father's wartime exploits, and those of his commander and close friend, Lieutenant Colonel Robert Blair Mayne. Thank you also for giving me access to your father's wartime letters, records, photos, memorabilia and other materials, which proved so useful in the research for this book.

Thank you to Scott Hackney, for sharing with me the private family archive of Charlie Hackney, including his unpublished and detailed account of the war years, and a plethora of associated materials from the Hackney family archives, and for all of our correspondence over the same. I am enormously grateful.

Thank you to Catherine Cary-Elwes, and family, for inviting me into your Oxford home and for sharing with me your father Oswald Cary-Elwes's wartime story, and also for allowing me access to the Cary-Elwes family archive. Our long correspondence during the gestation of this book was extremely useful, as were the materials and records you were kindly able to send to me. I am most grateful.

Very great thanks to Margaret Duncan, the daughter of Captain

George Duncan MC, for reaching out to me about your father's wartime story and for sharing with me your father's wonderful poetry from that time.

Thank you to Christine Gordon, the daughter of British and Irish rugby international George Ernest Cromey, for helping me tell the story of the springbok-hunting episode that happened during the 1938 British Lions tour of South Africa. Thanks to David Robson, for sharing with me the stories of how Lieutenant Colonel Mayne helped guide him as a young man in his life choices. Thanks also to Barbara Coffey, whose father, Dr Cole, was a close friend of Lieutenant Colonel Mayne's, and who shared with me her childhood memories. Thanks to Harold Hetherington for sharing with me the stories of how Lieutenant Colonel Mayne was in the habit of rounding him and his brothers up as young and somewhat wayward boys, and ensuring they did attend the local school.

Thanks also to Liam, for sharing with me the photos and diary entries of Eric Musk, one of Mayne's SRS raiders during the summer and autumn of 1943. Thanks once again to Amy Barkworth, the daughter of Major Eric 'Bill' Barkworth, for sharing with me his wartime reports concerning Hitler's 'Commando Order' and related materials.

Thank you, as ever, to my long-standing friend and reader of early manuscripts, and commentator thereon LRDG, SAS and SBS veteran Jack Mann. As you knew Lieutenant Colonel Mayne personally, your comments and remarks on an early draft of this book are treasured, as always.

Thank you also to the late Alec Borrie, SAS veteran, who served alongside Lieutenant Colonel Mayne and many others portrayed in this book, for speaking with me about his wartime experiences and memories. Again, such contributions from one who was there have been invaluable and I am hugely privileged and grateful for all his help and insight. Sadly, Alec passed away before this book could be published.

Thank you to Eric Lecomte and Arnaud Blond, for all the correspondence, help and assistance you were able to furnish concerning my research into the operations of the Free French SAS, and also for your kind invitations to France, to look into more of the same. This was invaluable and I am very grateful.

Huge thanks to Piers Lloyd Owen, for visiting me at home and bringing such a wealth of your father David Lloyd Owen's personal papers, photos and wartime memorabilia with you. That was a special highlight of my research, as were the fine conversations and recollections you were able to share.

Thank you to Ros Townsend, a specialist working with the fantastic charity PTSD Resolution, for reading an early draft of this book, and for sharing with me your expert perspective on the history of diagnosis and recognition of PTSD and your personal feedback and observations on the trauma suffered by Second World War veterans, and especially those serving behind the lines. This was invaluable, and I have leant on your analysis quite heavily. Thank you also to Colonel A. de P. Gauvain (Retired) FHGI, Chairman and CEO of PTSD Resolution, for all the help, support and advice you kindly extended to me in connection with the writing of this book.

Thank you to Joshua Levine, for sharing with me a pre-publication copy of your excellent work, *SAS: The Illustrated History of the SAS*, which includes a trove of never before published photographs of the unit in action in the Second World War.

Thanks as ever to Julie Davies, ace researcher and translator, for sharing with me the journey of discovery embodied in this book, and for your astute and pertinent observations, assessment and guidance; but most of all for your heartfelt enthusiasm that the full story of Lieutenant Colonel Mayne's wartime story, and that of his comrades, should be told. With this book it is continued.

Thanks are also extended to the following individuals, who are all experts in their own right on various aspects of Second World War history, and helped me in my research: Jonathan Woodhead, Michael Caldwell, Tom Hunter, Thomas Harder, Jimmy Russell, Will Ward, Paul Norman and Andrew Glenfield.

I also extend my warm thanks to my early readers: Paul and Anne Sherratt, as always, at the top of the list of 'thank yous'. Long may you keep providing me with such pertinent and telling feedback and comment. Sandy and Erica Moriarty, our wonderful neighbours just across the track – again, your detailed remarks, and your enthusiasm for this story, proved invaluable.

Enormous thanks to Henrik Beermann, who was born and raised in Schneeren, in Germany, for your kind and generous correspondence and conversations about the Schneeren episode of this story, and all things concerning the *Chroniken* and their purpose and intent. This proved hugely enlightening.

Thanks also to Mark Johnston, for sharing with me your dissertation on Lieutenant Colonel Mayne, '"The Bravest man never to have been awarded the V.C.": a re-examination', and for the correspondence we shared, and to your partner, Eimear, for reaching out to me in the first place about this.

Thank you, again, to Nina Staehle for your excellent research in Germany concerning this story and for your translations from German to English. As ever, with remarkable tenacity you unearthed some true gems concerning this story, and for that I am hugely grateful.

Huge thanks as always to Simon Fowler, my researcher in the UK – your hard work and insight were invaluable. Your work winkling out the files from where they were hardest to find, as always, was remarkable. Bravo!

Thanks again to my mother, Christine Major, for her refreshing thoughts and input into an early draft of this book. I hope it helped ease you through the trials and tribulations of what would seem to be 'long Covid'.

Thanks also to Paul Hazzard, long-standing reader and friend, for perusing an early draft and for your deeply perceptive comments. Thanks to John R. McKay, a fellow author and Second World War historian of great talent, for reading an early iteration of this book and for all your invaluable comments. It was great to have that support, as ever, my friend. Thank you also to Richard Domoney-Saunders for reading an early draft of the manuscript and for your comments and suggestions.

Thanks especially to SAS veteran Des Powell (with whom I co-authored *SAS Bravo Three Zero*), for it was immensely refreshing to have the thoughts and feedback of a more modern-generation 'pilgrim' – an SAS veteran – on this story of the SAS in its founding years. Well done, my friend, and massively appreciated. The legacy lives on in individuals such as yourself.

Thank you also to the Winston Churchill Fellowship, for backing me with a Fellowship many years ago, which ignited the spark in a young man to be curious about all things Winston Churchill, and especially the legacy of this extraordinary wartime leader.

I have benefited greatly in the research for this book from the efforts that the British, German and other governments, and related institutions, have put into preserving for posterity the archives from the Second World War era. The preservation and cataloguing of a mountain of papers – official reports, personal correspondence, telegrams etc. – plus photographic, film and sound archives are vital to authors such as myself, without which books of this nature could not be written. Devoting resources to the preservation of this historical record, and to making it accessible to the public, is something for which these governments and other institutions deserve high praise.

All at my publishers deserve the very best of praise for their committed, enthusiastic and visionary support of this project from the get-go. In the UK, Richard Milner, my long-standing editor and good friend, provided seminal guidance and feedback, as always. The wider Quercus team also deserve the highest praise, and especially Dave Murphy and Jon Butler. In the USA the publishing team at Kensington Books were superlative, as always. Thank you to all of you, but especially to Wendy McCurdy, Anne Pryor, Rebecca Cremonese, Barbara Brown, John Son, Elizabeth Trout, Lynn Cully, Jackie Dinas, Steven Zacharius and Adam Zacharius. Special mention must also be made of Kensington Books, for their excellent fundraising to support freedom and justice in Ukraine. Thank you also to Sophie Ransom, of Ransom PR, for your huge enthusiasm for this story from the very outset, and for working your special magic.

Finally, I need to extend my deep thanks and heartfelt gratitude to my family – Eva, David, Damien Jr and Sianna – who once again had to put up with 'Pappa' spending far too long locked in his study trying to do justice to this story. That I have – if I have – I owe to you all; to your forbearance, your love and support and kindness, and for putting up with me through it all.

This, of course, is a very special story for the Lewis family, if for no other reason than because of our deep links to Ireland, and because my wife has played a very hands-on and indispensable role in the research, archiving, writing and revisions of this book, not to mention overseeing the business side of things. This book has been a labour of love, and you stayed the course over the long years that it has taken to come to fruition, for which I am hugely grateful.

Acknowledgements on Sources

I am indebted to the following authors, who have covered some of the aspects of the story I have dealt with in *SAS Forged in Hell* in their own writing. As detailed in the Author's Note, I extend my deep gratitude to those who granted me kind permission to quote from their material. For those readers whose interest has been piqued by this book, these authors and their titles would reward further reading.

Peter Davis MC, whose book, *SAS Men in the Making* (edited by Paul Davis), is the author's diary from the time he spent serving with Lieutenant Colonel Robert Blair Mayne's squadron, including during training in the spring of 1943, and thereafter in Sicily and Italy, and is an excellent chronicling of this period of SAS history.

John O'Neill, the great nephew of Lieutenant Colonel Robert Blair Mayne DSO, and the author of *Legendary Warrior of the SAS Robert Blair Mayne DSO: The Original Who Kept the SAS Alive*, whose biography of his great-uncle relied on access to the O'Neill (Mayne) family archive, and is rich in biographical detail.

W. A. Deakins, whose book, *The Lame One*, is an autobiography of the author's wartime service, including his time spent with the SAS in North Africa, and Italy and Europe thereafter, and is based upon his detailed wartime diaries.

Derrick Harrison, whose book, *These Men Are Dangerous*, is a compelling account of the author's war years, and especially of his time serving with the SAS both in Italy, and thereafter in France, in the battle to liberate Nazi-occupied Europe.

I am also grateful to the following publishers, authors and estates for granting me permission to quote from their works (full details in the Selected Biography):

Roy Close, *In Action with the SAS*, 2005 – all rights reserved.

Roy Farran, *Winged Dagger*, 1986 – all rights reserved.

W. B. Kennedy Shaw, *Long Range Desert Group*, 2015 – all rights reserved.

David Lloyd Owen, *The Long Range Desert Group 1940–1945: Providence Their Guide*, 2001 – all rights reserved.

Malcolm James Pleydell, *Born of the Desert: With the SAS in North Africa*, 2015 – all rights reserved.

Gearoid O'Dowd, *He Who Dared and Died: The Life and Death of an SAS Original, Sergeant Chris O'Dowd, MM*, 2011 – all rights reserved.

Ian Wellsted, *With the SAS Across the Rhine: Into the Heart of Hitler's Third Reich*, 2020 – all rights reserved.

Selected Bibliography

Lorna Almonds Windmill, *Gentleman Jim*, Pen & Sword, 2011

Michael Asher, *Get Rommel*, Weidenfeld and Nicolson, 2004

——, *The Regiment*, Viking, 2007

Martin Dillon and Roy Bradford, *Rogue Warrior of the SAS*, Mainstream Publishing, 2012

Daniel Allen Butler, *Field Marshal*, Casemate Publishers, 2017

J. V. Byrne, *The General Salutes a Soldier*, Robert Hale, 1986

Dudley Clarke, *Seven Assignments*, Jonathan Cape, 1948

Roy Close, *In Action with the SAS*, Pen & Sword, 2005

Johnny Cooper, *One of the Originals*, Pan Books, 1991

Virginia Cowles, *The Phantom Major*, Pen & Sword, 2010

Peter Davis MC, *SAS Men in the Making*, Pen & Sword, 2015

W. A. Deakins, *The Lame One*, Arthur H. Stockwell Ltd, 2001

Margaret Duncan and Sue Knight, *Behind Barbed Wire*, privately published by Solway Print, 2021

Roy Farran, *Winged Dagger*, Arms & Amour Press, 1986

Raymond Forgeat, *Remember: Les Parachutistes de la France Libre*, Service Historique de l'Armée de Terre, 1990

Derrick Harrison, *These Men Are Dangerous*, Blandford Press, 1957

Stephen Hastings, *The Drums of Memory*, Pen & Sword, 1994

Robin Hunter, *True Stories of the SAS*, George Weidenfeld & Nicholson, 1986

Malcolm James, *Born the Desert*, Frontline Books, 2015

Nicholas Jellicoe, *George Jellicoe*, Pen & Sword, 2021

W. B. Kennedy Shaw, *Long Range Desert Group*, Frontline Books, 2015

Joshua Levine, *SAS: The Illustrated History of the SAS*, William Collins, 2023

Anon, *The SAS War Diary*, Extraordinary Editions, 2011

Damien Lewis, *Churchill's Secret Warriors*, Quercus, 2014

——, *SAS Ghost Patrol*, Quercus, 2018

——, *SAS Band of Brothers*, Quercus, 2020

——, *SAS Great Escapes*, Quercus, 2020

——, *The Flame of Resistance*, Quercus, 2022

B. H. Liddell Hart, *The Rommel Papers*, Harcourt Brace & Company, 1953

David Lloyd Owen, *The Desert My Dwelling Place*, Cassell & Company, 1957

——, *The Long Range Desert Group*, Leo Cooper, 1980, rev. edn 2001

Patrick Marrinnan, *Colonel Paddy*, Ulster Press, 1983

Carol Mather, *When the Grass Stops Growing*, Leo Cooper, 1997

Stewart McClean, *SAS: The History of the Special Raiding Squadron 'Paddy's Men'*, Spellmount, 2006

Patric McGonigal, *Special Forces Brothers in Arms: Eoin and Ambrose McGonigal*, Pen & Sword, 2022

Ben McIntyre, *SAS Rogue Heroes*, Viking, 2016

Ian McHarg, *Litani River*, www.litaniriver.com, 2011

J. Fraser McLuskey, *Parachute Padre*, Spa Books, 1985

Charles Messenger, *The Commandos 1940–1946*, William Kimber, 1985

Victor Miller, *Nothing Is Impossible,* Pen & Sword, 1994

Gavin Mortimer, *David Stirling,* Constable, 2022

Robin Neillands, *The Raiders: Army Commandos 1940–46,* Fontana, 1989

Gearoid O'Dowd, *He Who Dared and Died,* Pen & Sword, 2011

John O'Neill, *Legendary Warrior of the SAS,* Menin House, 2015

Hamish Ross, *Paddy Mayne,* Sutton Publishing, 2003

Gordon Stevens, *The Originals: The Secret History of the Birth of the SAS in Their Own Words,* Ebury Press, 2005

A. P. Wavell, *Other Men's Flowers,* Jonathan Cape, 1978

Adrian Weale, *Renegades: Hitler's Englishmen,* Pimlico, 2002

Ian Wellsted, *With the SAS Across the Rhine,* Frontline Books, 2020

Sources

Material quoted from the UK archive files listed below is courtesy of the National Archives, Kew. This book contains public-sector information licensed under the Open Government Licence v3.0.

ABBREVIATIONS

TNA – The National Archives, UK

Imperial War Museum

Documents

Notes Relating to Special Raiding Squadron, 1st SAS Regiment, Operations, July-October 1943, IWM Documents 25504

Private Papers of Captain M. J. Pleydell MC, IWM Documents 337

Private Papers of Sir Carol Mather MC, IWM Documents 17403

Private Papers of Mrs. A. M. Street, IWM Documents 6433

Private Papers of Winston Churchill, *Speech at Mansion House, 10 November 1942*, IWM Documents 24715

BBC The Archive Hour SAS Originals, IWM Catalogue Number
29806

Audio Archives
Bob Bennett interview, IWM Sound Archive 18145
Earl George Jellicoe interview, IWM Sound Archive 13039
Reg Seekings DCM MM, IWM Sound Archive 18177

Liddell Hart Centre for Military Archives
Street, Major-General Vivian Wakefield (1912–1970), GB 0099
KCLMA Street

Churchill Archives Centre, Churchill College, Cambridge
CHAR 1/369/3-4
CHAR 20/65/106-145
CHAR 20/205/49
CHAR 20/65/146-148

The National Archives, Kew
CAB 106/389 – Litani River
PREM 3/330/9 – Combined Ops
WO 311/1200 – Gavi POW camp reports
WO 331/7 – Hitler's Commando Order
WO 232 – War Office, Directorate of Tactical Investigations
WO 232/16 – Sicily Reports and Lessons Learned
WO 222/1568 – Locations of British General Hospitals during
WWII
WO 373/26 – Pleydell's MC Citation
WO-373-185-19 – French Awards Stirling/Jellicoe
WO-373-185 –French and American Awards for Stirling etc.

WO 373/92/123 – Recommendation for Award for Street, V W, the Devonshire Regiment

WO 218/222 – SAS WCIT Missing Parachutists

WO 218/160 – Middle East Commando A Squadron

WO 218/97 – 1 SAS War Diary Jan–Apr 43

WO 372-185 – CdeG citations

WO 218/107 – Light Repair Section

WO 218/106 – M Det 1943

WO 201/727 – Raiding Forces – Personal File of Lt-Col. J. E. Haselden

WO 201/748 – Agreement, Bigamy, Nicety: Reports

WO 201/765 – Raiding Forces: Signals in

WO 201/763 – OUT messages Jul–Nov 42

WO 201/764 – OUT messages Dec 42–Mar 43

WO 218/91 – Special Service War Diaries: Long Range Desert Group

WO 218/119 – HQ SAS Troops Norway

WO 171/766 – Raiding Forces IN Signals Dec 42–March 43

WO 201/765 – Raiding Forces IN Signals Jul–Nov 42

WO 373/46/23 – Raiding Forces

WO 218/119 – Operation Archway

WO 218/91 – War Diary 1 SAS 1943

WO 218/97 – Special Service War Diary 1940 onwards

WO 218/98 – Special Service War Diary 1940 onwards

WO 218/99 – War Diary Raiding Sqn 1943

WO 236/16 – Op Husky

WO 218/102 – Op Husky Signals

WO 128/176 – Taranto Sept '43

WO 218/119 – Op Howard

HS 9/1647 – Couraud

KV 2/626-1 – Douglas Webster Dt. Aubyn Berneville-Claye

KV 2/626-2 – Douglas Webster Dt. Aubyn Berneville-Claye

KV 2/627-1 – Douglas Webster Dt. Aubyn Berneville-Claye

KV 2/627-2 – Douglas Webster Dt. Aubyn Berneville-Claye

KV 2/77-1 – Theodore John William SCHURCH: deserted to the Italians and collaborated with them and . . .

KV 2/77-2 – Theodore John William SCHURCH: deserted to the Italians and collaborated with them and . . .

Other Published Sources

Max Arthur, 'Obituary: Reg Seekings', *Independent*, 3 May 1999

Ron Gittings, 'Tarnished Hero of the SAS', *Medal News*, April 2007

Jack Loudan, 'The Man Who Dared', *TV Post*, 23 August 1962

——, 'Braves Bullets to Save His Wounded Men', *TV Post*, 27 September 1962

Alastair McQueen, 'How the Spirit of Bravest SAS Hero Will Live On', *Express*, 1 March 1997

Margaret Metcalf, 'My father the war traitor', BBC News, 29 March 2002

Unpublished Sources & Miscellaneous

Amicale Belgian SAS Vriendenkring vzw, 'A Short History of the Belgian SAS in WWII', translated from the Flemish by Geert G., 2020

Anon, '.303 inch Incendiary', British Military Small Arms Ammo, undated

Anon, 'Blair "Paddy" Mayne', World Rugby Museum, 2013, Mayne family collection, undated

Anon, 'Major William (Bill) Fraser MC, 1917–1975', undated paper

Anon, 'Olympians Sports Gossip – Some Stories of Blair Mayne', Johannesburg Star draft article, 26 February 1942, O'Neill family collection

Anon, 'Robert Blair Mayne of Newtownards: A Commemorative Booklet', Rotary Club of Newtownards, Mayne family collection, undated

Anon, 'The Second World War: All RAF Aircrew Were Volunteers', Royal Airforce Museum, undated

Anon, 'Unveiling of the Memorial to Lt Col. Robert Blair Mayne DSO', Ards Borough Council, 2/5/1997, Mayne family collection, undated

Major Eric 'Bill' Barkworth, 'Report on the Commando Orders of 18.10.42 and 25.6.44 with Reference to Certain of the War Crimes Caused by Them', Barkworth family collection, undated

James Bruce, 'When You Go Home . . .', GCHQ official history, undated

'The End of the Beginning', International Churchill Society, undated

'Churchill's Government Defeats a No Confidence Motion in the House', International Churchill Society, 12 March 2015

Doug Goldsmith, 'Joe Goldsmith's War Diary', Goldsmith family collection, undated

Charles Hackney, 'A Soldier's Life', unpublished manuscript and notes, Hackney family collection, undated

Mark Johnston, '"The bravest man never to have been awarded the VC": a re-examination', LM Dissertation, MA Military History DL, undated

Omar Khayyam, 'One Moment in Annihilation's Waste', *The*

Rubaiyat of Omar Khayyam, first edition, The Lieder New Archive, undated

Major R. B. Mayne, 'Capo Murro Di Porco Op Orders & Report', Mayne family collection, undated

Rev. J. Fraser McLuskey, 'Between You and Me', eulogy for Lieutenant Colonel R. B. Mayne, Mayne family collection, undated

John Rodgers, B.A., Principal, 'Report for Term Ending 18th December 1925', Newtonards Academy, Mayne family collection, undated

A. J. Schofield, 'Special Raiding Squadron Sicily & Italy 1943', 1999

Index

Counselling Forces' Veterans & Reservists
registered charity no. 1133188

PTSD Resolution, Charity No. 1133188, provides therapy for the mental welfare of Forces' Veterans, Reservists and their families. Treatment is free, effective and delivered promptly and locally through a network of 200 therapists nationwide, and also by phone and internet during the pandemic. Contact www. PTSDresolution.org.

Founded in 2009, and with over 3,500 referrals to date, the charity delivers therapy in an average of six sessions, with 78% of cases seeing an improvement in reported symptoms to where the client and therapist agree that no further therapy is required.

The charity is one of the only organisations to provide therapy to veterans suffering with addiction issues or who are in prison – as well as to family members, including partners and children, who may experience the symptoms of trauma from living with a traumatised veteran.

PTSD Resolution has a unique 'lean' operation, with no salaried staff or assets – funds are used to deliver therapy and for essential research and public information.

Key features of PTSD Resolution's service:

Free, local, prompt and effective help for Veterans, Reservists & families suffering from mental health issues

Confidential, no GP referral is needed

Local help through a UK network of 200 therapists

Fast treatment, issues usually resolved in an average of six sessions

Easy to access – first session booked often in days

Compassionate: clients do not have to talk about events in their past

Cost-effective, £750 per programme – free to the people we help

Transparent, results are monitored and reported

No one is turned away: including HM prisoners and those with addiction issues

Cobseo members, working with other Forces charities (Cobseo, the Confederation of Service Charities, provides a single point of contact for interaction with Government, the private sector and with other members of the Armed Forces Community)

'Lean' charity management: we own no assets, have no salaried staff: donations are used for essential treatment, research and communications.

Who Dares Cares supports our Armed Forces, Emergency Services and Veterans including their families who are suffering from Post-Traumatic Stress Disorder (PTSD). It provides weekend retreat facilities where individuals and families can spend a weekend away from the daily grind and relax in fun activities, Walk, Talk and Brew Groups where they have teams of volunteers across the United Kingdom meeting with groups of people who maybe just want to clear their head and have the support of charity volunteers through participating in some gentle exercise or attending a PTSD awareness group or individual session to help provide a better understanding of what the signs and symptoms of PTSD are, how to manage symptoms and ways that families can better support in a way that is helpful to the individual. The charity recognises the importance of exercise as part of recovery and it works to encourage this and make this accessible for those who are struggling with PTSD and anxiety-related issues.

The charity was founded in Hamilton, Scotland in 2016 by two former serving soldiers, Calum MacLeod (King's Own Scottish Borderers) and Colin Maclachlan (Royal Scots and Special Air Service). After Calum and Colin met, sharing their own stories and becoming friends, bound by their own experiences, they both realised they could help so many other people, who were left 'alone' to deal with their experiences, thoughts and traumas. They decided to build a platform that would provide help and support to individuals and their families, all in the way of Who Dares Cares.

There are a number of volunteers that support the charity, all with varying skills, from military backgrounds to nurses, who offer help and support to all of their followers in many different ways. The volunteers are just that, volunteers. They are dedicated to the charity and give their time and effort to support other people in so many different ways. Without them, Who Dares Cares wouldn't be able to provide the dedicated support that it can.

Anyone with a service record and a history of PTSD should apply for support, even if you're not sure you meet the criteria; each application is assessed on an individual basis. For more details please email the Who Dares Cares Support Team Mailbox on wdc@who-dares-cares.com and if you wish to learn more about this amazing charity and how you can support its vital work, please visit www.who-dares-cares.com.

It is not about suffering from PTSD, it is about learning to live with PTSD!

Veterans In Action is an armed forces charity that helps veterans and their families who have suffered the effects of war or who have found the transition to civilian life difficult, focusing on the emotional and physical well-being of those involved to help them grow as an individual or family.

The charity was founded in 2009 by Billy MacLeod MBE, who had served in the Royal Engineers and who after looking at what was on offer for veterans in the UK looked further afield to the United States and Australia for inspiration.

The aim was to set an up an organisation based on the experiences and the camaraderie of serving in the Army and particularly the Royal Engineers and the tasks they carried out around the world, with the aim of helping ourselves by helping others.

A study in Australia was found called Wilderness and Adventure Therapy which became the basis of Veterans In Action's own unique ALIVE programme designed by the charity founder, which takes a non-therapy long-term approach to veterans' mental health, to help veterans and their families grow at their own pace, working alongside their peers on the projects run at the ALIVE Centre or off-site in the surrounding area or on long-distance expeditions.

Veterans In Action projects are based on the decades-old study of Post-Traumatic Growth. Veterans In Action's ALIVE CENTRE is the charity HQ and is ideally set on a beautiful private estate seven miles from Andover on the Hampshire/ Wiltshire border with beautiful walks through woodlands and the scenic Hampshire countryside. This environment helps veterans to de-stress as soon as they enter the estate and to feel 'safe' and relaxed in the quiet of the countryside.

From 2009 until 2016 Veterans In Action carried out a series of long-distance walks across the UK called the Union Flag Walks, with each walk forming a separate part of the Union Flag, covering a distance of 13,500 miles and with over 500 veterans suffering from PTSD taking part.

In 2017 the charity started a new project called Veterans Expeditions Overland where veterans strip and rebuild Land Rovers and prepare them to expedition standard. The vehicles are then used to undertake long-distance overland expeditions.

Due to the success of this project, it has now become the basis of all other projects that complement each other. All work on the vehicles and on expeditions is filmed by veterans on a project called Veterans In Focus where veterans learn to film and edit the footage for a YouTube channel called Veterans Expeditions Overland.

We know that veterans can achieve remarkable accomplishments and they possess a myriad of unique skills that when harnessed can be used on many different projects here at home, becoming valuable members of their community.

Veterans In Action is committed to helping veterans unlock the potential they have to make a difference throughout their lives, not only for themselves and their family but also their standing in the local community where they can develop projects to help others. This is the true definition of Post-Traumatic Growth.